BEST OF THE

OXFORD

★★★ AMERICAN ★★★

Ten Years from the Southern Magazine of Good Writing

Foreword **RICK BRAGG** ★ **MARC SMIRNOFF** Editor

HILL STREET PRESS ⅃ ATHENS, GEORGIA

A HILL STREET PRESS BOOK

Published in the United States of America by
Hill Street Press LLC
191 East Broad Street, Suite 209
Athens, Georgia 30601-2848 USA
706-613-7200
info@hillstreetpress.com
www.hillstreetpress.com

☆ Hill Street Press is committed to preserving the written word. Every effort is made to print books on acid-free paper with a significant amount of post-consumer recycled content. ☆ Hill Street Press books are available in bulk purchase and customized editions to institutions and corporate accounts. Please contact us for more information. ☆ No material in this book may be reproduced, scanned, stored, or transmitted in any form, including all electronic and print media, or otherwise used without the prior written consent of the publisher. However, an excerpt not to exceed 500 words may be used one time only by newspaper and magazine editors solely in conjunction with a review of or feature article about this book, the author, or Hill Street Press, LLC. Attribution must be provided including the publisher's name, author's name, and title of the book. ☆

Library of Congress Cataloging-in-Publication Data

Best of The Oxford American: ten years from the southern magazine of good writing / edited by Marc Smirnoff
      p.   cm.
    ISBN 1-58818-081-6 (alk. paper)
     1. American literature—Southern States. 2. Southern States—Literary collections. I. Smirnoff, Marc. II. Oxford American.
    PS551 .B39 2002
    810.8'0975—dc21   2002068458

ISBN # 1-58818-081-6
10 9 8 7 6 5 4 3 2 1
First printing

Contents

Foreword

My momma won't hardly eat restaurant food. It is the only area of her life in which she is a snob, this woman who grew up dragging a cotton sack with babies on her hip. Well, she also thinks there has not been a good movie actor since Alan Ladd, but that is not so much snobbery as just common sense. There really hasn't been much good on television since the last time Shane called Jack Palance a no-good Yankee liar.

But her feelings about food, which she knows the way some people know rocket science, are not a pretension so much as a conviction.

Restaurant food, she swears, has no taste.

"Some people," she said, "are just scared of the salt shaker."

I have heard it before. Old black women in New Orleans say it, a lot. They say you can't cook a damn thing if you're afraid—of the garlic, or the cayenne, or the other ingredients that make food and life worth the time they take to consume. For us, in the foothills of the Appalachians, it was salt. Cheap as dirt, but if you skimp, or leave it out, the supper table is just a flat place to pray.

But if you season it right, Lord, it is a place of pure joy, and when you close your eyes and say thank you, you actually mean it.

I don't claim to be an expert on writing, on telling stories, but I think it must be a lot like cooking.

Here in this collection are some of the best stories, articles, and poems to run in *The Oxford American,* by an assortment of its best writers.

Not one of them is afraid of the salt shaker.

RICK BRAGG

Introduction

"The Oxford American is a literary magazine, of general interest, established under the idea that it is time for a good general magazine to originate from the South. While in these parts many fine academic journals abound, our region lacks an invigorating magazine of mass appeal. It is in precisely this arena that *The Oxford American* is determined to excel. This magazine is written for the intelligent, and nonacademic, general reader. With the most exacting standards *The Oxford American* will publish many forms of excellent writing and artwork, including fiction, photography, humorous verse, essays, reviews, interviews, drawings, columns, reports, commentary, and more."

—The first paragraph of the editorial that appeared in the first issue of *The Oxford American,* Spring 1992.

How do you judge a person, a writer, a magazine—by the failures or the peaks? Well, in this book you only get to see *The Oxford American* in its shiniest Sunday best—which is not to imply . . . too much. Coming face to face with a profusion of candidates was what was most memorable about cobbling together this anthology. In all likelihood, we made a mistake in calling it *Best of.* Probably it needed to be called *Some of the Best of* or *Best of, Volume One.* But when Hill Street Press approached us with the idea, *Best of "The Oxford American"* was the obvious title that sprung to mind. After all, that's the kind of content they asked for. But between committing to that title (and seeing it carved into catalogs and ads and

Web sites) and hurling deep into the archives, I learned there were many more articles that deserved to be in this book but which we didn't have room for.

Have you ever coached a youth sports team? I have, and I learned promptly—and painfully—that because there are just so many positions out there on the field, good kids are inevitably benched. Nobody likes that—those kids, their parents, the cornered coach. Writers—thank God—are sensitive souls and I know enough about them to know that I am bound to prick the feelings of the many worthy ones who have written pieces for *The OA* that deserve to be in here. But impossible decisions *had* to be made, so we made them.

On the other hand, at least it is the case that we have this opportunity to wound a batch of writers by excluding them from this book. I mean it could have been worse: Think of how *my* feelings would have been hurt if, after re-reading ten years' worth of *Oxford Americans* for *Best of* fodder, I had not dug up enough candidates.

In any case, if anyone out there would like to know the titles of some pieces that just as easily could have been included in this book, please feel free to contact me at the magazine at P.O. Box 1156, Oxford, Mississippi 38655, or oxfordmas@watervalley.net.

The only way to do a magazine is with passion—overwhelming, death-defying passion. Everything else is secondary. Magazine people who first pipe up about ad pages and reader demographics and circulation projections and all the rest before getting to the subject of content—that is to say, people who are technically smarter magazine people than I—probably put out publications that . . . I can't read.

> "People here are bored and disgusted with the sentimental and clichéd depictions of the South that are rerun in the so-called Southern magazines of record. Those periodicals rarely portray the real life that is around. They rarely show a regard for ambitious and excellent writing. *The Oxford American* demands more of itself."—Ibid.

The grand epiphany of my life asserted itself when I was in my late teens.

Up until that time I had endured an insulting teenagehood: I was friendless. I was a bad student (which had me thinking I might be dumb). I got slapped around by bullies. I hyperventilated whenever a teacher called on me in class or a cute girl asked for a spare pencil. Etc.

That's the kind of baggage that if dragged around for too long could distort and even smother a person. But I got saved from it. Different sublime forces conspired to start me reading outside the dull curriculum. And this reading— from Sherlock Holmes who led me to *The New Yorker* which in turn led me to the writers and books discussed in *The New Yorker* prompted me to see the whole world, and myself, differently. The myself part is this: I began not to fret about the same old stuff (the isolation, the D grades, the bullies) and instead started to wrap my mind around the subjects the writers were grappling with. At the same time, I began to feel tinglings in my mind—the sensations, possibly, of an underdeveloped brain finally starting to expand.

The short of it is that I am utterly convinced, even if nobody else is, that the power of literature can do something so outright corny and magical as saving people. It can straighten us up (just like a military school does for some) and lead us to put things in better perspective. It can make us understand what is truly consequential and what is dross and dead and unworthy of our attentions.

It was fundamental to my vision of *The Oxford American* that we bring to it this belief that the best writing has the power *to effect personal change in the reader.*

E. M. Forster wrote "only connect." A simple enough directive but one hard to pull off. But when somebody does!

My hope is that the writing in this book connects with you in the way that Forster had in mind.

Naturally, I am thankful for the platform that this book provides for the magazine. I am also thankful for the many superb *Oxford American* contributors, and for all you great readers out there.

MARC SMIRNOFF

EDITOR, FOUNDER

Mr. Puniverse

WENDY BRENNER

YESTERDAY YOU SMELLED LIKE DETERGENT, having biked to work through the feeder bands of a tropical storm that was stalled just offshore in the Gulf. You clomped in like a draft horse, keys and change jingling, clean shirt steaming sweet ammonia and dripping all over the linoleum in the Xerox room, arms loaded with souvenirs from your recent vacation in a Midwestern state you refused to name: "A Midwestern state of mind," was all you would say.

The reporters and editors received trial-size jars of specialty barbeque sauce: Mackintosh-smoked, Jack Daniels-spiked, Ginseng Zinger, Grand Marnier Infusion. The custodial staff got a box of chocolates shaped like prairie dogs, proceeds to benefit the Midwestern Prairie Dog Relocation Project. For Mabel, the front-desk receptionist, a postcard of the famous fainting goats. For Kenny and Sonny, the other two photographers besides myself, car air-fresheners in the shape of the anonymous Midwestern state.

Kenny said he'd take Sonny's to him in the hospital. "Oh, yes, that's right," you said, your eyes meeting no one's.

After you had given everything out, you turned to me. My empty hands vibrated in anticipation—something was finally going to pass between us. I thought I might faint, like a goat.

"I'm still working on yours," you said. Your tone was both secretive and ironic, I thought, a little anxious but also triumphant, frustrated but resolute—sincere, yet more than a little recalcitrant.

"Is something wrong?" I asked.

"Ha!" you laughed, throwing back your large wet head, sending out an arc of storm-charged droplets. I watched one hit the bulletin board behind you and blur the word *operations* on a memo. The fluorescents flickered, went out, then blinked back on. "Whoa!" someone in the next room shouted.

"You just look a little anxious," I said. "Or, not anxious—worried. Worried."

Your hand moved across your gray-cratered chin and made an amplified, space-age sound. You said, "Well, it takes a worried man to sing a worried song." And then, backing away as if I had stepped too close, though I hadn't moved or even swallowed: "I'll try to bring yours tomorrow. Yours is special."

A wave of something went through me, tweaked my hyped-up aminos. I saw fish leaping out of the sea before a tsunami, strange fuzzy tendrils pushed out of the ground by the shifting plates of the earth. It didn't matter what the gift was. I could feel everything that was happening everywhere, and it was all for me.

My first photo shoot for the paper was the Mr. Puniverse Pageant, in which the editors had jokingly entered you, their colleague, as a contestant. I hadn't met you yet, but everyone was abuzz about the event, the fact that you were going along with it. "And, Jason, you're the perfect man to cover this," the editors said to me with genuine, mean-spirited excitement. "You'll make these dorks feel even more puny, get some great reactions." They were a giggling, sweaty, vengeful group, these editors. They reminded me to get some good shots of you for the bulletin board. "You'll know him—he'll be the old one!" they hooted.

Twenty years their—and your—junior, I had my killer summer tan still and was experimenting with a black-market protein powder that had doubled my muscle mass in a month and was probably veterinary steroids, which was fine with me. Smells and sounds were more intense, people got on my nerves more, but I was buff, I was ripped. I had no idea who you were. "Sure," I told the editors. "Whatever."

You did not win the title of Mr. Puniverse, didn't even place—while comically homely, certainly, you are not particularly skinny. Really, you didn't even make an effort. For your talent segment, you told one joke: *What's a potato's favorite TV show? M*A*S*H.*

The reporters from our paper cheered wildly.

Still, I found it hard to look away from you, to pay attention to the proceedings. You were scuffing around the margins of the stage, absent-mindedly stepping in and out of your sandals, keeping your eyes down, occasionally glancing up to grin at someone jeering you from the audience. Your gaze at those moments I found staggering. Clapton was playing on the p.a. system—*I've seen dark skies/Never like this/Walked on some thin ice/Never like this*—and the maddening animal smell of barbeque from the concession stand was rolling over me in waves. When I tried to take your picture, the power suddenly drained from my camera, and the shutter wouldn't budge. Luckily, I'd brought a backup.

The winner, the new Mr. Puniverse, was an albino biologist named Bultinck who stood six-two and weighed one hundred eleven. In the interview we printed, he said, "This is a real honor for me. I breed genetically specific mice, for which there is a pretty steady demand. I'm used to people thinking I'm weird." Energized by your presence, I got an inspired portrait of him, a happy freak naked from the waist up, the cold metal of the trophy he clutched making his nipples pop out. His figure appeared to be outlined in light, or hope, coming from some outside source.

Afterward, I pushed backstage, that song still playing in my head—*I've told you white lies/Never like this/Looked into true eyes/ Never like this—*

and offered you a ride back to the office in what I hoped was a neutral, businesslike tone. My parking meter, when we reached it, had apparently malfunctioned—in digital letters its screen said JAR. "Jar," you repeated, looking at me. I thought: *My god, your eyes.* Together, elbows knocking, we slid your Schwinn, a ladies' one-speed, into my backseat. I could hear the atoms in the cracks of space between us going crazy, buzzing like angry gnats.

Later, when I asked if you were bummed about losing the pageant, you said, "You can't always get what you want," and then gave me a look of nearly hysterical satisfaction. I would learn it was your habit to work popular song lyrics with a kind of feverish desperation into your conversation whenever possible, as if they were being pumped into you via secret radio waves and this was the only way to get them out of your system.

In fact, one question I frequently found myself wanting to ask you, later, was: "Didn't the electroconvulsive shock therapy help with the loose association?" But I would die before I'd remind you of something that hurt you.

Though you yourself never spoke of it, everyone at the paper knew and told several different versions of your troubled youth and unjust incarceration in a state mental institution, your close brush with, and lucky reprieve from, lobotomy. In one version, you had simply been a difficult teenager—for a year you refused to eat anything but Necco wafers, refused to read anything but the *Fantasy Baseball Index,* and in your free time snuck out of the house and climbed electrical towers. What choice did your affluent, dim-witted, voting-for-Eisenhower parents have but to commit you?

In another version, you tried to kill your father with a fencing foil. I found that version hard to believe, not because I couldn't imagine you as murderous, but because, in your own discordant, distracted, disintegrating way, you had too much style, too much real dignity for anything as idiotically self-important as fencing. You would have used your bare hands, I believe, or any simple firearm.

Common to all the versions was the length of your stay in the place—three years—and the reason for it: your parents moved across the country for your father's promotion, so you had to wait until you turned eighteen to sign yourself out. Office consensus was that you had come out crazier than when you went in, and this unusual bit of generosity on the part of your otherwise relentlessly critical colleagues—that they would grant you this—was, I thought, a measure of your personal power, your grace. It made my heart swell, like that of some idiot housewife, to think of it.

Never were they as hushed and reverent as when they spoke of your electroshock, how it made you smell roses even in your sleep and see people as cartoons, how it made your thoughts seem to come from a place like a luggage compartment located in the air ten feet above your head, how it made you forget your own name. I thought it must also have been the reason for your eyes—the layered, flickering darkness, the look, at one instant, of both reaching and refraining from reaching.

I couldn't think about it without the edges of my own body starting to crackle and tingle, not in sympathy but with the urge to hurl itself back through time and take your body's place, get between you and the source of the shocks, let the electricity mess with my simple, unspecial brain, my not-fragile self. I could have withstood it, I was sure, especially now with my new bulk. What good were my youth and strength doing anyone here, now? If only I had been there, I wanted to tell you, believe me, you would have come to no harm. Over my dead body.

That night, after the Mr. Puniverse Pageant, I dreamed I broke your bike. An accident—I was riding it, showing off for you, and the brake levers came off in my hands. The next night I dreamed that, together, you and I broke my TV, simply by standing in a certain proximity to each other and looking at it. In the dream, I understood that the TV was a sacrifice: if I didn't get to touch you, it was I who might die.

Though he was straight and shouldn't have been paying attention, Sonny, the senior photographer, quickly noticed me noticing you, and made sure I noticed. He would catch me in the men's room or the parking lot, pull me aside from nothing in particular, and say, *"By the way, he's not gay,"* in an obnoxiously pointed, fake-offhand manner, stroking his pubic-looking goatee with his ratty, precise little hand. Sonny von Cher, I called him to my friends. Straight photographers were, in my experience, a bunch of assholes, constantly needing to prove that they discerned hidden aspects of things, making it their life's work to unearth and destroy faith wherever they found it. Sonny was always pointing out examples of "unusual beauty" in a pompous, spiteful manner, as though he alone possessed the special power to recognize it, as though the rest of us, the masses, were too stupid and insensitive to appreciate or even know the real thing when we saw it.

Still, he had made his point. I brought it up on the way to Disney Gay Day with Owen, Kirk, Remy, Heath, Germain, Tab, Fidel, and Eddie in the Aerostar we had all chipped in to rent for the weekend.

"Why does Sonny care if you like this old ugly crazy straight guy?" Eddie said. "Does he want him?"

"No, Sonny's got a girlfriend," I said. "Though she does look like a boy. Or a praying mantis."

"Wait!" Owen yelled. "This guy you're in love with is old *and* straight *and* ugly? Maybe *you're* the one who's not gay!"

"He's not ugly *per se*," I said.

"He's not ugly, he's per se," Tab said.

"He's not ugly, he's my brother," Germain said.

"I'm telling you," I said. "I just have this feeling."

"Oh, please. Wake me up when we get to the Magic Kingdom."

As usual, Kirk was the only one who would take me seriously. We were lying in the back with the luggage, watching the string of sulphur-pink streetlights snake by in the sky. "Sometimes," Kirk said, "wanting what you can never have is the perfect spiritual position. Your faith develops, becomes an entity unto itself, takes on nearly physical reality—like the relationship we have with the dead, how the dead can sometimes seem more present than the living. Loving an absent partner is beautiful."

"It's not beautiful, it's pathetic," Remy said, leaning over his seat. "The guy is straight. Listen to what Sonny says. Forget about it."

"Who cares what Soon-Yi says?" Kirk said. "That doesn't mean anything.

"Maybe he is straight," I said, "but there's this look he gives me that just—I can't explain it."

"Communion," Kirk said.

"Spare me the *Touched-By-an-Angel* crap, will you?" Remy said. "Don't you remember what happened last year when Fidel hooked up with that 'bisexual' cardiac nurse guy?"

"Cancer care," Fidel said.

"Whatever. I personally don't have the time right now to sit up all night through Jason's nervous breakdown caused by some old freak who isn't even attractive."

"Okay, we won't call you," Kirk said. "God, Remy, you're, like, Touched By an Asshole. You think you're everything."

"I *am* everything," Remy said. "I'm *it.*"

Your image swam down to me from between the lights, flashed into me like a thought. I saw you again on the Mr. Puniverse stage, how you pulsed against my eyes as if you had been drawn in some darker, heavier medium than the other contestants, some radioactive kind of crayon. How you seemed the photographic negative of the boring joke that was being perpetuated there, and most other places, most of the time. How it hit me all at once that you were beautiful thinly disguised as ugly, the truth seeping out around your eyes and the vibrating edges of your person, the direct opposite of everyone else there, of most people I'd ever known, including, probably, myself.

Was I wrong, now, to believe you were taking a special interest in me? I thought of the way you stopped dead whenever we encountered each other in the corridor and held up your hands in a gesture of surrender; the way you spoke just a bit more loudly whenever I was working nearby, as if we were animals who had to track each other by sound; the way you sometimes appeared outside the darkroom, said my name, "Jason, . . ." but then nothing else, just stood there rubbing your chin, your eyes both bright and veiled, as if you were trying to remember the rest of the sentence.

"Besides," Kirk was saying, "Jason isn't having a nervous breakdown. Look at him, *hello,* he looks great. What have you been doing, Jason, lifting weights again? Your arms look bigger. Don't his arms look bigger? Look at his arms. Is it just me, or are your arms getting bigger? Jason?"

Everything I touched or even glanced at began to suffer surges and drains. Bulbs blew in every room of my apartment, and the coil on my toaster oven went cold. My water pressure fluctuated violently. New shoelaces snapped between my fingers; ink pens burst, unprovoked, in my pockets and desk drawers. My TV changed channels by itself, and my stereo suddenly picked up stations I'd never heard of, transmitted from cities hundreds of miles away. Downtown one day, a transformer I happened to walk by exploded, splattering the sidewalk behind me with hot oil. True, my body was growing so rapidly that I was bumping into things like an adolescent, having to adjust my conception of physical space, but I suspected something else at work, something that had visited me once before.

During one weekend when I was sixteen, the year I was coming out, the compressor in my mother's meat freezer, my Sunbird's alternator, and my Swatch battery all suddenly and mysteriously died. Then, our answering machine, which otherwise worked fine, stopped taking messages from Kim Falvey, the girl I was dating. Clearly, it was trying to help me. Some enormous invisible presence seemed very close to me then, bearing terrifyingly down, ripping out what I pictured as notebook subject-dividers in my brain. It peaked one night, and I made my parents kneel on the floor of my bedroom with me and pray, which they did without asking questions: they were good parents.

Kirk, whose father was a Masonic Perfect Master of the Fifth Degree, was actually hallucinating by the time he came out. On the way to school one morning, he said, he saw a giant hair ball driving a truck. To escape his family, finally, he wrote a letter to himself from an imaginary friend, Lance, in Pecos, Texas, inviting himself to come visit for the summer, but his hallucinations had become so convincing by then that he was devastated when he stepped off the Greyhound and Lance wasn't there to meet him.

"There's a proven link between repression and increased electrical activity," Kirk had said while we were waiting in line for Space Mountain. "How do you think a lie detector test works? So, the longer you hold it in, the worse it's going to get. Now, on top of that, you say this guy had electroshock. Very likely his altered electromagnetic field is messing up your gay-dar. Add to that your own increased chemical conductivity caused by the, ahem, 'protein supplement' you're taking, and interactive aberration seems inevitable."

"That sounds plausible, Kirk," I said, "but with all these environmental variables, how can anyone tell who they're in love with, or who's in love with them?"

"Look," Kirk said, speaking more loudly. "This much I know. This is fact, recorded history. The pendulum clock in the palace of Frederick the Great at Sans Souci stopped when the emperor died. Whatever's causing all this to happen—this force, or whatever it is, this wave, or frequency, this configuration of light and heat and matter, this juxtaposition of events and possibilities, this *thing,* whatever it is—it's trying to help you! You just have to have faith in it!" He had his hands on my shoulders and was yelling into my face. A jet roared right overhead then, so low it lifted my hair, and I stared up at its glaring silver underside, which appeared to be smiling at us. A moment later it was gone. Kirk looked worried. He said, "You saw that too, right?"

I wanted to confess, to tell you everything, but there was never the opportunity; Sonny, it had become clear, was trying to keep us apart. He gave me the most distant, time-consuming assignments—the renegade airport emu, the WHIP 102-FM Chevy Touch-A-Thon, the grand opening of the Hair Shanty two counties away—so I'd be out of the office all day. When I returned, after dark, you were always gone. And then you took your Midwestern vacation. The day after you left, the tropical depression pulled up to the mainland and parked there, a perpetual motion machine churning out line after line of storms, as if the world itself had stalled, as if change were no longer possible. It seemed I might never see you again—an unacceptable ending.

Kenny guffawed one morning when I told him where I was off to. "Let me tell you something, bro," he said. "No one's ever even *seen* that runaway ostrich. It's like a UFO, man."

My faith faltered, I'm sorry to say. I had to do something.

I caught Sonny in his cubicle, using a magnifying glass to scrutinize head shots of his Dilton Doily-looking girlfriend, and told him I needed his help. Rain was lashing the windows in ten-minute bursts, and I'd timed myself to approach his desk between them, during one of the eerie, swollen silences, thinking I'd be more likely to get Sonny to go along with me that way—I'd be in the flow, riding the waves of air pressure like a surfer, coasting in to the inevitable end. In the men's room mirror I'd made my face pleasant, expectant, like Mary Tyler Moore's normal expression. I only hoped that suppressing my intentions wouldn't cause a blackout or explosion before I had the chance to carry them out. "I'm having the damnedest time finding that emu," I said. "I need the benefit of your expertise."

Sonny laughed. "You want me to go out in this storm?"

"I'm going. Besides, I thought you said it came out when planes were grounded," I said. "Unless, you know, there is no emu. . . ."

"Oh, there's an emu," Sonny said. "I'll ride out on the tarmac with you, how's that? Show you where it nests. I've gotta go pick up my new lens anyway. But then you're on your own, bud. You're still the new guy, in case you've forgotten."

"Oh, no, never," I said. "Believe me, I feel fortunate."

In my car, he lit a cigarette and said, "You really need to get over this little crush on our Mr. Puniverse."

Something clanged in the engine. *Easy,* I thought. *Just hang on a little longer.* I said, "Sorry?"

"Come on, Jason, spare me."

"Well, we've become friendly," I said. "If that's what you mean."

"He's an interesting guy," Sonny said, his tone implying that he knew everything about you and that I knew nothing. "His father was editor-in-chief, years ago. Dead now. So we try to look out for him. Keep him out of trouble."

"And?"

"And so the last thing he needs—or the paper needs—is a gay stalker. Where's your ashtray?" Water slammed the passenger half of the windshield, as though aiming for him. "Hey, slow down," he said, "will you?"

"Sorry," I said. We were on the long, pine-lined entranceway to the terminal, a single supermarket-sized building, and the open sky over the runways was visible, striped with wide dark bands, like the shadows of giant fan blades moving in slow motion. I couldn't get there fast enough.

"Turn here behind the rental cars," Sonny said. "It'll take us right out on the tarmac. I hope you've been paying attention to what I've said. I don't care what you do at home, behind closed doors, but I hope you're listening to me. We had forty-five applicants for your position."

"You want to protect him from me," I said, steering to where he was pointing. "Right? *You* want to protect *him* from *me*." I cut the engine, and it knocked twice, some thunder rumbling along with it. We were at the edge of the gate's concrete skirting, facing out on the empty runways, and beyond them the thick stands of longleaf pine and palmetto scrub, from which the bird would supposedly emerge. A lone prop jet sat at the gate, unattended. I pulled my camera bag from the backseat, pretended to rummage in it. There was the little gun Owen had lent me—shiny, pretty.

"I'd watch the sarcasm if I were you," Sonny said.

"Watch the birdie, watch the sarcasm," I said. Blood rushed and beat in my ears, building in tempo. Sonny was glaring at me, stroking his scraggly chin, and it occurred to me that he might be sneakily appropriating your gestures, one by one, even as he proclaimed himself your protector.

"Look, it's let up," he said finally. "Let's get out there, okay? I don't have all day."

We marched along single file in the drenched grass, parallel to the tree line, his black-jeaned butt twitching self-righteously in front of me. The words I planned to say hurtled through my head.

"You didn't come this far last time, did you?" he said.

"I could never have come this far without you," I said.

"Okay," he said, stopping and brushing his hands together, as though he'd just finished a dirty job. "I'm out of here. I'll grab a cab, and why don't you just not come back in at all, okay?"

"I'm sorry," I said. "I don't think I understand." Thunder boomed as the next band of dark moved in.

Sonny glanced at the sky, then down at his shirtfront, which was beginning to speckle. "Look, I don't want some kind of showdown," he said. "Why don't you just do the honorable thing, the graceful thing—"

"Graceful!" I said. "This *is* a showdown." It was time. "This is a showdown about beauty," I began, but he had already turned his back and was heading for the terminal, his feet slapping into a jog. "Wait!" I yelled. "You f—ing coward!" The wind had picked up, and I didn't think he'd heard me. *You are the enemy of beauty!* I was going to say. *If beauty is to survive, you must be destroyed!* I broke into a run behind him, not to catch up, as I knew he couldn't match me for speed, but because the storm was suddenly enormous, almost upon us. Funny, I thought, it sounds like a locomotive.

Something huge and black and silver was bearing down, crackling and roaring like a metallic bear, moving faster than both of us. *You!* I thought, returning from your vacation just in time—but the planes weren't flying, and you weren't due back until the next day. Still, I knew it was going to help me, and I tilted my head back to greet it, grateful, relieved—I wouldn't need the gun. There was a pause in the noise, like an intake of breath, and then the lightning smacked down a few yards in front of me, knocking Sonny sideways. His body seemed to hang in the air for a moment as the charge exited it, and then it folded and fell, almost slowly, like a used-up helium balloon, making no sound when it hit the ground.

"Thank you," I said, out loud.

The light had gone back up in the sky and was pulsing on and off there, a signal meant just for me. Rain sliced down finally. I heard the sirens start back at the terminal—the trucks would reach us in seconds, I knew, so I didn't have to do anything, nothing was required of me. I stood there with my hands dangling, like a beautiful girl, helpless, guiltless, perfect.

Before the authorities could get there, though, a figure crashed out of the trees beside Sonny's body, a shape moving tentatively, then quickly toward me, tall and impossibly skinny and outlined in light, a familiar silhouette. *Bultinck?* I whispered. But it whooshed right past, feathers rustling, the smell of burned flesh and roses fluttering in the air behind it.

January/February 1999

My Hand Is Just Fine Where It Is

WILLIAM GAY

WORREL WAS SITTING ON THE STONE STEPS drinking his third cup of morning coffee when he saw the Blazer turn off into his driveway. The softwood trees were beginning to green out in a pale transparent haze but the hardwoods were bare yet and he could see the red Blazer flickering in and out of sight between their trunks, the bright metal of its roof flashing back the sun like a heliograph. He'd seen it come a hundred times before, but its appearance was still as magical as something he'd conjured by sheer will, and he hoped the magic held through even such a day as this one threatened to be.

He rose from the steps when he heard Angie downshift for the hill and drank the last of the coffee and tossed out the dregs. He set the cup on the edge of the porch. When she parked the Blazer in the yard he was standing with his hands in his pockets. It was March and the wind still had a bite to it around the edges and he leaned slightly into it with his shoulders hunched.

She cut the switch and got out and stood by the car. She wore dark glasses and pushed them up with a forefinger as if she'd have a better view of him. She looked at him with a sort of rueful fondness.

I didn't know if you'd be ready to go or not, she said.

Yes you did.

Well I don't know why. I can't see why you want to come with me.

I don't want to even talk about it, he said. Are you ready?

She smiled. Ready as I'll ever be, she said.

She slid back under the steering wheel and he came around to the passenger door and got in. She had the motor going but was waiting for him to kiss her and he took her into his arms and kissed her mouth hard. When he moved his face back from hers, her green eyes were open. She always looked at him as if he were the only one who had the answer to some question she had been thinking of asking.

Well, she said. I won't even ask if you're glad to see me.

She felt thin in his arms. He could feel the delicate bonework of her shoulder through her flesh, through the silk of the blouse she wore. She'd been thin ever since he'd known her and he always tempered the strength with which he held her but now she seemed thinner. If he held her as tightly as he wanted, he felt he'd crush her. Yet the flesh of the face turned toward him looked new and unused, scarcely touched by the abrasions of the world or its ministrations.

Where's Hollis?

He had to work. They didn't want to let him off.

The son of a bitch, Worrel said.

Don't say that. He offered to take off anyway and go with me.

The son of a bitch, Worrel said again.

He doesn't know the whole story anyway, Angie said. He just thinks it's tests. I couldn't say the word *malignant*. You're the only one who knows everything.

She said she loved him and he had no cause to doubt it. They were like a drug in each other's veins. A crazy badnews drug, their hands trembled with the hypo, the needle prodded for an uncollapsed vein. The drug they used was rare and dangerous with unknown and catastrophic side effects—you couldn't buy it, it had to be stolen under cover of darkness when other folks were asleep or their attention had wandered.

If he didn't call or if he made no effort to see her, she came to see about him. She always seemed a little harried, almost distraught, glad to see him still there. It was as if she expected to see the house open to the winds and him gone without a trace or a word of farewell, gone to Africa to search for diamond mines or to South America to save souls. But Worrel had given up on prospecting and had come to feel each soul responsible for its own salvation and he was always there. In bed she'd cling to him and call his name as if she were trying to call him back from the edge of something. Warn him.

There had been a time when she was going to leave Hollis for him but the violence of his own recent divorce had sobered her, given her pause. There were other lives to be considered. Hollis had said in no uncertain terms there would be a custody battle. She was not in a good position for one. Hollis was in an excellent position. He was a good provider and a steady worker, and he was also faithful, or at least discreet. Angie and Worrel had started out careful and discreet but the power of the drug had surprised them and things had gotten out of hand: at some point, like drunken teenagers trashing a house, they had kicked down the doors and smashed the windows and sprayed their names on the walls in ten-foot-tall graffiti.

Everything fled from Worrel in the aftermath. Everything: house and car and vindictive wife. Disaffected and disgusted children fleeing at a dizzying pace like animals scuttling out of the woods from the mother of all forest fires, little scorched and smoking Bambis and Thumpers hellbent for elsewhere, and Worrel himself seized in the soft grasp of her flesh, scarcely noticing.

He studied her profile against the shifting woods of late winter sunlight, a little stunned at the price he had paid for so tenuous and fragile a portion of her life, though he never doubted she was worth it.

They were driving out of Ackerman's field and nearing Nashville when she glanced over at him. Did you find a place yet? she asked.

Since the affair had begun Worrel had become an addict of shading and nuance, decoding her speech as if there were always hidden meanings. What she'd asked could have meant, *Have you found a place for me and the kids?* or it could have meant, *Have you found a place we can be without your ex-wife coming in and screaming at us?* But it did not mean either of those things. All it meant was, *Have you found a place?* and he discarded it.

I may move in with you and Hollis, he said.

She glanced from the road to him, half a smile, half a grimace. It's not funny, she said. When are you going to stop treating everything as if it were a joke?

Maybe when everything stops being a goddamned joke, he said.

The last of the traffic lights had fallen away now and she didn't need her right hand for shifting, so she reached and grasped his left, pulling it over to the console between them. Her hand uppermost, her fingers laced with his. She squeezed it hard, then just drove clasping it loosely, her fingers calm and cool against his own. There was something oddly comforting about it, and Angie seemed to feel it as well, for climbing into the hills where perhaps she should have downshifted, she just drove on, the transmission laboring and vibrating until they'd made the grade.

If you need your hand to drive just take it back, he said.

She smiled at him, her face an enigma behind the dark glasses. My hand is just fine where it is, she said.

He turned away and looked at the countryside, aware of the scarcely perceptible weight of her hand, and watched Tennessee roll up—bleak trees, buttercups on the shoulder of the road, the leached funeral silks of winter, the cusp of promised spring the world hung onto.

They had been friends before they had been anything else and they could talk or they could ride in comfortable silence. Mostly they rode in silence, Worrel's mind turning up images of her as you'd turn up pages in an album of photographs and, in the one he looked at most, her eyes looked as they did in the moment before he kissed her the first time. He'd known he was going to and was glad he'd waited until her eyes looked the way they had. As if they'd been simultaneously asking and answering a question. They'd stepped together and Worrel felt as if she'd slammed against his chest, as if they'd stepped onto some narrow ledge of unreckonable height. Looking down made you dizzy and you might plummet later in the next second, though not now; now seemed not only enough but all there was. Later there were other kisses: in hallways, in the moment before a closed door opened, in the moment between the wash of headlights on a wall and the slam of a car door, in the moment when footfalls announced someone was coming but he wasn't here yet. In these tawdry moments are worlds, universes.

The night before they went to the motel for the first time she twisted his mouth down to hers and said against his teeth, I think you're trying to corrupt me. He didn't deny it.

It was seventy miles to Nashville and today it seemed too short a distance. After a while they joined the insectlike moil of traffic and she needed her hand back. She was a good driver, effortless, unpressured, and she didn't even have to look for street signs to find the medical center. She'd been there before.

In the thin watery light, the Athens of the South perched atop its hills like something from a dream. The red Blazer went through the narrow canyons between the buildings with ten thousand other red Blazers negotiating the narrow canyons and everything began to look unreal.

The pale transparent light off the facades of the buildings imbued them with meaning so that they looked to Worrel like monuments erected and fled by some prior race finer than the present folk who milled about like maggots working in flesh.

She parked in front of the medical center and they got out. She looked at her watch. We don't have time for lunch before my appointment, she said. Do you mind waiting until we get through here?

Of course not, he said. I'm not even hungry.

Well, she said, uncertain, looking at the building.

They walked toward it. The marble veneer glittered in the sun. It looked like an enormous mausoleum. The statuary on the lawn looked like relics replevied from a tomb so long hidden from the daylight that the thought of time and its unspooling made Worrel dizzy.

He sat in the waiting area with a roomful of other people. Nothing looked right. Maybe he was coming down with something. The pictures on the wall were wrong. A Dali print, a Bosch. Watches melted, marvelously detailed folk were flayed. The pictures seemed part of some surreal scheme to acclimate him to the horror to come.

The people did not seem right either. Everything about them rang false, even their clothing seemed strange, either years out of style or years ahead of its time. When they spoke some of the voices were pitched too high, others dragged endlessly like audiotape moving slower and slower. Their emotions were out of sync, their anxiety too hyper, their stoicism simply cold indifference.

She'd left her purse for him to mind and dangling it by the strap he went outside and smoked a cigarette. He seldom left the country and his eyes were drawn almost against his will to the jumbled skyscrapers and high-rise apartments. Everything seemed leaned toward some common center, the hazy pastel buildings collapsing on themselves. In the sepia light the city looked as strange as some fabled ruin on the continent of Lemuria.

He put the cigarette out in an urn half-filled with sand and went back inside the waiting room and took up a copy of *Newsweek*. He tried to read an article on a new survey of sexual habits but the sheer amount of work that had gone into producing the magazine he held in his hands made him tired. Lumberjacks had felled trees that had been shredded and pulped to make paper. Ink had to come from somewhere. Other folks ran presses, stacked the glossy magazines, delivered them; the U.S. Mail shuttled them across the country. Not to mention the people with cameras and word processors, people with curiosity and the knowledge to ask the questions to satisfy it. The magazine grew inordinately heavy; all these labors had freighted it with excess weight. He could hardly hold it. All the information was encoded in bits that swarmed like electronic insects and the words flew off the page like birds. He sat staring at an advertisement for a red Blazer that he was convinced was the very truck that had brought him to Nashville.

When she came through the doorway back into the waiting room, days seemed to have passed. He'd laid the magazine aside and sat clutching her purse. Reaching it to her he pretended not to study her but he did all the same. Having learned nuance and shading he'd become adept as well at interpreting her body language. Her smile was a little bright, her movements a little mannered: she'd put on the restraints and maybe screwed them down a notch too tight.

Ready? she asked.

More than, he said, scanning the room one last time as if he'd mark it as a place to avoid, remember all these miscast faces should he ever encounter them in old movies on late-night TV.

They went out. The cars in the parking lot glared under the sun. He felt hollow and enormous inside.

She was reaching for the door handle of the Blazer when he stopped her with a hand on her arm.

Wait, he said.

Wait? For what?

He was silent a time. Tell me something, he finally said.

I guess there's not much to tell.

Was it bad?

She had her lower lip caught between her teeth. About as bad as it gets, she said.

He thought for a moment her eyes looked frightened then he saw that more than fear they showed confusion. She looked stunned, as if life had blindsided her so hard it left her knees weak and the taste of blood in her mouth. He wanted to cure her, save her, jerk her back from the edge as she'd tried to do for him.

But all he could say was, Do you want me to drive?

I'm fine; she said. I can always drive. I like to drive.

Behind the wheel she searched her purse for the keys. I'm starved, she said. Are you hungry?

Yes, he lied.

Where do you want to eat?

She had the keys, the Blazer caught on the first crank, then sat idling. She studied him intently.

I don't care, he said.

You must care.

I don't care, it's nothing, it's just food. Hell, it's just food. He knew she thought that a barbaric notion but that was just the way he felt.

Where was that little Italian place we went to? You had the veal, they had these great salads there. Terrific salads. What was the name of that place?

I don't know.

You must know. The salads had the little cherry tomatoes?

Goddamn it, he said, suddenly angry. They all have the little cherry tomatoes.

She knew him, she wasn't fooled, she didn't take offense. She smiled. I can find it, she said. We'll just drive around; I'll know it when I see it.

I still don't see what it matters.

It matters to me, she said. It was the first time we ever went out to eat. You know, in a nice place. You bought me a bottle of wine you couldn't afford.

As she drove back into the street, she kept looking at the buildings, cutting down narrow crooked alleys, taking sidestreets that seemed to go nowhere you'd want to be—as if the place where they had the cherry tomatoes would materialize before her, between the tacky country music souvenir stores with their ceramic Roy Acuffs and price-tagged Minnie Pearl hats and the interminable pawnshops in whose dust-moted windows guitars hung by their necks like arcane beasts taken as trophies.

The day was waning, the light stingy and oblique. The sun flared behind the buildings and lent them a stark undimensioned quality. After a while they were hopelessly lost. The city looked strange even to her. They didn't speak. It began to seem to Worrel that they had sought and found their own level.

They trickled down sunless corridors and burst capillaries until they were in the city's dark heart. A city within the city where the blood slowed and thickened and clotted in viscous smears of alizarin crimson dried to burnt sienna around the edges. The tires of automobiles bore it away in fading hieroglyphic slashes. Neon flared, the air had grown heavy with the drone of flies. BAR BAR BAR, the neon repeated. 20 NAKED GIRLS 20. Brands of beer seemed to have the significance of the names of prophets on graven tablets.

Finally she pulled the Blazer to the curb and cut the switch and stared uncertainly about her. They had parked next to a vacant lot. Dead weeds tilted askew by the winds, the sun caught in broken wine bottles. The husk of an Eldorado sat so stripped and demolished it seemed to suffer obsolescence on an epidemic scale. A brown dog came out of the weeds and stood staring at them as if it had news of their coming. It was starved to the point of emaciation, just something that stood for a dog, a concentration that might possibly reconstitute a dog, a dog decocted in smoking electric chambers by a mad doctor who'd seen a dog once long ago and conjured one up with only the vagaries of memory as a recipe.

Adjacent to the vacant lot was a row of buildings constructed of umber-colored brick. Between two of them a narrow two-story house was wedged so tightly it seemed to have no sides of its own, simply its wooden frame front and tin-roofed porch hung parasitically between the brick walls, the rococo gingerbread trim of the porch paint-lorn and rotting. A swing dangled motionless from rusted chains. The front window had been stoned out and covered with a metal sign that read CLABBER GIRL BAKING POWDER. A cracked sidewalk led to the street through packed earth encysted with bottlecaps. Venus flytraps grew in car-tire planters serrated as if pinked by enormous shears.

The streets were full of drifters who seemed to be looking for something that they had lost. The homeless by choice and by circumstance held in common their disconnectedness and the selfsame look of threat in their faces, danger loosely contained, like lightning in a voltaic jar. They looked listless and numb as sleepwalkers, they moved as if the air itself offered hindrance to their passage. A man with shoulder-length blond hair stood on the high concrete steps of the parasite house and had occasional commerce with these streetfolk. He wore a quilted vest from whose cargo pockets he dealt glass vials of some iridescent liquid, smoky and volatile as nitroglycerin. The drifters paid him with bills that he folded onto a thick sheaf of like bills and he treated the money casually as if it were of no moment in itself but simply some happenstantial by-product of the transference of the vials. Occasionally he'd speak into a cellular telephone while watching Worrel with narrowed blue eyes.

Worrel looked away. He felt the uneasy knowledge that at any moment everything could alter. The air felt heavy and volatile, the way it does before a summer storm.

He turned to look at her. Her head was lain back against the upholstery. Her eyes were closed. Perhaps she slept.

He had no doubt that at some point he'd be confronted; it was a given, a law of nature. If she did not drive away, if he did not get under the wheel and take charge himself. Apparently he was not going to. Apparently he was going to sit here and look blankly back into the eyes that locked momentarily with his then slid away, until someone motioned for him to roll down the glass and he did and someone said, in a spray of spit, a reek of splo whiskey, in white-hot crackhead clarity, *What is it with you, motherf—er? And who the f— do you think you're looking at?*

Until the day waned and the light pooled and drained westward and the streetlamps came on and until the pace of the streets altered and moved in a loose disjointed rhythm and fierce chromatic colors that seared the eye and until the day's possibilities became probabilities and then dead certainties and they were hauled from the Blazer and humiliated, made to plead for their lives, urinating on themselves and soiling their clothing while the last vestiges of human dignity fled. Credit cards gone, money gone, pristine Blazer stripped and burned. Surely they'd slit his throat and rape her fair white body, slit her throat and rape his own fair white body, shoot them full of drugs that would send them at warp-speed past any conception of reality the mind was prepared to deal with, snuff them in a blinding flash of light that was the very essence of ecstasy. Their bodies would be found in garbage-strewn alleys, septic hypodermic needles dangling from their veins like fey ornaments, or their bodies would drift pale and bloated in the currents of the Cumberland River until they turned up stranded on silt bars like worn-out whores their pimps had no further use for.

Bring it on, Worrel told their sullen faces. Let me have it, you sons of bitches. You goddamned amateurs. There's nothing you can do to me half as bad as this.

He thought of the people waiting for Angie, beginning to wonder where she was. The kids at the grandmother's, the husband probably wondering why there was no supper on the table. He suddenly felt weary and omnipotent, like a troubled god: he knew something they did not yet know, something that was waiting for them like a messenger with a finger on the doorbell and a telegram in his hand. They did not know, any of them, that they were living in the end times of bliss. The last belle epoque. Not the kids at Granny's, whining where is Mama, not the husband bitching about the fallow table.

They did not know that they were going to have their world blown away, walls flung outward and doors ripped from shrieking hinges, trees uprooted and riding the sudden hot wind like autumn leaves, the air full of debris like grainy old eight-millimeter footage of Hiroshima. A cataclysm that would leave the floor of their world charred and smoking, inhospitable for some time to come.

Just for a moment, though, he was touched by a feeling he could not control, that he had not sought and instantly tried to shuttle to some dark cobwebbed corner of his mind. He wanted to forget it, at the very least deal with it later.

He had felt for an instant a bitter and unconsoling satisfaction that terrified him. Where she sat eyes closed with her fair head against the seat she seemed to be fading in and out of sight like someone with only a tenuous and uncertain reality, going at times so transparent he could see the leather upholstery through her body, her face in its temporary repose no more than a reflected image, a flicker of light off water.

At these moments, all that was real was the grip of her hand, the intent focused bones he could trace with the ball of his thumb. All that was holding her back were the fingers knotted into his own. She was sliding away, fare-thee-well-I'm-gone, vanishing through a fault in the weave of the world itself, but until this moment ended and whatever was supposed to happen next happened, he was holding on to her. Everybody was hanging on to her, all those grasping hands, but for the first time no other hold was stronger than his own.

November/December 1999

Anthropology

ANDREA LEE

(MY COUSIN SAYS: DIDN'T YOU THINK ABOUT WHAT THEY WOULD THINK, that they were going to read it, too? Of course Aunt Noah and her friends would read it, if it were about them, the more so because it was in a fancy Northern magazine. They can read. You weren't dealing with a tribe of Mbuti Pygmies.)

It is bad enough and quite a novelty to be scolded by my cousin, who lives in a dusty labyrinth of books in a West Village artists' building and rarely abandons his Olympian bibliotaph's detachment to chide anyone face to face. But his chance remark about pygmies also punishes me in an idiosyncratic way. It makes me remember a girl I knew at Harvard, a girl with the unlikely name of Undine Loving, whom everybody thought was my sister, the way everybody always assumes that young black women with light complexions and middle-class accents are close relations, as if there could be only one possible family of us. Anyway, this Undine—who was, I think, from Chicago and was prettier than I, with a pair of bright hazel eyes in a round, merry face that under cropped hair suggested a boy chorister, and an equally round, high-spirited backside in the tight Levi's she always wore—this Undine was a grad student, the brilliant protégé of a famous anthropologist, and she went off for a year to Zaire to live among Pygmies. They'll think she's a goddess, my boyfriend at the time annoyed me by remarking. After that I was haunted

28

by an irritating vision of Undine: tall, fair, and callipygian among reverent little brown men with peppercorn hair: an African-American Snow White. I lost sight of her after that, but I'm certain that, in the Ituri Forest, Undine was as dedicated a professional who ever took notes—abandoning toothpaste and toilet paper and subjecting herself to the menstrual hut, clear and scientific about her motives. Never even fractionally disturbing the equilibrium of the Lilliputian society she had chosen to observe. Not like me.

Well, of course, I never had a science, never had a plan. (That's obvious, says my cousin.) Two years ago, the summer before I moved to Rome, I went to spend three weeks with my Great-Aunt Noah, in Ball County, North Carolina. It was a freak impulse: a last-minute addressing of my attention to the country I was leaving behind. I hadn't been there since I was a child. I was prompted by a writer's vague instinct that there was a thread to be grasped, a strand, initially finer than spider silk, that might grow firmer and more solid in my hands, might lead to something that for the want of a better term I call *of interest*. I never pretended—

(You wanted to investigate your *roots*, says my cousin flatly.) He extracts a cigarette from a red pack bearing the picture of a clove and the words *Kretek Jakarta* and lights it with the kind of ironic flourish that I imagine he uses to intimidate his students at NYU. The way he says *roots*—that spurious '70s term—is so shaming. It brings back all the jokes we used to make in college about fat black American tourists in polyester dashikis trundling around Senegal in Alex Haley tour buses. Black intellectuals are notorious for their snobbish reverence toward Africa—as if crass human nature didn't exist there, too. And, from his West Village aerie, my cousin regards with the same aggressive piety the patch of coastal North Carolina that, before the diaspora north and west, was home to five generations of our family.

We are sitting at his dining table, which is about the length and width of the Gutenberg Bible, covered with clove ash and Melitta filters and the corrected proofs of his latest article. The article is about the white-washed "magic houses" of the Niger tribe and how the dense plaster arabesques that ornament their facades, gleaming like cake icing, are echoed faintly across the ocean in the designs of glorious, raucous Bahia. He is very good at what he does, my cousin. And he is the happiest of scholars, a minor celebrity in his field, paid royally by obscure foundations to rove from hemisphere to hemisphere, chasing artistic clues that point to a primeval tropical unity. Kerala, Cameroon, Honduras, the Phillipines. Ex-wife, children, a string of overeducated girlfriends left hovering wistfully in the dust behind him. He is always traveling, always alone, always vaguely belonging, always from somewhere else. Once he sent me a postcard from Cochin, signed, "Affectionately yours, The Wandering Negro."

Outside on Twelfth Street, sticky acid-green buds are bursting in a March heat wave. But no weather penetrates this studio, which is as close as a confessional and has two computer screens glowing balefully in the background. As he reprimands me I am observing with fascination that my cousin knows how to smoke like a European. I'm the one who lives in Rome, dammit, and yet it is he who smokes with one hand drifting almost incidentally up to his lips and then flowing bone-lessly down to the tabletop. And the half-sweet smell of those ridiculous clove cigarettes has permeated every corner of his apartment, giving it a vague atmosphere of stale festivity as if a wassail bowl were tucked away on his overstuffed bookshelves.

I'd be more impressed by all this exotic intellectualism if I didn't remember him as a boy during the single summer we both spent with Aunt Noah down in Ball County. A sallow bookworm with a towering forehead that now in middle age has achieved a mandarin distinction but was then cartoonish. A greedy solitary boy who stole the crumbling syrupy crust off fruit cobblers and who spent the summer afternoons shut in Aunt Noah's unused living room fussily drawing ironclad ships of the Civil War. The two of us loathed each other, and all that summer we never willingly exchanged a word, except insults as I tore by him with my gang of scabby-kneed girlfriends from down the road.

The memory gives me courage to defend myself. All I did, after all, was write a magazine article.

(An article about quilts and superstitions! A fuzzy folkloristic excursion. You made Aunt Noah and the others look cute and rustic and backward like a mixture of *Amos 'n' Andy* and *The Beverly Hillbillies*. Talk about quilts—you embroidered your information. And you mortally offended them—you called them black.)

But they *are* black.

(They don't choose to define themselves that way, and if anybody knows that, you do. We're talking about a group of old people who don't look black and who have always called themselves, if anything, colored. People whose blood has been mixed for so many generations that their lives have been constructed on the idea of being a separate caste. Like in Brazil, or other sensible countries where they accept nuances. Anyway, in ten years Aunt Noah and all those people you visited will be dead. What use was it to upset them by forcing your definitions on them? It's not your place to tell them who they are.)

I nearly burst out laughing at this last phrase, which I haven't heard for a long time. It's not your place to do this, to say that. My cousin used it primly and deliberately as an allusion to the entire structure of family and tradition he thinks I flouted. The phrase is a country heirloom, passed down from women like our grandmother and her sister Eleanora and already sounding archaic on the lips of our mothers in the suburbs of the North. It evokes those towns on the North Carolina–Virginia border, where our families still own land: villages marooned in the tobacco fields, where—as in every other rural community in the world— "place," identity, whether defined by pigmentation, occupation, economic rank, or family name, forms an invisible web that lends structure to daily life. In Ball County everyone knows everyone's place. There, the white-white people, the white-black people like Aunt Noah, and the black-black people all keep to their own niches, even though they may rub shoulders every day and even though they may share the same last names and the same ancestors. Aunt Eleanora became Aunt Noah— Noah as in *know*—because she is a phenomenal chronicler of place and can recite labyrinthine genealogies with the offhand fluency of a bard. When I was little I was convinced that she was called Noah because she had actually been aboard the Ark. And that she had stored in her head— perhaps on tiny pieces of parchment, like the papers in fortune cookies— the name of every child born since the waters receded from Ararat.

I was scared to death when I went down to Ball County after so many years. Am I thinking this or speaking aloud? Something of each. My cousin's face grows less bellicose as he listens. We actually like each other, my cousin and I. Our childhood hostility has been transmogrified into a bond that is nothing like the instinctive understanding that flows between brothers and sisters: It is more a deeply buried iron link of formal respect. When I was still living in Manhattan, we rarely saw each other, but we knew we were snobs about the same occult things. That's why I allow him to scold me. That's why I have to try to explain things to him.

I was scared, I continue. The usual last-minute terrors you get when you're about to return to a place where you've been perfectly happy. I was convinced it would be awful: ruin and disillusion, not a blade of grass the way I remembered it. I was afraid above all that I wouldn't be able to sleep. That I would end up lying awake in a suffocating Southern night contemplating a wreath of moths around a lightbulb and listening to an old woman thumping around in the next bedroom like a revenant in a coffin. I took medication with me. Strong stuff.

(Very practical, says my cousin.)

But the minute I got there I knew I wouldn't need it. You know I hate driving, so I took an overnight bus from the Port Authority. There isn't a plane or a train that goes near there. And when I got off the bus in front of Ball County Courthouse at dawn, the air was like milk. Five o'clock in the morning at the end of June and ninety percent humidity. White porches and green leaves swimming in mist. Aunt Noah picked me up and drove me down Route 14 in the Oldsmobile that Uncle Pershing left her. A car as long and slow as Cleopatra's barge. And I just lay back, waking up, and sank into the luxurious realization that you can go home again. From vertical New York, life had turned horizontal as a mattress: tobacco, corn, and soybeans spreading out on either side. And you know the first thing I remembered?

(What?)

What it was like to pee in the cornfields. You know I used to run races through the rows with those girls from down the road, and very often we used to stop and pee, not because we had to, but for the fun of it. I remembered the exact feeling of squatting down in that long corridor of leaves, our feet sinking into the sides of the furrow as we pulled down our Carter's cotton underpants, the heat from the ground blasting up onto our backsides as we pissed lakes into the black dirt.

The last time before my visit that I had seen Aunt Noah was two years earlier at my wedding in Massachusetts. There she elicited great curiosity from my husband's family, a studious clan of New England Brahmins who could not digest the fact that the interracial marriage to which they had agreed with such eager tolerance had allied them with a woman who appeared to be an elderly white Southern housewife. She looked the same as she had at the wedding and very much as she had when we were kids. Eighty-three years old, with smooth graying hair colored intermittently with Loving Care and styled in a precise 1950s helmet that suited her crisp pastel shirtwaist dresses and flat shoes. The same crumpled pale-skinned face of an aged belle, round and girlish from the front but the profile displaying a blunt leonine nose and calm predator's folds around the mouth—she was born, after all, in the magisterial solar month of July. The same blue-gray eyes, shrewd and humorous, sometimes alight with the intense love of a childless woman for her nieces and nephews but never sentimental, never suffering a fool. And, at odd moments, curiously remote.

Well, you look beautiful, she said when she saw me get off the bus.

And the whole focus of my life seemed to shift around. At the close of my twenties, as I was beginning to feel unbearably adult, crushed by the responsibilities of a recently acquired husband, apartment, and job, here I was offered the brief chance to become a young girl again. Better than being a pampered visiting daughter in my mother's house: a pampered visiting niece.

Driving to her house through the sunrise, she said: I hear you made peace with those in-laws of yours.

Things are okay now, I said, feeling my face get hot. She was referring to a newlywed spat that had overflowed into the two families and brought out all the animosity that had been so dutifully concealed at the wedding.

They used excuses to make trouble between you and your husband. He's a nice boy, so I don't lay blame on your marrying white. But you have to watch out for white folks. No matter how friendly they act at first, you can't trust them.

As always it seemed funny to hear this from the lips of someone who looked like Aunt Noah. Who got teased up North by kids on the street when she walked through black neighborhoods. Until she stopped, as she always did, and told them what was what.

The sky was paling into tropical heat, the mist chased away by the brazen song of a million cicadas. The smell of fertilizer and drying earth flowed through the car windows, and I could feel my pores starting to pump out sweat, as if I'd parachuted into equatorial Africa.

Aunt Noah, I said, just to tweak her, you wouldn't have liked it if I'd married a black-black man.

Oh Lord, honey, no, she said. She put on the blinker and turned off the highway into the gravel driveway. We passed beneath the fringes of the giant willow that shaded the brick ranch house Uncle Pershing built fifty years ago as a palace for his beautiful childless wife. The house designed to rival the houses of rich white people in Ball County. Built and air-conditioned with the rent of dark-skinned tenants who cultivated the acres of tobacco that have belonged to Noah and Pershing's families for two hundred years. They were cousins, Noah and Pershing, and they had married both for love and because marrying cousins was what one did among their people at that time. A nigger is just as bad as white trash, she said, turning off the engine. But honey, there were still plenty of boys you could have chosen from our own kind.

(You stayed two weeks, my cousin says, jealously.)

I was researching folkways, I tell him, keeping a straight face. I was hoping to find a mother lode of West African animism, pithy backwoods expressions, seventeenth-century English thieves' cant, poetic upwellings from the cyclic drama of agriculture, as played out on the Southeastern tidal plain. I wanted to be ravished by the dying tradition of the peasant South, like Jean Toomer.

(My cousin can't resist the reference. *Fecund Southern night, a pregnant Negress,* he declaims in the orotund voice of a Baptist preacher.)

What I really did during my visit was laze around and let Aunt Noah spoil me. Every morning scrambled eggs, grits, country ham, and hot biscuits with homemade peach preserves. She was up for hours before me, working in her garden. A fructiferous Eden of giant pea vines, prodigious tomato plants, squash blossoms like Victrola horns. She wore a green sun hat that made her look like an elderly infant, blissfully happy. Breakfast over and the house tidy, we would set out on visits where she displayed me in the only way she knew how, as an ornamental young sprig on the family tree. I fell into the gratifying role of the cherished newlywed niece, passed around admiringly like a mail-order collectible doll. Dressing in her frilly pink guest room, I put on charming outfits: long skirts, flowery blouses. I looked like a poster girl for *Southern Living*. Everyone we visited was enchanted. My husband, who telephoned me every night, began to seem very far away: a small white boy's voice sounding forlornly out of Manhattan.

The people we called on all seemed to be distant relatives of Aunt Noah's and mine, and more than once I nearly fell asleep in a stuffy front room listening to two old voices tracing the spiderweb of connections. I'd decided to write about quilts, and that gave us an excuse to go chasing around Ball County peering at old masterpieces dragged out of mothballs, and new ones stitched out of lurid polyester. Everybody had quilts, and everybody had some variation of the same four family names. Hopper, Osborne, Amiel, Mills. There was Gertie Osborne, a little freckled woman with the diction of a Victorian schoolmistress who contributed the "Rambling Reader" column to the *Ball County Chronicle*. The tobacco magnate and head deacon P. H. Mills, tall and rich and silent in his white linen suits. Mary Amiel, who lived up the road from Aunt Noah and wrote poetry privately printed in a volume entitled *The Flaming Depths*. Aunt Noah's brother-in-law Hopper Mills, who rode a decrepit Vespa over to check up on her every day at dawn.

I practiced pistol-shooting in the woods and went to the tobacco auction and rode the rope-drawn ferry down at Crenshaw Crossing. And I attended the Mount Moriah Baptist Church, where years before I had passed Sunday mornings in starched dresses and cotton gloves. The big church stood unchanged under the pines: an air-conditioned Williamsburg copy in brick as vauntingly prosperous as Aunt Noah's ranch house.

After the service, they were all together outside the church, chatting in the pine shade: the fabled White Negroes of Ball County. An enterprising *Ebony* magazine journalist had described them that way once, back in 1955. They were a group who defied conventional logic: Southern landowners of African descent who had pale skins and generations of free ancestors. Republicans to a man. People who'd fought to desegregate Greensboro and had marched on Washington yet still expected their poorer, blacker tenants to address them as Miss Nora or Mr. Fred. Most of them were over seventy: their sons and daughters had escaped years ago to Washington or Atlanta or Los Angeles or New York. To them I was the symbol of all those runaway children, and they loved me to pieces.

(But then you went and called them black. In print, which to people raised on the Bible and the *McGuffey Readers* is as definitive as a set of stone tablets. And you did it not in some academic journal but in a magazine that people buy on newsstands all over the country. To them it was the worst thing they could have read about themselves—)

I didn't—

(Except perhaps being called white.)

I didn't mean—

(It was the most presumptuous thing you could have done. They're old. They've survived, defining themselves in a certain way. We children and grandchildren can call ourselves Afro-American or African-American or black or whatever the week's fashion happens to be.)

You—

(And of course you knew this. We all grew up knowing it. You're a very smart woman, and the question is why you allowed yourself to be so careless. So breezy and destructive. Maybe to make sure you couldn't go back there.)

I say: That's enough. Stop it.

And my cousin, for a minute, does stop. I never noticed before how much he looks like Uncle Pershing. The same mountainous brow and reprobative eyes of a biblical patriarch that look out of framed photographs in Aunt Noah's living room. A memory reawakens of being similarly thundered at, in the course of that childhood summer, when I lied about borrowing Uncle Pershing's pocketknife.

We sit staring at each other across this little cluttered table in Greenwich Village. I am letting him tell me off as I would never allow my brother or my husband—especially my husband. But the buried link between my cousin and me makes the fact that I actually sit and take it inevitable. As I do, it occurs to me that fifty years ago, in the moribund world we are arguing about, it would have been an obvious choice for the two of us to get married. As Ball County cousins always did. And how far we have flown from it all, as if we were genuine emigrants, energetically forgetful of some small, dire Old World country plagued by dictators, drought, locusts, and pogroms. Years ago yet another of our cousins, a dentist in Atlanta, was approached by Aunt Noah about moving his family back to Ball County and taking over her house and land. I remember him grimacing with incredulity about it as we sat over drinks once in an airport bar. Why did the family select him for this honor? he asked, with a strained laugh. The last place anyone would ever want to be, he said.

I don't know what else to do but stumble on with my story.

Aunt Noah was having a good time showing me off. On one of the last days of my visit, she drove me clear across the county to the house where she grew up. I'd never been there, though I knew that was where it had all begun. It was on this land, in the 1740s, before North Carolina statutes about slavery and mixing of races had grown hard and fast, that a Scotch-Irish settler—a debtor or petty thief deported to the pitch-pine wilderness of the penal colony—allowed his handsome half-African, half-Indian bond servant to marry his only daughter. The handsomeness of the bond servant is part of the tradition, as is the pregnancy of the daughter. Their descendants took the land and joined the group of farmers and artisans who managed to carve out an independent station between the white planters and the black slaves until after the Civil War. Dissertations and books have been written about them. The name some scholars chose for them has a certain lyricism: Tidewater Free Negroes.

My daddy grew tobacco and was the best blacksmith in the county, Aunt Noah told me. There wasn't a man, black or white, who didn't respect him.

We had turned onto a dirt road that led through fields of tobacco and corn farmed by the two tenant families who divided the old house. It was a nineteenth-century farmhouse, white and green with a rambling porch and fretwork around the eaves. I saw with a pang that the paint was peeling and that the whole structure had achieved the undulating organic shape that signals imminent collapse.

I can't keep it up, and, honey, the tenants just do enough to keep the roof from falling in, she said. Good morning, Hattie, she called out, stopping the car and waving to a woman with cornrowed hair and skin the color of dark plums, who came out of the front door.

Good morning, Miss Nora, said Hattie.

Mama's flower garden was over there, Aunt Noah told me. You never saw such peonies. We had a fish pond and a greenhouse and an icehouse. Didn't have to buy anything except sugar and coffee and flour. And over there was a paddock for trotting horses. You know there was a fair every year where Papa and other of our kind of folks used to race their sulkies. Our own county fair.

She collected the rent, and we drove away. On the road, she stopped and showed me her mother's family graveyard, a mound covered with Amiel and Hopper tombstones rising in the middle of a tobacco field. She told me she paid a boy to clean off the brush.

You know it's hard to see the old place like that, she said. But I don't see any use in holding on to things just for the sake of holding on. You children are all off in the North, marrying your niggers or your white trash—honey, I'm just fooling, you know how I talk—and pretty soon we ugly old folks are going to go. Then there will just be some bones out in the fields and some money in the bank.

That was the night that my husband called from New York with the news we had hoped for: his assignment in Europe was for Rome.

(You really pissed them off, you know, says my cousin, continuing where he left off. You were already in Italy when the article was published, and your mother never told you, but it was quite an item for the rest of the family. There was that neighbor of Aunt Noah's, Dan Mills, who was threatening to sue. They said he was ranting: *I'm not African-American like they printed there! I'm not black!*)

Well, God knows I'm sorry about it now. But really—what could I have called them? The quaint colored folk of the Carolina lowlands? Mulattos and octoroons, like something out of *Mandingo?*

(You could have thought more about it, he says, his voice softening. You could have considered things before plunging into the quilts and the superstitions.)

You know, I tell him, I did talk to Aunt Noah just after the article came out. She said: Oh, honey, some of the folks around here got worked up about what you wrote, but they calmed right down when the TV truck came around and put them on the evening news.

My cousin drums his fingers thoughtfully on the table as I look on with a certain muted glee. I can tell that he isn't familiar with this twist in the story.

(Well—he says.) Rising to brew us another pot of coffee. Public scourging finished; case closed. By degrees he changes the subject to a much-discussed new book on W. E. B. Du Bois in Germany. Have I read about that sojourn in the early 1930s? Du Bois's weirdly prescient musings on American segregation and the National Socialist racial laws?

We talk about this and about his ex-wife and his upcoming trip to Celebes and the recent flood of Nigerian Kok statues on the London art market. Then, irresistibly, we turn again to Ball County. I surprise my cousin by telling him that if I can get back to the States this fall, I may go down there for Thanksgiving. With my husband. Aunt Noah invited us. That's when they kill the pigs, and I want to taste some of that fall barbeque. Why don't you come too? I say.

(Me? I'm not a barbeque fan, he says. Having the grace to flush slightly on the ears. Aren't you afraid that they're going to burn a cross in front of your window? he adds with a smile.)

I'll never write about that place again, I say. Just one thing, though—

(What?)

What would you have called them?

He takes his time lighting up another Kretek Jakarta. His eyes, through the foreign smoke, grow as remote as Aunt Noah's, receding in the distance like a highway in a rearview mirror. And I have a moment of false nostalgia. A quick glimpse of an image that never was: a boy racing me down a long corridor of July corn, his big flat feet churning up the dirt where we'd peed to mark our territory like two young dogs, his skinny figure tearing along ahead of me, both of us breaking our necks to get to the vanishing point where the green rows come together and geometry begins. Gone.

His cigarette lit, my cousin shakes his head and gives a short, exasperated laugh. (In the end, it doesn't make a damn bit of difference, does it? he says.)

March/April 2001

Memorial Day

MARK RICHARD

THE BOY MISTOOK DEATH FOR ONE OF THE LANDLADY'S SONS come to collect the rent. Death stood leaning against a tree scraping fresh manure off his shoe with a stick. The boy told death he would have to see his mother about the rent, and death said he was not there to collect the rent.

My brother is real sick, you should come back later, the boy said.

Death said he would wait.

They had sent the boy's brother home from the war in a box. When the boy and his mother opened the box, the brother was not inside. Inside the box was a lifesize statue of a woman holding a seashell to her ear. A messenger's pouch hung around the statue's neck. Hide this for me, the note in the pouch read. Love, Brother.

Then came the brother a week later. He was thin and yellow and sorry-looking, too weak to fend off his mother when she struck him, too weak to be held. The mother and the child carried him into the house and put him to bed.

The next morning, a black healer woman walked down the white shell driveway and straight into the house to squeeze the older brother's guts and smell his breath. She looked over her shoulder at the high weeds and the statue box and the bitter, brown gulf beyond and she said This place flood flood flood. Stink, too.

The mother bathed the brother with an alcohol sponge and the black healer woman twisted his spine to break his fever. The brother saw monkeys in the corners of the ceiling that wanted to get him, their mouths full of bloody chattering teeth. The black healer woman and the mother fought with the brother and told the child to Get out! when he came in to tell them that someone was waiting in the yard.

It was not unusual that the child could see death when the mother and the healing woman could not. Once at a church picnic the child had seen Bad Bob Cohen walk through the softball game and past the barbeque tables with a .22 rifle slung barrel down over his shoulder on a piece of twine. The child had watched Bad Bob walk right past where mothers and small children were splashing on the riverbank, had watched Bad Bob reach up and select two sturdy vines to climb up, and Bad Bob had turned and looked at the child, feeling him seeing him, and Bad Bob had nodded because they both knew that Bad Bob was invisible, and then later when the deputy and the road agents came to the picnic looking for Bob no one had seen him and no one would have believed the child if he had said he had, so he said nothing. Also, one Easter, the child had seen an angel.

Tell them they have to wait, the mother said. The rent's not due until tomorrow.

You have to wait, the child told death sitting in a tree. Death ate a fortune cookie from his pocket. His lips moved while he read the fortune to himself.

I'll come back tomorrow, death said finally, jumping down from the tree.

The black healer woman stood on the porch and said she would keep death from the doorstep as long as they had faith in Christ Jesus Our Savior and a little put-away money to cover her expenses coming down the long white broken shell driveway to their house. Death, that day, was wearing white pants and a white dinner jacket, a small, furled yellow cocktail umbrella buttonholed in his lapel. There were three good scratches across death's cheek from the beautiful woman who had not wanted to dance the last dance with death aboard a ship somewhere the previous evening. I don't get much time off from this job, death confided in the child under the tree. Work work work. I am much misunderstood. I actually have a wonderful sense of humor and I get along well with others. I'm a people person, death told the child. Death climbed the front porch steps to make faces behind the black healing woman. Death folded his eyelids back, stuck out his tongue, then pinched his cheeks forgetting about the scratches. Ow! death said. The black healer woman did not hear death nor see death but to her credit, she shivered when death blew on the back of her neck.

The child followed the black healer woman and his mother into the back bedroom where his brother stank. The black healer woman burned some sage cones and rubbed charcoal on the brother's temples and on the soles of his feet to draw out the fever.

How come you don't work? the black woman said to the child.

He's just a child, the mother said. The mother was stripping the brother's bed around them to boil the sheets on the stove.

When I young, I work, said the black healing woman.

I can make baskets from reeds, the child said.

What do people need reed baskets for when they give wooden ones away for free at the tomato fields, said the woman.

When the brother sat up and shouted Get the monkeys! the black healing woman said to him Your little brother here going to get them monkeys, your little brother going to get them monkeys and put them under baskets, under *wooden* baskets, she said to the child. Won't no *reed* basket hold no monkey, she said, and the brother lay back down.

Here's the rent money, the mother said. I don't want anybody to come in the house while we get your brother's fever down. The child said Yes ma'am. He took out the messenger pouch his brother had sent home in the box with the statue. It was not a purse. It had two long pockets and a waterproof pouch in case you had to swim a river. The child put the rent money in the waterproof pouch because it had two good snaps on it.

When the landlady's son came to collect the rent, death told the child to ask for a receipt.

I want a receipt, the child told the landlady's son.

You want to be evicted? the landlady's son said. You want us to throw your sorry asses out on the highway?

Don't worry, death said, he's afraid he might catch what your brother has. He won't go in the house. Tell him you want a proper receipt, tell him to bring a proper receipt for the rent.

Before the child could say all that the landlady's son said Give me the money I bet you got in that purse!

It's not a purse! the child said and yanked back on the strap.

All right, I'll be back tomorrow, said the landlady's son.

Death sat on the edge of the porch and lip-read a new fortune cookie. It looked like a word near the end hung him up.

That's a good one, death finally said, and he crunched the cookie in his big white teeth.

The brother's tongue grew fuzzy and his ravings were barking up the bad neighbor's dogs down the road all night.

The black healer woman came out on the porch.

You get me a shoebox of scorpions, what I need, she told the child. Try get me white ones. They stronger than the piddly brown ones. Go on and get me them.

They had scorpions in the woodpile, scorpions in the sandbox, scorpions in the clothes-pin pouch, scorpions in the cinderblocks where they burned trash, scorpions under the bathroom sink, scorpions in the icebox water tray, and scorpions in the baby crib. They didn't have a baby anymore, so it was all right.

I wouldn't fool with scorpions, death said. Some people are highly allergic. It's a neurotoxin thing in the stinger, death said. Death followed the child around trying to find a shoebox. The child could not find a shoebox. He had an old wooden-style cigar box. The lid was broken.

I wouldn't use that cigar box, it's got no lid, death said. The child said he could see that.

The child took the rent money out of his waterproof pouch and put it in his pocket. He cut a good stick and found three brown scorpions and one white scorpion by lunchtime. He put the scorpions in the messenger pouch and snapped it shut carefully so not to crush them, and shook the bag down every time before he opened it so he would not get stung. He had never been stung before and had heard it was ten times worse than a wasp, maybe fifty times.

It looks to me like your brother's got a neural infection that may be at the stem of his brain, death said. Of course, that's just a layman's guess.

The child was beginning to tire of death hanging around so much and talking talking talking. Death never seemed to shut up. Down where the bitter brown gulf water foamed dirty, death talked about time zones and the speed of light. Under the big yard tree, he talked about pine cones that broke open their seeds only when they burned. Under the brother's window looking in on the mother and the black healer woman, death said the brown statue of the girl holding the seashell to her ear was pedestrian terra cotta.

I bet it's valuable, the child said, and death said Yeah, maybe as a boat anchor.

The mother took back the rent money to fetch a real doctor. The landlady's son came by with a friend who smelled like vomit and the friend who smelled like vomit threw a dirt clod that hit the child in the mouth. The landlady's son kicked open the front gate. The child had forgotten he had taken the rent money out of the messenger pouch so he held on to its strap until the landlady's son broke it and said Here's your receipt, and he rabbit-punched the child twice in the ear. The landlady's son and the friend who smelled like vomit roared off in their car with the messenger pouch, taking with them, inside the pouch, the little yellow furled fruit cocktail umbrella, twelve white scorpions, and thirty, maybe even fifty, brown scorpions in the waterproof pocket. Death laughed in the treetops.

Death flocked down beside the child. He said maybe the scorpion cure would have worked and maybe it would have killed the brother outright. It would have depended on if the black healer woman could figure a good way to extract the neurotoxin and put the brother into moderate shock to break the fever. I guess it could work, maybe in a laboratory, death said, and the child, holding his ringing ear, said You just want an easy way to take my brother from me, and death said the child had completely misunderstood him. That was all right, because he was much misunderstood, death began again, and maligned, and the child left death in the front yard making speeches, and to the child's one good ear, it all sounded like wind in the stovepipe.

The doctor hardly thought it worth breaking a car axle to drive down and look at the brother, so he took the rent money for his trouble walking and said to bathe the brother in alcohol and put these sulphate powders in honey tea. The doctor gave the brother a shot and on his way out said the child needed some fish oil but did not give him any.

You find them scorpions for me? the black healer woman whispered after the doctor had gone.

I had a bunch that got away from me, the child told her. She said to get her a new bunch unless he wanted his brother to die. Tonight, she said. The black healing woman had no faith in the shot or the sulphate or doctor. She said she had seen him swing little newborns by their heels against tree trunks back where the real white trash lived. Go get them scorpions and get them quick, she said.

Death sat on the levee pipe and watched the child weave a reed basket. Death said baskets done well like that could fetch maybe two, three dollars from tourists. Of course, the child would have to learn to weave the popular check-cross design, and not just the standard lanyard double-tuck.

This is for scorpions, the child said. The child said he noticed death had not come around the house when the doctor came, and death laughed and said he liked doctors, that you could make a career following doctors. No, death said he had just had an appointment that had taken a little longer than he had planned for, and he offered the child a fortune cookie.

No thanks, said the child, weaving his basket.

Death read his fortune. Sometimes these things are incomprehensible, he said, and he let the little white paper float away.

That night the brother broke the mother's jaw. Punched her right in her damn monkey teeth, red and chattering at him.

No one knows their time. The brother recuperated and returned to the war, and afterwards, operated a small, profitable import business until his death at age fifty-eight from smoke inhalation. He had been trying to retrieve an old three-legged dog from a warehouse fire.

The man who smelled like vomit died of emphysema at age seventy-two living on the benevolence of the state. The state ridded itself of Bad Bob Cohen at age forty-one with a lethal injection.

It is believed among the black healing woman's family, and among those to whom she administered, that she was commended by God, that God spared her from death entirely, that He lifted her directly into heaven, for one day she simply disappeared.

The mother died seven years after the older brother recuperated. Her jaw did not heal well and her weight dropped to slightly below normal for her height, diet, and hereditary dispensation. The mother's passing away at age forty-eight was generally ascribed to grief, from finding her youngest remaining son at the edge of the hot brown gulf. According to the deputy and to the coroner who drove the station wagon to fetch the body, it appeared that the bottom of the reed basket the child had been carrying had flung itself open somehow, as if whoever had made the basket had folded the reeds backwards, upside down into the spiraling center instead of outward to the edges, and the action and weight of several hundred scorpions inside the basket had broken through the bottom. The child had been stung too many times to count. The neurotoxin, to which the child was highly allergic, had caused his windpipe to close, and when they found him at the edge of the gulf, he had already turned blue, his protruding tongue black and flyspecked. It was as if the child had run down to the gulf while being stung to drink the bitter water and could not drink, could not force down what he thought he felt he could not swallow, and only death had seen him try, death saying to him Run to the water and drink, come on, run with me to the gulf and drink, and the child had taken death's outstretched hand because he was beginning to stumble, and death encouraged him Run with me! and the child ran with death and finally he was no more, for death had taken him.

As for the landlady's son, he is one of many who have long since been forgotten.

1997

Flight Patterns

CYNTHIA SHEARER

1958

MY FATHER STANDS IN THE DOORWAY. I'm next to my mother with my cheek pressed against her gray wool skirt. "Go, go, go," seems to be what they are saying, and they are angry. My mother is crying, so I cry also, afraid of things I don't even have the words to name yet.

He goes. The house seems to relax. Now we all sleep in one room, and my baby bed is beside the fireplace. We seem to eat crazily: cold cornflakes for lunch when there is no money and steak for supper when there is. I learn that it is terrible that I need new shoes. It makes my mother tired and tearful. Needing anything is bad, so I stop needing anything.

My red-haired sister Allie seems to be in charge of what I learn about the world. One day we steal eggs from a nest she has found across the tracks at an old black woman's house. Under her tutelage I learn who in town has new puppies or old dirty magazines in their tool sheds. Once on a summer morning she discovers our father's car parked at his mother's house, which is two blocks from ours. His mother will not speak to us, but she lets us in. He wakes up to find us staring down at him. We are wearing matching playsuits with giraffes on them.

"Don't you like our new clothes?" we say, but we cannot get him to say our clothes are pretty. It has something to do with our mother being the one who bought them. I am three by now, my sister is five.

I sit in a chair by the door while she sings him piano lesson songs and makes him laugh. He has a nickname for her, "Red." I feel safer being an observer than a participant.

Another day my sister takes me to a little room in our house that has always been padlocked. She has picked the lock with my mother's nail file. "Look," she says, opening a tall packing crate, strewing the floor with the bright confetti of shredded comics. She hoists out a brandy snifter as big as her head. It has a circle of roses etched around its rim. When she lets me hold it, I drop it. Its shards will remain there on the wood floor for several years.

This becomes our secret, that we burrow and tunnel through boxes stacked to the ceiling. There are golf clubs in a leather bag fuzzy with mildew, and a rotting brown leather bomber jacket. Light, airy water-colors of the villages of Bermuda, fringed with oleander and hibiscus. Uncountable long-stemmed cocktail glasses, which we break having imaginary tea parties. We're more accustomed to the cheap thick crockery from the local grocery store.

We pass the summer ruthless in the wreckage of our mother's former life. We break the tortilla holder shaped like a floppy sombrero. More booty: a box of evening dresses, tulle-festooned, satiny-slippery. We fight over a green paisley one studded with green brilliants. I settle for the strapless pink and blue one with the rustling skirts. Damask napkins down my front: instant bosoms. Black lace mantilla over my head: Bat Masterson's girlfriend.

We venture outside in our regalia, carrying champagne glasses for effect. The kids from the housing project in what used to be our grand-father's peach orchard are not amused. "That ain't yours," one little boy says. "And it is a sin to drank."

We know that we are poor, and that they are poor, but we live in a big white house, and they live in cramped little dark ones. We know that we are smarter than they are.

Our secret seems to be out. My brother investigates the room. By sundown he has used three sterling silver platters for BB gun targets and 78 rpm records for flying saucers.

"These are mine," my brother says, pulling out two heavy wooden propellers. "They were on Daddy's airplane. I remember them. They were on my wall in Bermuda." He drives the propellers into the soft earth, like a conquistador staking claim. It seems to me that he has a bigger claim on the earth than I do, partly because he can remember more of the time that is prehistory, when our mother and father were capable of talking to each other.

Our mother, when she finally notices, simply makes us throw everything back into the room and tells us to stay out of it. Of course, we don't. A teak and bamboo teacart makes a terrific entry in a soapbox derby, and a burgundy damask and lace tablecloth is just the thing for a stray mongrel to have her puppies on.

Some months later, my brother calls me to come listen to a record he is playing on the record player my father left behind. I hear music playing, and what I remember to be my father's voice talking.

"Daddy's talking about being shot down in the war," my brother explains and I look into his face and wonder why he has bothered to notice me.

There is a big red book in our living room, with black and white photos of soldiers in it. Once my brother thumbs through it and shows me our father, sitting on the front row of officers, his legs crossed easily, squinting into the sun. For a long time, I am confused. I think that World War II is still going on, that my father is there, and they play a lot of saxophones in the background there.

1963

Sometimes my father comes to take us to a town nearby to eat at a restaurant called The Purple Duck. I love these times because I can sit in the backseat of his Rambler station wagon, smelling his old fishing things in the back, hearing the conversation of my older siblings pass over my head. Their presence deflects his attention from me, and I feel safe watching them.

One early fall afternoon I come flying out of my third-grade classroom at 3:10, and I see the Rambler. I run up with my sister, and she explains that she has a piano lesson for the next hour. His smile fades, but he says he will take me fishing. He takes me to his brother's pond, out in his little brown wooden boat.

He doesn't give me a fishing pole to hold. When I speak, he hushes me. I sit facing him, with hands in the lap of the green party dress bought a few years earlier to go with my sister's red hair. I am worried that he is angry at me for wearing the dress. I study the whorls in the varnished wood of the boat seat between us. It begins to get dark, and my back begins to hurt.

On the way home, he stops at an old well. "Bet you've never had well water before," he says in a mild rebuke of my mother. He draws up an old metal bucket and reaches behind the well and takes a dinged-up metal dipper and hands it full of cold water to me. While I am drinking it, he says in his clowning-around voice, "You'll never drink water this good anywhere else. I'm tellin' you like a friend. I used to haul so many buckets of water for my mama when I was your age, I felt like Paul Bunyan's ox." He studies my face for a reaction. "I've had water from all over the world, but it was never as good as this."

When I'm getting out of the car at our house, he hands me the string of small, slimy fish he caught. "Give these to your mother," he says, and closes the door and drives away.

This excites me. A string of fish is a joyous thing in the houses behind us, and I have seen the men come home and hand the fish to the women, who float them in red-rimmed white dishpans, then cut off their heads, slit open their bellies, and throw the little orange hot-dog-looking things to the cats. Then they cook the fish in big deep black skillets. I have even seen a big deep black skillet in the secret room of my mother's house.

My mother scowls when I hand her the fish. *"More* work for me to do," she says angrily, and throws the fish, still on the string, out into the backyard. She curses our house, our clothes, our life. "He could have been a *general.*"

1968

My mother decides to dose us with more truth as we get older: My father is not with us because he doesn't love us. He loves to drink and dance with lots of different women. He once told her that he had better things to do with his life than to raise children. He has sudden unexplained absences, and he hangs around Navajo Indian reservations when he disappears. He was given a choice of retiring from the Air Force at the age of forty-one or being court-martialed. That was the year we all crashlanded in my grandfather's house in Georgia, in the little town where he and my mother both grew up. In a drawer in her bedroom are manila envelopes of old Defense Department photos: my parents greeting Eisenhower, Churchill, and Anthony Eden as they step onto the tarmac at Kindley Field in Bermuda, my father accepting golf clubs upon retirement. My father is saluting and serious in these; my mother's face is seraphic as she beholds Eisenhower.

My brother and I press my mother for information. She tells us that she used to read the Bible when he was in the air. We ask her about my father's separation and retirement papers, with all the details such as the women he was seen with outside bars and hotels, and the time he left the tanks empty in the planes when he flubbed an alert as Deputy Base Commander at Egland Air Force Base in 1957.

"Sounds like a setup job to me," my brother comments.

He is twenty-one and a draft resistance counselor at the University of Georgia.

"The alert came through, and they couldn't get the planes off the ground," my mother shrugs, as if that is the only explanation needed.

My brother and I look at each other: the imaginary enemy was coming, and there was imaginary fuel in the planes: off with his head.

My brother is 4-F, having blown out an eye with a cherry bomb when he was seven, while my mother and father were attending the Army-Navy game. Now it is summer and he is home from college. He and the one other long-haired boy in town spend evenings on our front porch facing Main Street, discussing the act of war. My sister is in Savannah with my father for the summer. She is the only one who sees him.

One night as we sit talking on the porch a young man with short hair runs shirtless, shoeless, and shrieking down Main Street and into the woods. We begin to hear screen doors slamming up and down the street—the men coming out from their suppers and TVs to go see who is screaming in the woods—so my brother goes, too. We can hear voices, calls and shouts, in the woods for a while. Then my brother comes back.

"It was Mickey Vance," he says. "He got drunk at the Two Spot and thought he was back in Vietnam."

"These people," my mother says with a snarl, and takes a long drag off her cigarette. "They don't know what a real war is. World War II. Now there was a *real war.* This war is a moral atrocity." She retires to her bedroom, with stacks of the *Atlanta Journal* and paperback Faulkner novels heaped in the place where most women would have installed a new man.

By the end of the summer my sister has returned, wearing long sleeves and pants, even in the swampy south Georgia heat. Her first night back, she and my mother sit in the kitchen crying and talking long after I have gone to bed. The next morning my mother explains to me privately that my sister's legs and back and arms are covered with old brown bruises. She had been out in an elegant Savannah restaurant with my father, who became drunk and combative with the waiters. She became afraid of him. She called a policeman to drive her to his girlfriend's house. He found her there and beat her. When he sobered up, he bought her a new wardrobe and took her and the girlfriend to Hilton Head, to let the bruises heal.

"Don't talk about it," my mother tells me. "We are not going to talk about it again."

My sister goes to a Methodist revival that fall, the kind where for one week out of the year everyone is fixated on the idea of being saved from something terrible. She goes down the rabbit hole of religion, never to resurface in quite the same incarnation that we knew her.

One day as I am leaving school, I see my father's new silver Chrysler parked in front of the school. He is waiting outside for us. My sister runs to meet him. I hang back by the holly bush that grows beside the book room. What will it be this time? I can see my sister chatting with him, animated. I step between two girls I hardly know, and I walk right past his car, pretending to be so interested in what the girls are saying that I have no time to notice that he's there. And so he is out of my life for a few more years.

1977

Now I'm twenty-one. I live alone in a little rented house on the edge of a cotton mill district, with the scrawls of previous tenants' children still on the bare pine walls, and the apparently stolen tombstone of one James T. Hughes, late of the Spanish-American War, as the front stoop.

My father has cruised into my college town with his new Winnebago, and his old silver Chrysler for me. It is his one rite of fatherhood to give each of us a used car when we become seniors in college. It's my turn now. I have come to identify him with Nixonian politics, the military industrial complex, male chauvinism, and all the other bugaboos of the decade. I have seen him perhaps three times in the previous ten years, and always within the safety of my brother's presence. But now my brother is a newspaperman in Athens, Georgia.

He and his wife have invited me out to dinner. It's as nice a restaurant as can be had in that town, with a lengthy wine list. His wife waits for him to tell the waiter what we will all have for dinner. I order a cheeseburger, so I can offend him twice over by ordering something inelegant, and ordering it myself. I am waiting for him to give me the line that he always gave my sister, that real ladies always wait to have men order for them. If he does, I will walk out.

My father makes a big issue out of ordering the most expensive wine on the list. I make a big issue out of not drinking any. I keep a closer eye on his highball glass than the waiter does. I know the precise number of blocks to the little mill house. I know the precise number of blocks to my boyfriend's apartment. I know the drill that seems to have been dormant in me for a long time. I just don't know precisely where the boundary is that my father has to cross before I will walk free of him forever. I even know the precise objects in my house I would crack his head open with if he ever so much as lifts a hand to hurt me. It is a fantasy I have had ever since my sister's bad summer with him. But for the moment in the restaurant, I'm navigating under a different plan: always know my precise position: where the available exits are in relation to how drunk he is getting. Keep money and keys in pocket, not purse. Like any good guerrilla, I know how to watch and wait.

He drinks prodigious amounts, but he doesn't seem to get drunk. He drives me home and we say good-bye. I assume that it will be for quite some more years, and that the next I hear from him will be through his elegantly scripted postcards from places like Tempe or Gallup.

He shows up at my door the next morning, toolbox in hand. "I have work to do here," he says and proceeds to nail shelves around. Bizarre places: thereafter I will think of him when I crash my head after brushing my teeth. He makes a pretty lamp out of a dime-store basket, hangs it over my garage sale table, and puts a dimmer switch on it. My mother's anger is also in me; that he would think a dimmer switch to dine by is a necessity of life, when most nights I come home alone to wash the waitress smell of grease and nicotine off me so I can study.

He bumbles around my house, recognizes my refrigerator as one that used to belong to my mother's mother, and hails it like a long-lost friend. I notice that he is not drinking. He quotes poetry to impress me, now that I am an English major. He used to be an English major, at West Point, he says, and this throws me. Nobody ever told me that.

I tell him about finding some old textbooks of his in my mother's house, with foldout maps of Civil War battle plans. He quotes poetry that I don't know. He has to identify it for me. "Ever read Wilfred Owen?" he asks. "Sigfried Sassoon?" I shake my head. He tinkers with the lock on the refrigerator, while I hold the handle he's removed. "That's okay," he says. "They also serve who only stand and wait." He glances back at me to see if I know what I'm hearing, and I don't. It's final exam week at the university, and I am cutting class as we stand there.

"Uh, Dryden," I say.

"Nope," he says. "Don't you do your homework?"

That night I pick up a box of greasy fried chicken, and we shove my books and papers aside to eat together, dirt-smudged and tired. I feel good, I feel easy with him. I feel like I am meeting myself coming and going. He grew up in the same schoolyard that I did, played house in the same crooked oak roots. "Garthel Vickers and I used to raid your mother's acorn piles and shoot them in our slingshots." We both learned to swim in the Alapaha River by diving off the same cypress stump. We bicycled over the same sidewalks, bought penny candy in the same grocery store. We both tried to breathe the same air as my mother as long as we could, and then we left.

By the second nightfall, I have cut another day of exams to accompany my father to the hardware store while he indulges in an orgy of shopping for me. Jumper cables, gas can, pliers, hammer, fire extinguisher, deadbolts, window locks, flyswatter, hibachi. Everything he seems to be appalled that I don't possess. His wife joins us, bearing a Porterhouse steak. He goes down the block to buy scotch. She produces linen napkins, silver, and crystal that travel battened down in the Winnebago with them from Nova Scotia to Vancouver. "He won't eat with paper napkins," she says in her martyr's whisper. "He gets very angry with me if. . . ."

"He ate greasy chicken last night off paper towels," I answer, slapping my cheap forks onto the table.

She looks puzzled and betrayed. "He just drinks too much and I don't think I can go on—"

"That's why my mother threw in the towel," I say. "He broke her nose twice."

"The sun is now retreating over the yardarm," he grins from the doorway. He begins to grill the steak, making a great effort to show me the correct way to do it, out of some need to impart something useful to me. "Just look at this woman," he says, pointing to her. "Doesn't she look just like one of those fine carvings on the prow of a Swedish ship? This is no ordinary woman you're looking at. This is my mate." He pulls her up to dance around the room to a Stevie Wonder record he has fished out of his Winnebago.

I watch him drink his way into the late hours, though I have another final exam the next day. His speech becomes grandiloquent. He tells me fantastic stories: how he delivered a baby in a taxicab on the New Jersey turnpike.

But you vanished when I was being born, I think.

But I have become a connoisseur of fine lies and a sucker for fantastic stories and grandiloquence, so I listen amiably, sifting out who he is by seeing what it is important for him to lie about. I have relaxed, I no longer keep my eye on his glass or the door. "Tell me about when you were shot down over New Guinea," I say, companionably.

"Ancient history," he says, waving his hand, deflecting the thought.

Soon they depart in the Winnebago, out of my life again. I am tired. I have had little sleep in three days. I go back to my professors whose classes I have been AWOL from and explain that my father, an alcoholic, had showed up unexpectedly, and that I had chosen to spend the time with him. They let me make up my exams.

I got a postcard from my father some months later in handwriting so stark, lean, and elegant that it makes me ache to know the person who produced it: "The sight of thirteen Winnebagoes belly up in an arroyo can give one a healthy appreciation of the value of the left turn signal. —Dad." On the front: the Hotel del Coronado, resplendent in sunshine, clouds, and airbrushed stucco.

1985

I am at this stage of divorce: I need a supervisor in my life, telling me that it's time to eat or sleep, and that I am going to survive. My lawyer's secretary has watched me ink over line item after line item on my divorce papers, the way someone might watch a fox gnaw off its leg to get out of a trap.

"Do you drink?" she asks.

"Not really," I joke. "But I usually catch on real fast."

"Well, come with me and Susie tonight. I know a guy you'd like a lot. He's divorced, too."

But I'm avoiding men. They might sense how like a recently sprung ex-con I am: suspiciously pale and gaping and blinking in the sudden light of their presence: *gee, when did they take the tail fins off the Cadillacs?*

I go to a little café around the corner where the men have learned that I will drink my two margaritas in solitude. I sit there wearing my first bikini tan in six years, the junkyard dog who is quieted by the proximity of the human species. But no real contact, please.

Then I go home.

I sit there in my first divorced dusk.

I remember that it was dusk that did me in in the first place, made me marry so I would have a man to cook for at dusk.

I sit like I'm washed up on an empty island somewhere, waiting for the Lilliputians to arrive.

I call my mother. She can't understand why I would leave a man who is neither a drunk nor violent, so she tells me about her new dahlias. I call up my brother, working late at his newspaper. "Shit, shit," he repeats like a mantra. I call my sister and ask her to tell me about Jonah and the whale, like, what exactly did Jonah *do* with himself once he got out of that belly.

"He praised God," she says, without missing a beat.

My own personal guess is that he found a small tight cave and stayed there curled into the fetal position for a while.

After several calls around the country, I find my father. He is at something called the Trophy Bass Lodge in Georgetown, Florida, where he goes when he and his wife have had enough of each other's company for a while. I can hear a jukebox in the background, a heavy honky-tonk beat, and the rich human complaint of the saxophones. I want to *be there,* with all the old men and their fish bait.

My father's voice is all scotch-warm and wise through the eight-hundred-some-odd miles of telephone cable.

"In a divorce," he says, "the potential for holocaust is real. But who you are has taken you this far, and who you are will take you any place you want to go. Just cultivate a sense of ironic detachment."

He squires his sentences around like Gene Kelly dances with women: a masterful turn here, a droll pause there, an incremental repetition of the fun parts. "Hate is a form of mental laziness," he says, and I know that he is referring to my mother, who has nursed her wrath along with her dahlias for years. "It means you can't grasp the big picture." He lets that sink in. "There is a young woman here that I watch," he continues. "She gets out in the middle of Lake George in the biggest goddamn boat around. And she is the mistress of her own vessel. The rest of us old geezers just get out of the way. You got to be like that babe in the Bayliner boat. You can't pay too much attention to that skinny cat playing that sad violin offstage—it'll mess up your sense of comic timing. You got to be like that babe in the Bayliner boat. Ironic detachment."

We agree to meet for a visit at Warner Robbins Air Force Base in Georgia, on his way to a West Point class reunion. He blows into the place in a slightly smaller Winnebago, his old one having been declared too large to be legal. He and his wife meet me outside the gates, to get me in. The sentry does not salute him; my father chews him out, indicating the colonel's star on his windshield. The kid knows the drill and apologizes profusely.

My father is ready to hit the bar at the Officer's Club as soon as he has checked us into to the VIP suite. "He's not well," his wife whispers to me as we both stand at the same bathroom mirror applying makeup, dressing for dinner. "We talked about divorce all the way up from Winter Park. He just drinks entirely too much and I don't think that I can go on—"

Shit, shit. I tune her out with my brother's mantra. I am nervous. It has been many, many years since I have slept under the same roof as my father. I notice where all the exits are. I remember that my brother always parks his car head out when he visits my father, ever since the time in 1973 when he showed my father a joint rolled in flag paper and had to make a fast retreat. Not because of the grass, but for desecrating the flag. I put my car keys and my money in my skirt pocket, and we head for the bar.

I explain to my father the problems of my job, of milking the federal government for strategic studies money when you are a thousand miles from Washington.

"All you need are the ideas," he points to his temple. "Nobody has a monopoly on the truth." He has had three scotches to my one margarita, and his words are attaining that drunken cadence that mesmerizes me on the phone. I drink faster, to catch up to where he is.

"Ideas," he says tapping his temple. "Go do your homework. Wars don't start in Washington. Wars begin out in radioland. Do you know that? Do you know what I'm talking about? You know why I went to West Point in 1935? Because I was tired of giving my mama my shoeshine money to feed me with." His wife's face softens, and I wish in that moment to know all the things about him that she knows.

"You don't need Jaynes, just get a map. Look for the places where the people are fed up with being unfed. Look for where the malcontents mass along the borders. Look at that dude out in that jungle, Homo sapiens *human being,* and he suddenly starts digging *Dallas* on his neighbor's satellite dish, and his baby needs a brand new pair of shoes. War. Two, five, ten years down the road,"

"But I work for people who just want to make speeches about rivet patterns on Japanese Zeroes," I reply.

"A Zero is a worthy thing to study," he says. I sense that he is tired of the discussion. He waylays a group of pilots coming into the bar. "Lissen," he says to them, at that stage of drink where you are open to whatever might flower around you. "I have a female member of the species Homo sapiens *human being* here who is bugging the goddamn hell out of me with questions about aircraft." His voice has turned into a parody of Shirley Temple. "Do you gentlemen know anything about such things, and would you care to field questions for a while?"

It turns out that they are Thunderbirds. My father has to find out all their names, ranks, and hometowns. Only one of them is drinking, the one from Red Cloud, Nebraska, who almost bought it this afternoon when a bird flew in front of his intake vent right before he chandelled.

"Lissen," my father coaches him, leaning forward, "lissen, Lieutenant Thackeray Phillips of Red Cloud, Nebraska." My father points to the band. "You hear those funny noises in the air? Those little ruffles and flourishes and beating of tom-toms? That stuff is called music. Take a *lissen* to that stuff, man."

The lieutenant leans backwards, enduring his second indignity of the day—being told how to act by an old geezer. His politeness is standard Air Force issue.

My father is in his element, eloquent in the altitudes of alcohol. "And it is quite imperative that when you hear that stuff in the air that you get up and dance, shake a leg, trip the light fantastic. What are they teaching you in flight school? Get up and fly, man. There are females in the world languishing." He gets up to demonstrate, pretending to pat the fanny of a stout woman dancing with her back to us, escorted by a dignified old general-looking fellow.

My father's wife shoots me a look: *help* and I go dance with him. I am at that stage of drink where I can't tell which is the soft-petaled thing opening, the universe around me, or me. My father is portly, but graceful. We dance, pausing only to have new drinks. The band does a cover of Springsteen's "Pink Cadillac," and we find that it is magical, to dance to a saxophone joke about Adam and Eve. If nobody can touch us, it's because we've become the same person. I am him, young; he is me, old. We circle each other, smiling like *Hello, me. Long time no see.*

He can boogie like a college boy, or samba like a sailor, or float around as graceful as a glider, no feet, nothing to tie him down to earth. His wife sits patiently, looking exactly like something carved on the prow of a Swedish ship. The club is closing down; the waiters have all the chairs upside down on the tables. We have not only skipped dinner, we have closed the place.

My father and I sit down a minute, oblivious, admiring each other's funny freckly hands. "I have your hands," I say, and there is a very thin membrane of something tough inside me holding back a lifetime of tears waiting to spill on his calluses. We vow that if all else fails in my life, we will simply go into the fish bait business together in Key West.

"Look at this," he calls when we are walking back to our rooms. He jumps up on a three-foot-high retaining wall that scallops the sidewalk we're on. "Can you do this?" He walks it all the way back, agile as an alley cat. He is seventy and has had more scotch and sodas than I could count. I am thirty, have had three margaritas, and I want to curl up on the sidewalk and lay me down to sleep.

When he kisses me good-bye the next morning, I smell the fresh scotch. He's still cruising along holding altitude, coasting over the tops of the heads around him.

Later I describe it all to my mother, omitting my margaritas.

"He used to do that every weekend," my mother says. We are standing in her prize dahlia bed. "He broke my nose one time because I asked him for money to buy groceries."

I cut her off before she can get to the part where I am conceived in what essentially amounts to an act of rape, and where he disappears for three weeks when I am due to be born, and how she almost dies having me, and how he beats her up when I am two weeks old. I know it all already and keep it filed in the same place in my mind where he, in perpetuity, beats my sister Allie in an elegant pastel Savannah apartment, or burns my brother's hand with an alabaster cigarette lighter to teach him not to disturb the symmetry of the coffee table items.

"She was talking divorce, as usual," I say.

"I really feel for that woman," my mother surprises me. She's been doing a lot of that lately, now that I have joined the sacred sisterhood of the divorcées. She prunes off a dried dahlia. "I used to pray that he would die," she says. "I used to pray that his plane would crash."

I want a drink, I think. *The potential for holocaust is real.*

When I get back home my father mails me a photocopy of a letter, dated June 1942, that he wrote to a Santa Fe woman, reprinted in an Albuquerque newspaper. It described to her the last moments of her husband, his navigator, one Winston Eight Horses, late of the Navajo tribe and the Battle of the Coral Sea, after they were shot down by a Japanese Zero off the coast of New Guinea. He told her how much the man had loved her and named the precise latitude and longitude of the spot on the sea where the plane went under.

I want a drink when I have finished reading it. I have several. I sit in the wisteria and drink my margaritas and listen to Benny Goodman. Pretty soon I feel like I've got squatter's rights to the stars, and I can handle the massive dose of history that I have been given. He knew the drill. Know your latitude and longitude the moment you begin descent. Try to pry that member of the race that Custer conquered out of that fuselage, the one who was telling your white face where to fly.

1986

When I walk into my mother's hospital room, my brother takes one look at my face and thinks up a phony excuse to walk with me down the corridor. We wander without really knowing where we are, and I tell him that the doctor used the word "terminal," and in that moment I understand what it must be like to bayonet someone who's been trained not to flinch. I tell my brother everything the doctor has told me, everything from the futility of surgery to the availability of little old polyester ladies who have no better thing to do than come keep the death watch and plump the pillows. He takes a long, even breath. "We better get in there," he says, "Or she'll start getting paranoid."

We weave back through the sterile honeycomb of labs. "Look," he whispers, eyeing a shrunken old white lady asleep in a wheelchair, twisted in the fetal position. She is clutching a pink plastic baby doll. They have matching lipstick, fire-engine red, and matching wildly thatched hair. "Dada art," he whispers to me. I love him fiercely, proud to be breathing the same air that he breathes.

Back in my mother's room, he turns in a passably good performance of the man he was a few moments before. "Jesus, Mother," he teases, rummaging through a Whitman Sampler someone has brought to her. "You've hogged all the goddamn Brazil nuts."

A few days after Christmas when I am trying to answer my mother's mail, I find a lush, expensive Christmas card from my father. To her. "Wishing you a joyous and peaceful Nativity," the card reads. No note, just a signature. I study an illustration on the card, a blue and silver and green sketch of a Bayliner boat hauling a fresh cut tree across a frothy glittering lake. Maybe ten seconds elapse before the scream makes its way up out of me.

She can't hear me, though. She's already floating on Demerol. "Look at that," she says to me, indicating the wine-colored asters that are blossoming on the back of her hands. Her eyes say it all: *I am old, can you believe it?* The phone rings. She is oblivious, enchanted by the antiquity of her own hands.

It is my father. Ah, I think. Nice bit of closure here. He will talk to her. He will tell her he is sorry. She will tell him she is sorry. They will not die hating each other.

"There are certain documents I must have," he says, breathless at some automatic-pilot alcohol altitude where the air is thin. "You need to know the truth, and the truth will set you free."

She is sitting on the side of the bed, picking at the buttons of her nightgown, convinced that they are pills she is supposed to take.

"You have not always been told the truth by your mother," he says and I see her smiling beatifically at *Wheel of Fortune.*

"I have to go help Mother," I say. "Nobody has seen those papers in years. I'll look and call you back tomorrow." But he hasn't heard anything I've said because he hasn't stopped talking. He is still talking about the truth setting me free as I put the phone back in its cradle.

I try to persuade my mother to lie back down, and the phone rings again.

"This. Is. Your. Father. Speaking. You. Do not. Hang up. On. Your.

Father." He is saying, full of what registers in my mind as rage and hatred.

I slam the phone down. *Come on, come on, old man. Your moment with me has come.*

The phone rings again. It is his wife, ever sweet-voiced. "He asked me to see if I could get you on the line. There seems to be some problem with the line," she says.

"It's not the line," I say.

I write my father a letter that night, my kamikaze rage burning me up before I finish: *Last time I heard, phone conversations were intended to be dialogues, not monologues. If you want conversation with me now it will be sober, and you will do me the courtesy of listening when I tell you something. You never stuck around long enough to notice it, but I am the toughest and meanest of your offspring. I am the most like you. If you give my mother one moment more of grief during what is left of her life, one of us will live to tell about it, and it won't be you.*

Soon I go next door to my aunt's and ask her to come show me how to give a bath to someone who can no longer move a muscle. She is a nurse. She says, "I remember the first time I saw you. You were nineteen days old. You were a sorry-looking sight when you stepped off that plane. Your mother had a black eye from where he'd gone after her—"

"Why?" I ask.

"Some trouble they had in Bermuda. He didn't think that you were his baby."

I want a drink. I want altitude, solitude. Solid Alcoholtude.

In the last days my mother goes back in her mind. She welcomes Winston Churchill, she has tea with Queen Elizabeth. The pain intensifies, and she goes back to 1921 or so, calling for the old local doctor who took her tonsils out. *Go tell Dr. Moore,* she beseeches me, her face full of bewilderment at the war that is being fought inside her. *He will fix me.* She goes further back: *A, B, C. One, two, three.* She goes back to an infant's rosebud-mouthed whisper, and then she's gone.

My brother and I break the seal on a bourbon bottle before we ride out to the cemetery to show the funeral home man where to dig.

1988

I come to, in my hospital room, to the sound of my new husband's voice. He is cradling our newborn daughter in his hands, crooning to her, "What are we going to do? Your mother can't stay awake, and she walks like an old Chinaman." I know that I am smiling at him, but I don't know much else, except that I have recently acquired some horrific memories, and there is a thin, thin gauze of drug between me and immense pain.

I swim up out of the Demerol long enough to hear him singing to our daughter, easing her troubled passage into earth because Mommy is momentarily blotto. The nurse is holding her out to me. My first sight of her: tiny hands clasped like a mezzo-soprano in a mouse opera might, and it's like they are giving me my very own papoose to have, and from it are issuing whimpers of bewilderment at being born into the species Homo sapiens *human being,* the bright lights, the big loudspeaker. But she seems to know who I am and where to go for lunch.

My husband stands by to catch her if I am too woozy to hold her, and I push the blanket aside to inspect her fully.

She has my father's face.

It's like a fist of love slamming up through me, slowly through the Demerol. It's like the heel of God upon my neck, to give it to an infant I love with ferocity. It's like being inducted into some secret chapter of species Homo sapiens *human being.*

I uncurl the little fists. The thumbs are my husband's, a familiar arc in miniature. "Look," I say. "She has your hands." I am quite relieved by this.

My husband calls my brother and sister to tell them of the birth.

He does not call my father, because I don't want him to. In the first year of my daughter's life I don't want to see or talk to my father for reasons that don't have anything to do with me. I have this child, and she is too helpless to know where the exits are. Every time I look into her face, I see my father as an infant, too, and I feel like I am learning to love him from his own infancy. But I feel an obligation to my daughter to filter my father out of her life the way I stopped drinking coffee and alcohol.

I do not question why I must do these things, and my husband doesn't question it. I seem to be flying on instruments anyway. I can hear some other woman's baby cry in the supermarket, and the milk will rush into my breasts, staining my blouse. I cannot read newspapers; they will pipe wars and rumors of wars into my house. One night after several weeks of awakening every hour or so at night to nurse the baby, I dream I am the ragged mother coyote I saw once, milk-swollen, trotting oblivious alongside buzzing traffic, in transit either to her babies, or her next meal, or lost.

1990

My father's wife calls a few days before he dies. "Don't let him know I called you," she says. "But can you please call him? He has talked and worried about you all day. But don't tell him I suggested it. He gets so angry if—" she trails off.

My father has ripped out his IV tubes a week before and thrown his TV through his window. I dial the hospital number that she gives me, at the appointed time when she will be there to act surprised and hand the phone to him.

Who is this weak old man I'm talking to? He acts like we just saw each other days before. The truth is, we've each been locked into our respective aeries of outrage for so long we hardly remember what the original fracas was.

He tells me he understands why I haven't brought the baby to see him. "You've got a good thing going," he says, already sambaing with the angels at 200 cc's of morphine a pop. "I didn't want to spoil it for you," he says. "Man. Woman. Baby. Winter. Fire. There is probably nothing else, sweetheart. Nothing else but love."

He mentions the time I walked past him in the schoolyard. The tears are like acid in my eyes.

I keep waiting for something that feels like apology from him, for what he did to my sister. He seems to be fishing for what feels like an apology from me. He tells me how he used to park his car a few blocks down from the house to watch me ride my tricycle up and down the sidewalk.

I do not believe this. I am no longer a sucker for a good story.

"You used to stop and make imaginary phone calls in the crepe myrtle bush," he says.

The crepe myrtle bush.

There is no choice but to believe.

It is a terrible frightening thing, to feel the cold floes of old anger loosening, creaking.

Within days I'm sitting with my brother and sister in a cemetery in Savannah, and even though I am expecting the salutatory gunshots, they give me the confusion of fight or flight. I want to rise up and gore the enlistees with their own bayonets. When they fold the flag and give it to my brother's young son, as per final instructions of the deceased, I want to scream, *No, don't fill his peaceable little head with your dreams of aerial ascent.*

"The sun is now over the yardarm," his wife says, back at the motel where we are staying. She produces a silver flask of scotch. I keep trying to get my brother and sister to listen to a tape of Clifton Chenier doing "In the Mood." As if that will evoke our father's presence. They don't want to hear it.

So I hang back like a junkyard dog in my expensive dress and my high heels, sorry that my father was not around to take it all in. He would have loved the spectacle: the opportunity to chew out the soldier in the honor guard whose left shoe was not spit-and-polish perfect. He would have marveled at the nicest piece of Dada my brother and I have ever seen: a funeral wreath of red, white, and blue carnations, shaped like a B-17. From the old geezers at the Trophy Bass Lodge, Georgetown, Florida. I am sorry that he is not here now to have a drink with us after we have taken off our shoes.

—It wasn't a B-17, was it, I would tell him. It was a Flying Fortress.

—Oh, really?

—Well, your brother told me that your name is in this book called *Heroes of World War II*, and—

—*I made that up.*

—I figured. Never could locate it. So I looked up the Battle of the Coral Sea, matched your dates and coordinates with what I found, and figured that you were one of the scouts sent out looking for the Zeroes. You were within three miles out of Port Moresby at eighteen thousand feet when one came at you. He wrote in his bomb report later that he knocked out your tail and your left wing. All of the crew were alive when the plane pancaked, but he kept strafing you. You told a Melbourne newspaperman who interviewed you that every time he came back over, you would dive as deep as you could and think of all the women you had to get back to. When the Zero left, you swam to shore, alone. The natives passed you from tribe to tribe until you made it to base. It took two weeks. You weighed ninety-eight pounds and had dengue fever.

On the morning that your father got the telegram saying you were missing in action, your brother, a C-240 transport flyer on leave, just happened to read in the *Atlanta Constitution* that you had made it back. That was the first time he ever saw your father cry. The second time he saw your father cry was later when your baby brother, a tail-gunner on a B-25 was shot and killed by MP's outside a Negro nightclub in Montgomery, Alabama, for refusing arrest after going AWOL. He was eighteen. You called him Red, and he had enlisted when he was sixteen. When they found out his age, they had sent him home, but he just enlisted again in the next county.

You were given the Silver Star for gallantry in action. Red was given a quiet soldier's burial, with none of your other three brothers present. You all told your mother he'd been killed in combat, and she never knew the difference. You were all flying bombing missions or talking airplanes down out of the sky on radios or trying to fly food into the Pacific theater. You were a local luminary, the light of which blinded you and Mother both to the fact that the potential holocaust is real. Did you know that she used to read the Bible and pray while you were in the air?

—*How do you know all this?*

—I do my homework.

—*Then you ought to know that a B-17 and a Flying Fortress are the same animal. Not bad though, for a dame. It was more like ten thousand feet than eighteen. I musta lied.*

—Tell me about the time you threw the TV through the hospital window.

—*Ancient history. Lissen at that music. Mercy. I refuse to believe that a child of mine cannot learn to samba. Come here.*

And I'd come there. And I'd look at him and say *Hello, me. Long time no see.*

Summer 1992

Death in New Orleans, A Romance

BILLY COLLINS

Long into the night my pencil
hurried across the page,
a young messenger boy
doing his nervous little errands,
making lines,
making comparisons—
the world is like this, the moon like that,

the mind, I even wrote, is like a wire birdcage
hanging from a stand
with a wooden perch and a tiny mirror,
home of a single canary,
I went on,
always the same one, the same song every day,
then quiet under the floral hood of night.

Always the same blue and yellow feathers,
I continued,
blue for the past, yellow for the future,
I added for symbolic weight,
and on the day I die,
I wrote, curving toward the elegiac,

the wire door will swing open
and the bird will fly out the window
into the looping ironwork of the city,
circling up over the silent, latticed buildings
and into the clouds and stars,
I typed,

leaving my body behind,
slumped upon a café table,
my empty head down in a pool of wine,
the waiter and two customers
bending over me with obvious concern.

January/February 2000

Erskine Caldwell: The Journey from Tobacco Road

HAL CROWTHER

> Darling Jill felt the returning surge of savage excitement grip her. . . . She
> stood it as long as she could, and then she ran and fell at his feet, hugging
> his knees and kissing him all over. Will laid his hands on her head and
> stroked her hair. She stirred jerkily, rising to her knees and thrusting
> her body between his legs, and locked her arms around his waist. Her
> head was buried against him, and she hugged him with her arms and
> shoulders. It was only when she could find his hands that she lay still
> against him. One after the other she kissed his fingers, pushing them
> between her lips and into her mouth. But after that, she was still not
> satisfied.
>   ". . .What time is it?" he asked after a while.
>
> —GOD'S LITTLE ACRE

ERSKINE CALDWELL PUBLISHED THIS IN 1933, when most American readers were
too shocked to laugh. Will is neither husband nor lover to Darling Jill,
you understand—he's her brother-in-law, and across the room his wife
(her sister) sits calmly in a rocking chair during the entire performance.

The adoration of Will Thompson is a set piece no one but Caldwell
would have attempted. Will, a cotton mill worker, symbolizes the
working-class superman, like those giants with sledgehammers on Soviet
propaganda posters. He's about to be martyred heroically in an uprising

against the mill bosses. The sexual force field of such a colossal manhood is so powerful that no woman could deny her sister's need to enter it. On the previous page, Will has invoked his proletarian divine right to rape another sister-in-law, the exquisite Griselda, whose sexual aura is as irresistible as his own.

It's entertaining to imagine how Will Thompson might go over with contemporary critics, who replace class struggles with gender wars and purge the canon of testosterone titans. Postmodern criticism, which has congealed around a notion academics call "the frailty of the author" (the writer as a sort of helpless pointer on the Ouija board of literature), has no tools to deal with Erskine Caldwell.

He was a rogue wave, a one-man literary movement. No theory can account for him—or for the critical success that launched him. *God's Little Acre* was compared to the fiction of Twain, Faulkner, and Balzac. Caldwell was hailed as a genius by Malcolm Cowley, Lewis Mumford, and Jean-Paul Sartre and was championed by H. L. Mencken and Ezra Pound. As late as 1960 he was under serious consideration for the Nobel Prize. Saul Bellow, for one, believed that he should have had it. To Brooks Atkinson, czar of New York's drama critics, Caldwell was "a demonic genius—brutal, grimly comic, and clairvoyant." What Caldwell and his once-exalted reputation demonstrate most convincingly is the chronic frailty of the *critic*.

Caldwell died in 1987 at eighty-three, and a few months later Dartmouth College opened its collection of his papers to researchers. Several biographies have been written. Dan Miller's, from Knopf, is the first released by a major publisher. It's a book that deserves attention— not because Caldwell deserves resurrection but because there's no case study anywhere that sheds more light on the perverse way literary reputations are made and unmade in America. To understand how completely Erskine Caldwell has vanished from the literary firmament, all we need is Dan Miller's confession that it was not until he was twenty-seven that he first heard Caldwell's name.

That seems incredible to some of us a generation older, to whom Erskine Caldwell was a name as familiar as Joe Louis, Harry Truman, or Arthur Godfrey. When he hit his second peak in the early '50s, Caldwell had already sold a world-record fifty-five million books in hardcover and paperback editions (now seventy million plus). The paperbacks, with their sordid, suggestive cover art—leering rednecks touching the crotches of their overalls, swooning farm girls with huge breasts spilling out of ragged blouses—were a part of every private library. Often they were the most private part, slipped under mattresses and concealed under stacks of *Saturday Evening Posts* where the kids, it was hoped, couldn't find them (though we always did).

The scholar's gold mine that drew Miller and the others to Dartmouth turned out to be a fairly nasty old landfill. What Miller's research reveals about Caldwell is almost uniformly disturbing. The writer was cruel, hypocritical, conniving, greedy, self-absorbed to the point of obtuseness, a man of few friends who betrayed the few he had.

He was a possessive, manipulative, abusive husband to at least three of his four wives. He beat, terrified, and neglected his children. He became a sad and sloppy drunk. His lone moral asset, a gift from his father, was a well-developed social conscience. But this passion for the underdog, black or white, evolved into a lucrative industry for Caldwell and the source of some of the dreariest, most predictable fiction in all the bleeding-heart canon.

The key to Caldwell's net worth as an interpreter of our times probably lies in his repeated declaration that he was "a writer, not a reader." It happens that I've heard this strange boast from a number of writers. One, who need not be named here, has also been touted for the Nobel Prize.

A writer who boasts that he doesn't read is like a fish who boasts that he doesn't need water. It won't be long before we're holding our noses. Since Caldwell described himself as a nonreader, and since his fiction putrefied in a manner consistent with total intellectual isolation, we don't need to exhume his library card to prove that he was one of those poor fish. James Baldwin, a critic who wasn't taken in by Caldwell's reputation or his radical credentials, declared him dead as a writer in 1947, when Caldwell was forty-four. "Unless we hear from him again in accents more individual," Baldwin wrote, "we can leave his bones for that literary historian of another day."

Dan Miller makes the most of these old bones, acknowledging that the dogs have buried them in some places you'd hate to dig. By 1960 Caldwell was a bitter hack reduced to selling stories to slick T&A magazines like *Playboy, Cavalier, Dude, Swank,* and *Gent.*

Miller has dealt honestly with Caldwell's sorry character and the pitiful quality of most of his fiction. But he shies away from the great mystery of Caldwell's reputation. With a humility altogether fitting in a biographer so young, Miller declines to challenge the literary lions of the '30s who welcomed Erskine Caldwell to their pride. He generously decides that there must have been magic in the early novels that somehow vanished from all the rest.

I'm too old to be so humble. Though Caldwell published twenty novels and more than one hundred stories, his critical reputation rested largely on the merits of *Tobacco Road* (1932) and *God's Little Acre* (1933). Miller's book compels us to read or reread them. They're quick reads, especially *God's Little Acre.* And they will astonish you; if they impress you, then you and I operate on different aesthetic assumptions.

They're literary Frankensteins, of crude materials crudely stitched together. Jonathan Daniels of the Raleigh newspaper clan hailed *God's Little Acre* as "one of the finest studies of the Southern poor white which has ever come into our literature," which must be one of the most obtuse critical assessments ever rendered in print. It raises the possibility that Daniels, from a family with a notably low incidence of pellagra, had never encountered a Southern poor white face-to-face.

Dan Miller documents conclusively that Caldwell, born and raised in rural East Georgia, the son of a well-educated but often indigent Presbyterian minister, encountered any number of poor whites. That seems to indict him more hopelessly, because the characters in his novels are the same grotesque stereotypes immortalized on hillbilly postcards. They teach us as much about poor whites as the minstrel shows taught us about black people. And subsequent experience—the hookworm belt became his "beat" as a well-paid left-wing journalist—never seemed to deepen or sharpen Caldwell's perceptions.

Ignorant of the fact that lust is one of the first casualties of extreme hunger, he created starving subhuman characters and endowed them with rampaging superhuman libidos. Caldwell's sharecroppers sniff and rub and lick and mount each other as unself-consciously as rutting dogs or lab rats. But, like the worst of Henry Miller, it's all phallic fantasy, projections of the author's personal pathology.

Dan Miller reports that the young Caldwell was fascinated with "the obscene." It's a cruel thing to say, but some of his novels are so misbegotten I wonder if perpetual tumescence diverted a critical supply of blood from Caldwell's brain. Though sex was his obsession, he was no Rabelais. Even in the permissive '90s, "disgusting" is the only word for the infamous turnip scene that kept the Broadway version of *Tobacco Road* running for eight years.

How did the critical establishment of the '30s mistake this coarse stuff for literature? They weren't entirely blind. Above all Caldwell was a crank, an odd duck. His radical admirers, like Mike Gold of *The Masses*, knew there was something queer about him—the way he tossed farce and tragedy together as if he couldn't tell the difference, as if he knew a bold recipe for fiction no one else had attempted.

Critics questioned his strange shifts of tone and chided him for his superficial grasp of politics. But they never questioned his integrity as a witness. Caldwell's South, a land of terrified Negroes and degraded sharecroppers starved by heartless capitalists and landowners, was precisely the one required by the Marxist worldview. The Marxist popular subtheme of sexual liberation didn't hurt Caldwell either.

My guess is that New York radicals knew as much about Georgia as they knew about Suriname, and like ancient cartographers were only too ready to populate the unknown regions with fabulous monsters. Caldwell was a fellow traveling Southerner who specialized in monsters. Of course there was never anyone in Georgia like Ty Ty or Darling Jill. There were worse—inbred, pellagra-hollowed Kallikaks shortchanged by the economy and the gene pool—but the gregarious, philosophical Ty Ty Walden would sound like a New York actor to the likes of them.

It was the Bolshevik PC of the day that made a prophet of this palpably flawed and unreliable witness. But it created a man without a country. Caldwell was spoiled and misled by the Northern Left and disowned by most Southerners, who naturally hated to see themselves portrayed fornicating like rabbits on amphetamines. He left the South when he was twenty-seven and never really returned, cutting himself off from any source of inspiration that might have compensated for his lack of intellectual curiosity.

The gullibility of those radical critics raised up a myopic giant with feet of red clay. It also legitimized stereotypes that plague the South to this day. There should be a lesson in humility here for academic critics who threaten to take over literature entirely. Here's a proposition I think I could prove: The average critic is much more distracted by tribal conventions, and by intellectual fads and fashions, than any first-rate writer.

Erskine Caldwell's precipitous fall doesn't seem as cruel if we acknowledge, as I do, that his rise was a big mistake. His vision of the South may be no more misleading or dishonest than the visions of

Margaret Mitchell, the Fugitives, "the Richmond-Charleston School," or any of the other romanticizers and apologists Caldwell so detested. But it was a crackpot, sometimes almost lunatic vision elevated by frail critics to a most improbable authority. It devolved into a dismal, unvarying formula.

Dan Miller, a good writer, has done us a great service by reopening this dusty old file. Now it's time to close it. Many Southerners said all along that Erskine Caldwell was the joint creation of dumb Yankee critics and smart Yankee businessmen who made a mountain out of a dunghill. Time has eroded that unsavory mountain in a very appropriate fashion.

August / September 1995

Letter from Sister: What We Learned at the P.O.

TONY EARLEY

I HAVE A THEORY—perhaps unformed and, without question, unsubstantiated—that most bad Southern writing is descended directly from Eudora Welty's "Why I Live at the P.O." Welty's story smacks of a certain now-familiar sensibility, rife with caricature, overstated eccentricity, and broadly drawn humor, that has come to represent Southern writing and, through that representation, the South itself.

It would be difficult, if not impossible, to read much Southern fiction and not come upon story after story faithfully cut from our landscape and culture, using the template provided by Welty in 1941. The characters in "Why I Live at the P.O." possess the prototypical, colorful Southern names that, in the musical sound of their regional specificity, have come to promise colorful Southern doings: Papa-Daddy, Uncle Rondo, Stella-Rondo, Shirley T., Sister. They eat green-tomato pickle and, on the Fourth of July, sport about in flesh-colored kimonos while impaired by prescription drugs. They live in Mississippi. They grow long beards and illegitimate children and mismatched sets of breasts.

In delicious, honey-coated accents they utter the delicious, honey-coated statements, void of any real importance, that fall sweetly on the ears of book-buying lovers of stereotypes everywhere. "Papa-Daddy," Stella-Rondo says, when she's looking to stir up trouble, "Papa-Daddy! . . . Sister says she fails to understand why you don't cut off your beard."

Uncle Rondo, after he has donned Stella-Rondo's flesh-colored kimono and illegally ingested God knows what prescription narcotic (he's a pharmacist), cries, "Sister, get out of my way, I'm poisoned."

So faithfully have the conventions of "Why I Live at the P.O." been copied by succeeding generations of writers, so dominant has the regionally identified literature laid out by the story become, that Welty might well have titled it "How to Exploit the People of the Nation's Poorest Region and Get a Really Big Book Advance." All of which is at least shameful, if not artistically criminal, because "Why I Live at the P.O." is a bona fide work of genius, not only one of the best short stories produced by a Southern writer, but one of the best stories by any writer, anywhere.

The genius of "Why I Live at the P.O." lies not in the story that the narrator, Sister, tells us—which is, without question, broadly told, colorful, eccentric, and side-splittingly funny—but in the story Sister does not know she is telling us. In her hysterical attempt to win us over to her side in a seemingly inconsequential family dispute, Sister inadvertently reveals the emotional and spiritual burdens that she and the members of her family must pull through their lives. Stella-Rondo has been abandoned by a traveling salesman who might or might not be her husband, leaving her to raise a daughter who might or might not be illegitimate. Uncle Rondo is a shell-shocked veteran of World War I who once had a breakdown because one of his nieces broke a chain letter from Flanders Field. Mama is a tired woman—a widow, one presumes—who knows that she must spend the rest of her days caring for, and keeping peace among, the rapidly aging daughters she can't marry off; her senile father; and her shell-shocked, drug-addled brother. Papa-Daddy's rages are directed not so much at Sister, but at what a colorful writer who wasn't from around here famously called the "dying of the light" (Sister tells us he's "just about a million years old").

And Sister, poor Sister. She thinks she is simply justifying to us her reasons for choosing to live in the second smallest post office in the state of Mississippi. But what she doesn't know she is telling us is that she is horribly alone, that she realizes she will spend the rest of her life in a tiny, tiny place, with no chance of escape, unloved and unmarried, dependent upon the charity of her family. Her monologue to us, unbeknownst to her, is at once a comedic tour de force and a heartrending cry in the wilderness.

While these aren't new critical insights, they are, I think, important ones. The bright surface of "Why I Live at the P.O." is so extraordinarily attractive that it is easy to see why it has been so often imitated. But it is also easy to see why, if only the surface of Welty's story is imitated, the result is but a shallow and often exploitative parody of a great work of art. It is easy to make up characters who live in double-wide mobile homes, wear beehive hairdos and feed caps, never put a "g" on the end of a participle, have sex with their cousins, voted for George Wallace, who squint and spit whenever an out-of-towner uses a polysyllabic word; who aspire only to own a bass boat, scare a Yankee, have sex with their cousins again, burn a cross, eat something fried, speak in tongues, do anything butt nekkid, be a guest on a daytime talk show, and make the next payment on a satellite dish that points toward Venus and picks up 456 separate channels on a clear day. What is difficult is to take the poor, the uneducated, the superstitious, the backward, the redneck, the "trailer-trash," and make them real human beings, with hopes and dreams and aspirations as real and valid, and as worthy of our fair consideration, as any Cheeverian Westchester County housewife.

While I can forgive our brothers and sisters from other parts of the country for taking pleasure in, or even creating, a Southern literature based on stereotype, I find it harder to forgive Southerners who do the same thing, particularly if they are capable of writing with greater understanding but choose not to. What Welty's more cynical impersonators choose to ignore is that the eccentricities portrayed in "Why

I Live at the P.O." are character-specific and not indicative of any larger pattern of regional or cultural behavior or belief. The humor in the words "Uncle Rondo" arises not from the words themselves but from the way Sister says them.

While the sound of Sister's voice has become the matriarch of all the shrill, self-absorbed voices we hear in Southern fiction, yammering on about nothing at all, we should remember that her voice is also one of agenda and calculation. Sister wants to make her family look bad; she wants us to believe that they are stupid and that, in their stupidity, they have treated her unfairly. What worries me is the possibility that Sister's voice, with all its layers of complexity, will become lost in the din raised by its imitators, and that din will become, if it hasn't already, the only voice we hear in our heads when we think about the nature of the word "Southern."

I am often asked if I consider myself a Southern writer, and, to be honest, my answer depends on—to borrow a line from Owen Wister's *Virginian*, one of the most famously one-dimensional Southern stereotypes—whether or not my questioner smiles when he calls me that. If he means, do I make fun of my characters because they are Southern and because there is a bottomless market for that sort of thing, then the answer is no. But if he means, do I consider myself someone who at least attempts to portray the people of my native region in all their complexity and diversity and Christ-hauntedness and moral ambiguity, the answer is yes, I consider myself a Southern writer.

And as a Southern writer—even one who tends to be as thin-skinned, testy, and self-righteous about this issue as I am—I have been tempted to lower the IQs of my characters, name them Something-or-Other Bob, and stick their illiterate backsides to a Naugahyde La-Z-Boy in order to make myself popular and sell some books. The real danger arises when too many of us at once give in to this invidious urge. In creating our own literature, a Southern literature, we often go for the quick laugh, the easy buck, the cardboard character. When we do that, we eat away the foundation of that literature from the inside. My fear is that, eventually, because of our willingness to feed on, without replacing, the tenets and traditions and subjects given to us by our predecessors—Welty, Flannery O'Connor, and William Faulkner, most prominent among them—Southern writing will collapse and bury all of us, leaving only kudzu, grits, and a certain vaguely familiar voice to mark the spot.

January/February 1999

Homage to Halliburton

SUSAN SONTAG

BEFORE THERE WAS TRAVEL—IN MY LIFE, AT LEAST—there were travel books. Books that told you the world was very large but quite encompassable. Full of destinations.

The first travel books I read, and surely among the most important books of my life, were by Richard Halliburton. I was seven, and the year was 1940, when I read his *Book of Marvels*. Halliburton, the handsome, genteel American youth, born in Brownsville, Tennessee, who had devised for himself a life of being ever-young, ever-adventuring, was my first vision of what I thought had to be the most privileged of lives, that of a writer: a life of endless curiosity and energy and countless enthusiasms. To be a traveler, to be a writer—in my child mind they started off as the same thing.

To be sure, there was a good deal in that child mind that prepared me to fall in love with the idea of insatiable travel. My own parents had lived abroad most of my first six years—my father had a fur business in northern China—while my sister and I remained in the care of relatives in the States. As far back as I can remember, I was already conducting a rich dream-life of travel to exotic places. But my parents' unimaginable existence on the opposite side of the globe had inspired a too precise, and hopeless, set of travel longings. Halliburton's books informed me that the world contained many wonderful things. Not just the Great Wall of China.

Yes, he had walked on the Great Wall, and he'd also climbed Etna and Popocatépetl and Fujiyama and Olympus; he'd visited the Grand Canyon and the Golden Gate Bridge (in 1938, when the book was published, the bridge counted as the newest of the world's wonders); he'd viewed Lenin's tomb and rowed into the Blue Grotto; he'd made it to Carcassonne and Baalbek and Petra and Lhasa and Chartres and Delphi and the Alhambra and Masada and the Taj Mahal and Pompeii and Victoria Falls and Jerusalem and the bay of Rio and Chichén-Itzá and the Blue Mosque in Isfahan and Angkor Wat and, and, and. . . . Halliburton called them "marvels," and wasn't this my introduction to the notion of "the masterpiece"? The point was: the faraway world was full of amazing sites and edifices, which I too might one day see and learn the stories attached to them. Looking back now, I realize that *Book of Marvels* was a prime awakener of a good part of my own ardor and appetite.

The year before I read *Book of Marvels,* in 1939, Halliburton had ventured a trip under sail in that quintessentially Chinese vessel, a junk, from Hong Kong to San Francisco, and had vanished somewhere mid-Pacific without a trace. He was thirty-nine years old. Did I know he was dead when I was reading his *Book of Marvels*? Probably not. But then, I'd not entirely taken in the death of my own thirty-three-year-old father in Tientsin, which I learned about in 1939, when my mother returned from China for good. And a sad end couldn't taint the lessons of pluck and avidity I took from Halliburton's books. Those books—from *The Royal Road to Romance*, his first, published in 1925, to *Book of Marvels*, his last; I eventually read them all—described for me an idea of pure happiness. And of successful volition. You have something in mind. You imagine it. You prepare for it. You voyage toward it. And then: you see it. There is no disappointment—indeed, it may be even more captivating than you imagined.

Halliburton's books convey in the most candid and ingenuous—which is to say, unfashionable—way the "romance" of travel. Enthusiasm for travel may not be expressed so giddily today, but I'm sure that the seeking out of what is strange or beautiful, or both, remains just as pleasurable and addictive. It has certainly proved so for me. And because of the impact of those books read when I was so young, my more enviable sightings throughout grown-up life, mostly by-products of opportunity or obligation rather than pilgrimages undertaken, continue to bear Halliburton's imprint. When I finally did walk on the Great Wall, and lined up in Red Square to see Lenin's tomb, and was shat on by monkeys in the Taj Mahal, and wandered in the ruins of Angkor Wat, and wangled permission to spend a night in a sleeping bag on the rosy rocks of Petra, and surreptitiously climbed the Great Pyramid at Giza before daybreak, I thought: I've done it. They were on his list. Truth is, though San Francisco is anything but an unusual destination for me, I never drive across the Golden Gate Bridge without recalling where it figures in Halliburton's book. Even a place I've assumed isn't very interesting and haven't visited, Andorra, remains on my interior map because he went there. And when Machu Picchu or Palmyra or Lhasa or Fujiyama comes to mind, I think, I haven't done that. Yet.

The cult of youth that animates Halliburton's books could hardly have meant something to a seven-year-old. But it is the association of travel with youth, beautiful youth, that seems most dated now. As an undergraduate at Princeton just after the First World War, Halliburton succumbed to the spell of *The Picture of Dorian Gray*; and throughout his brief life his beau idéal remained Rupert Brooke, whose biography he hoped one day to write. Even more remote than these references is Halliburton's assumption that he is bringing news to his readers, that what will entice and seduce are his words—not the photographs in the books, many no better than snapshots: the author standing in front of the Taj Mahal and so forth. Today, when lust for travel is awakened primarily through images, still and moving, we expect the sights, many of them all too familiar, to speak for themselves. Indeed, we've seen the famous sights unrolling in color long before we actually travel to see them.

Halliburton's travel narratives are stocked with people: guides, facilitators, scam artists, and other locals. The busy world that he encounters fills his mind. Today it is possible to travel solo, without traveling, to vacancy itself. The distraught heroine of Don DeLillo's new novel, *The Body Artist*, logs on to her computer at odd hours to watch a live-streaming video feed from the edge of a little-used, two-lane road outside Kotka, Finland, where a Webcam is always trained on asphalt. "It emptied her mind and made her feel the deep silence of other places."

To me, travel is filling the mind. But that means it empties my mind, too: I find it almost impossible to write when I am traveling. To write I have to stay put. Real travel competes with mental traveling. (What is a writer but a mental traveler?) When I recall now how much Halliburton's books meant to me at the beginning of my reading life, I see how the project of traveling infiltrated, perfumed, abetted my nascent dream of becoming a writer. When I acknowledge to myself that I'm interested in everything, what am I saying but that I want to travel everywhere. Like Richard Halliburton. . . .

March / April 2001

#

RICK BASS

AS A KID, I WAS WILD ABOUT ALL TURTLES. I have no idea what it was about them that drew me so. At the time, I would have known nothing of the archetypal values ascribed to them, such as endurance and world-genesis. I was especially wild about the gothic grotesqueries of snapping turtles. I adored their savage appetites, was fascinated by their infinite belligerence, and took awed solace in their hideous land-bound clumsiness. Here was a creature, a dinosaur really, that appeared supremely dispossessed in the world—unglamorous, unfriendly, even plain plug-ugly—and yet it thrived like a king, seeking out the muddy depths where other turtles could not prosper or would not go. The larger ones, I had read, could measure over three feet long, and might weigh in excess of a hundred pounds. They were eaters of fish, snakes, other turtles, and even ducks. It was said that their bite was powerful enough to snap a broomstick, or sever a finger, and that once they bit, they would not turn loose until thunder boomed. The real behemoths never came to the surface, I'd heard, except once a year to breed and lay eggs, but I would occasionally luck onto one of their smaller progeny, which made the most satisfying, aggressive pets. They ranged in size from a golf ball to a frying pan, and even the smallest, with their baleful red eyes and hissing malevolence, gave an observer pause. Though I never saw one of the true giants in its depths, it was a source of deep pleasure to me to know that they were down there, secure in their element, titanic.

The one time I did see a giant snapper, it was not in its element, but in transition. I viewed it for only a few minutes, but what a glorious and heartrending few minutes they were.

I was twelve or thirteen years old, in the full grip of my turtlemania. Some weekends my parents would travel out toward the town of Katy, Texas, in the prairie. Katy was then only a hamlet, rather than the sterilized suburban strip mall it has since become. My parents played golf at a club called Jersey Meadow, only recently carved out of prime bayou woodland, and it was one of my great joys to be allowed to fish and dip net in the water hazards of the golf course.

I've never experienced better fishing in my life, nor a more exhilarating general fecundity. The bass and bream bit harder and fought better, as did the sleek, potbellied catfish. There were giant bullfrogs everywhere, and vast populations of polywogs, and entire nests of snakes (and not just the sissy little garter snakes, but water moccasins, too, the real thing, as dark as charred wood and as thick around as a man's wrist). There were swirling inky swarms of newly hatched catfish fry, wandering chaotically across the surface in amorphous rafts composed of hundreds of individuals, a sight so exciting to me that I would often leap fully clothed into the water with my dip net, no matter the water's depth, hoping to scoop up one of the half-inch catfish. (It was such a magical sight that I still dream of it to this day. The last time I dreamed it, my youngest daughter, four years old, was with me, and I was trying to explain to her what she was seeing in the dream: that the clumsy, drifting, loose, wiggling sprawl was actually about five hundred newborn catfish all swimming together for protection, in their first few days of life. . . .)

And there were, of course, turtles, of all possible species, in every possible size, and on a good day, I might be fortunate enough to catch one. It isn't as easy as you might think, if you haven't tried it. Capturing the terrestrial box turtles was simple enough, but the aquatic turtles were as quick as lightning.

They couldn't resist basking, however, and I would slither on my belly toward a log on which ten or twenty of them might be perched, sunning themselves, frozen like statues. Crawling like a commando, hoping to evade the twenty pairs of sentinel eyes, I would make a quick charge at the end, and try to net the slowest one as they all slipped off the log into the water. Once they fell in, they usually went straight to the bottom, but occasionally in its panic one would land upside down and might linger on the surface for half a second, righting itself, and that was when I had a chance, if the handle on my dip net was long enough.

It was dusk, and storming, as it can storm only in the subtropics in late spring and early summer: violent bursts that tear green limbs from trees and flood streets and knock out power lines, dropping four or five inches of rain in a couple of hours, and above and through it all, the wonderful crackling and roaring of thunder and lightning.

We were driving out of the club in the downpour. As we wound our way along the little road, beneath the boughs of ancient live oaks, I glanced out at one of the putting greens and saw, in the dimming light, the silhouette of my desire—the perfect shape of it manifested as if into archetype and then magnified tenfold: a snapping turtle that seemed to be the size of a small Volkswagen, lumbering across that verdant lawn of civilization, tumultuous rain hammering against her shell as she dragged her immense bulk, nearly too much for the land to bear, from the depths of a pond up toward a sand trap, where she might have intended to lay her eggs. (I did not stop to think of that at the time; I knew only that by the most miraculous of flukes, I had sighted my life's quarry—a quarry I did not even know I had been pursuing until I saw it—creeping across that manicured grass, gargantuan and lovely in its hideousness.)

Even my parents were impressed. We stopped and viewed her from the car as we might the nearsighted rhinoceros or tame garbage-bears at some drive-through safari park, and then I was out the door and running toward the turtle, and my parents snatched up their umbrellas and bailed out of the car and came running after me.

As I joined the massive turtle, she hunched upon her hind legs, hissed and spat, but then trudged on resolutely, making good time for such a labored and ponderous gait, dragging that huge spiny tail behind her like a log.

Her feet were as broad as a wolf's, with claws like a bear's. Had she not been so ferocious, I would have tried riding on her shell, as I had sometimes done with the immense but gentle Galapagos tortoises at the zoo.

It was her head that was most spellbinding. It was easily the size of a man's head, and her eyes were as large as oversized marbles. The three of us were mesmerized by this strange new inhabitant of the earth, and I pleaded with my parents to let me take her home. I could tell they sympathized with the immensity of my discovery, but they realized also the impossibility of caring for and feeding such a monstrosity in the suburbs, and they were adamant in their refusal.

I sobbed in anguish as we tracked the mythic creature on her charmed and steadfast path. "We could put her in the trunk," I pleaded, and even grabbed hold of her long tail in an attempt to show my father that it was possible, that she could be transported.

This was a mistake. With a savage hiss she jacked her hind end up and dug deep into the turf with those powerful forelegs, and as quick as a ferret she whirled and snapped at me. I was barely able to release the tail and leap back in time: She had the power of a sumo wrestler and the speed of a rattlesnake.

I took another step back and watched as she re-oriented herself with whatever magnetic tack she had been following, and then, with thunder booming and lightning flashing and rain howling, we resumed following her. My parents were holding up their umbrellas in vain attempts to stay dry in the storm, and as the three of us walked in procession behind and flanking the astounding reptile, it might have seemed to a distant observer that we were exercising the animal, taking it for a walk on a leash, or perhaps even letting it pull us. Glimpsed between lightning bolts, as darkness fell quickly now, we must have looked like characters from *The Addams Family*, and I suspect a passerby would not have been inclined to stop and ask if we needed any help.

We followed her all the way to another flood-swollen pond, into which she disappeared gracefully—as gracefully, I could see in a boom of lightning-flash, as a ballerina. I was still crying in my frustration, still arguing with my parents right up until the very end, and I recall being very angry at them for a long time, though by now I have completely forgiven them. And I've never forgotten the wild power and savagery of that sudden head-strike, when I gripped the turtle's tail.

March / April 2000

from Fire Notes

LARRY BROWN

IT WAS A LOVELY SUMMER AFTERNOON, about three or four in the afternoon, and
the line of stopped cars we had been passing for the last two miles made
a steady rushing sound in the windows of the fire truck, and the wreck
was below us, finally in sight, about a mile away, at the bottom of a very
steep hill, and we were doing sixty-five, and we had no brakes.

Uncle Wright and I had already braced ourselves to be killed. I felt
fairly sure that we were going to die, and the only thing I was wondering
was how many of the people who were driving the parked highway
patrol cars and the fire trucks and the ambulances at the bottom of
the hill where the wreck was were going to die, too, when we slammed
into them, at sixty-five. The truck I was driving weighed many tons and
it was full of water and I knew that the brake shoes had "faded away"
from the drums from the repeated use of them and I was bearing down
on the brake pedal with everything I had and the truck wasn't slowing
down any. Down below us, there was a sea of flashing blue and red lights
and stopped traffic stretching away as far as the eye could see. A truck
was overturned in the middle of the road, and I told Unkie that we
weren't going to make it. Like I said earlier, it was a fine summer evening,
but I never believed all that Indian shit about it being a good day to
die. I did not want to slam into that parked group of emergency vehi-
cles and I knew that Unkie didn't want me to either. I pumped the pedal

and it didn't give anything back. I downshifted and the sound of the parked cars kept rushing in the windows. We had already driven nearly twenty miles to this wreck, passing cars, hogging the road, running people off the road, and I had come upon it a little too fast. I told Unkie that I thought the only chance we had was to pull the MicroBrake just before we got there, which would lock all the tires down if there was anything left. I kept downshifting, slowing down, pumping the brake. It still didn't feel like I had anything, and suddenly I was given a miracle, because the pedal suddenly had something under it, and we slowed down some and I downshifted some more and we swung in nonchalantly beside the wreck and parked without telling any of the assembled rescue people how close they had come to another disaster.

You never know what to expect. You just get out and deal with whatever they have called you to. You are the professional, that is your job. There is always a victim to be extricated, sometimes a crushed and dying person whose life hangs in your hands. What we were looking at that day was a large truck that had been carrying a load of loose lime. It had swerved to miss an oncoming car, and the truck had flipped. There were several tons of lime on the road. The trailer wheels were on the ground, but the frame had twisted and the cab was upside down with the roof resting on the highway centerline. The driver had come out with the windshield and was up and walking around. His wife, or his woman, or whatever relationship she was to him, was inside the cab, underneath it.

Most wreck victims are in shock when you get there. They're walking around in a daze, or lying on the side of the road with a blanket over them, if somebody is there who knows how to treat for shock. This man, a black man, was in shock, and up and walking around. I could see the woman through the large hole where the windshield had been. She had on a red shirt and a pair of blue jeans. There were a whole lot of people standing around watching. There always is. I dropped down on my belly in the broken glass and diesel fuel and crawled under the truck with her.

She was a young black woman, probably less than thirty. She was flat on her back and her main problem was that she was caught by the dash in the one place a lady surely ought not to be caught, and pinned effectively with her legs on either side of the sharp ridge of the dash. She had a broken nose, and aside from that, and aside from being terrified, she seemed to be all right.

I talked to her and told her that we were going to get her out. I held her hand. She gripped my hand with a strength born out of fear. I told her that I had to feel her, that I had to check for broken bones, for her to please not think anything about it, that I was a fireman, that I was trained in my job and I had to check for what injuries she might have. She squeezed my hand and told me that she understood. She said Don't leave me. I said I won't.

How would I have been if I had been in her place? A truck upside down on top of me? She was pretty cool. I checked her legs and arms. Nothing seemed to be broken. I asked her if she had any internal pain. She said nothing was hurting her but her nose. And this other, she said. I kept holding her hand. I told her that help was on the way, but that was a lie. I knew we hadn't brought a damn thing with us that could lift that truck off her. So we just laid under there and talked. She told me what had happened, how the wreck had happened, how it had happened so fast. It was very hot, and we were both sweating. I could see the faces of ambulance attendants peering in the broken windows at us.

What we needed was a crane and we didn't have one on Engine Eight. I told her that I had to leave for a few minutes, but that I'd be right back. I crawled out from under the truck and stood up. Traffic was completely blocked for miles each way. I called Unkie over to the side and told him that her ladyhood was caught tight and we were going to have to jack the truck up or something. I asked him what he wanted to do. He was the shift chief, I was just a lieutenant. He said he guessed we'd better get the Ram Tool out of the truck.

We did that and all it did was blow a gasket. She kept looking at me with those eyes while I lay next to her and jacked the handle of that thing until it blew the gasket. A doctor arrived. Some young boy working on one of the ambulances told the doctor he thought she had a flail chest. That was bullshit. He hadn't been under there and checked her. I crawled back under and lit her a cigarette when she asked me for one. She wanted to know was it any danger smoking under there. I told her that diesel fuel had a low flash point. We laid under there and smoked a cigarette together.

I said Listen. I'm going to try and move you. I told her I didn't think her hip was broken. She said she didn't think her hip was broken, either. I told her I was going to try and slide her out from under that dash. I told her that if it started hurting her, for her to tell me. She said she would.

I tried and tried. I hooked my hands in her belt loops and pulled and pulled, but there was no moving her. She was embarrassed, and she giggled a little, maybe from shock, maybe from this white boy lying under a smashed truck with her trying to get her vagina unhung. Mutually we decided that we weren't doing any good. When I crawled back out that time, it looked like traffic was backed up all the way to the Union County line.

Miracles happen sometimes. We'd already had one, but I never expected two. A convoy of National Guard trucks was backed up somewhere in the line and they had a crane. The highway patrol moved them into position and they parked next to the wreck. I crawled back under there with her and told her what was about to happen, that they were going to wrap a steel cable around the cab of the truck and tighten it up and that I was going to hold on to her and slide her out the second the pressure lifted. I think she dreaded that. I think maybe she thought they might lift it a few inches and then drop it back down on her and crush her. I didn't tell her that I thought that might happen, too. The cable came in, and I passed it around the body of the truck, and sent the hook back out, and they tightened it. We didn't say anything. The cable creaked. The truck shifted. She squeezed my hand. There was the groaning of metal. The dash lifted a few inches and I grabbed her belt loops in my hands and slid her backwards, and suddenly many hands reached in and caught her with me and we pulled her out into the highway and she was free.

We stood around for a while. They attended to her and she was able to stand. She was crying, but from happiness, glad to be alive, and she came over to me, this black woman who had lived and not died, and she put her arms around me, and she hugged me. I think maybe now that there might have even been a gentle kiss on my cheek. I know that she stood off from me for a second, just before she climbed into the ambulance, with her arms on my shoulders, and looked at me.

Unkie came over and said, You did good, Brown.

We catch the next light on green and we the blue lights of the police cars and the red lights of the ambulance and we slow down and pull in and stop the pumper in the middle of the street, put the pump in gear, apply the parking brake. I pick up the radio mike and report that we're 10-7, engaged in an assignment, and then I report what I'm looking at, which is a car on the right hand side of the street pointed the wrong way and halfway wrapped around a telephone pole at the edge of the sidewalk. Mac is out and pulling on his coat and gloves. Henry Hill arrives behind us in the rescue truck. I hand up the mike and get out, pull on my gloves, get my helmet from the compartment, and walk over and look into the car. The passenger door is open and a nurse is in the seat with a young man who is lying across the bucket seats, jammed tight against the shifter, covered with blood, his legs twisted behind him in the smashed remains of the driver's door. The nurse is jabbing a piece of surgical tubing down his throat, shouting: "Breathe, baby, breathe!"

Henry is getting the entry saw out of the rescue truck and I walk back to the pump panel and pull the lever that opens the booster line, a coiled one-inch hand line that's on a reel above the pump panel, and then I throttle the engine up and watch the pressure gauge until the needle sits steady at two hundred pounds and then I walk off and leave it. Mac pulls the line down with one hand and takes it over to the car and lays it down in the street. Henry is bringing the saw and I go back to where the nurse is working on the boy. The nurse looks up at me and tells me that we've got to do something quick and I say that we'll do all we can, lady. The boy is trying to breathe and she has almost as much blood on her as he does. He probably has internal injuries, something ruptured in his chest, and she keeps saying that he's going to die before we can get him out. Here is this thing facing me again, this human and fragile thing called life wasting away before my eyes, and I am the one who has to decide what to do about it.

This is in the early eighties, before the city ever got convinced that we needed to spend seventy-five hundred dollars for a Hurst Tool, the Jaws of Life, and all we have is the Ram Tool, which is not worth a shit in a situation like this, in a wreck of this magnitude. It's only a hand-pumped hydraulic tool with various attachments. It won't pull a car apart like taffy the way the Hurst Tool will. All we've got is the Ram Tool and the saw, so I walk around to the other side of the car where the door is bent into a U-shape against the telephone pole. For a moment I consider moving the car, calling a wrecker and yanking it off the pole, but then I tell Henry that we need to try and cut the door off. An incredible number of people are standing around watching us. I wish they'd all go away and let us do our work but they're not about to do that. Hell no. This is too good to miss. They're going to stand right here and watch every f—up we make.

Henry gets the saw running and noses the carbide blade into the door and a shower of orange sparks starts flying around in a circle. We keep the hose ready in case gasoline ignites and I already know this isn't going to work. The whole weight of the car is against the door and we won't get it off without cutting down the pole. It doesn't look possible. It doesn't look possible that the boy could have gotten himself into this kind of shape. It looks like he's going to die right here with all of us trying to prevent it. I tell them to keep sawing and I go back around to the other side of the car where the nurse is screaming for the boy not to die, shouting things at me, I don't know what, I don't listen, I don't care what she's saying, I'm looking at this car and trying to figure some way to get the boy out of it as fast as I can. I lean over her with my flashlight and look at his legs. They're somewhere in that door behind him and the saw is running on the other side of the door, lighting up Henry's face and the goggles he has on. The boy breathes a little and then his breath catches in his chest and he makes that strangling noise again and she jabs the thing down his throat again. I can see that it's clogged with bubbles of air and blood and she keeps saying that we've got to do something, do something right now. She's about to get on my nerves and I wish to hell I did know what to do.

I get back out and look at the position of his body. And then I see it. He's got to come straight up. He's got to rise vertically out of that car like somebody levitating. The nurse tells me that they've got to call the rescue unit and I tell her this is it, lady, this is the rescue unit and it's the only one you're going to get. I don't tell her that I've been to the State Fire Academy to learn this shit, I don't show her my First Responder patch, I don't tell her that if the city would open up its billfold I'd carve this car up like a Christmas turkey. I just go around to the other side and tell the guys who work with me to cut off the saw and let's get the windshield out.

We cover the nurse and the patient up with a blanket and then we take two fire axes and start chopping through it, going around the edges, trying not to get glass splinters in our eyes, trying to remember to keep our face shields down. Sometimes adrenaline takes over and we forget, grab hot things or sharp things with our bare hands, suffer wounds we don't know about until later. We go all the way around the top of the windshield and down both sides and then push it out over the hood and throw it into the street like a dirty carpet. Then I'm up on the hood and reaching down through the hole for the shifter he's lodged against, that has his body hung. I push on it with all I have and it won't give. Somebody takes the blanket off the nurse and her patient and she's still working with him and he doesn't sound any better. I push against the shifter but it won't move. I say, Mac, come here, help me. He crawls up beside me and lies down. I tell Mac that he's hung against the shifter, that we've got to bend it out of the way, but I'm not strong enough. I tell him to put his hand on mine on top of the shifter and he does. We push. Mac is strong as an ox and it starts to give. We push and strain, as hard as we can, and Mac is nearly crushing my hand with his, but the shifter gives and bends over in the floor until it's away from him and not holding him. Somebody has pushed the wheeled stretcher up near the car and we all reach and lift while somebody puts traction on the patient, just in case he has a broken neck, and we slide the half-backboard behind him and strap him and out he comes, onto the stretcher, the nurse walking beside him still jabbing the thing in and out of his throat, the respirator inside the ambulance only a few seconds away now, and they strap him down and load him up and get in with him and the doors slam and the ambulance screams down the street, the lonely wall of it washing over us until it fades away down toward the hospital.

Thanks, Mac, I say. I'm glad that he is so strong. I'm glad the boy didn't die. I understand why the nurse had no patience with me.

We roll up our shit and we go back home. No thanks is needed from anybody. The city thanks us twice a month.

Now we are gathered in a little church in the woods, and the yard of the church is filled with muddy cars and muddy fire trucks and we have all driven up a muddy road and we are here to say our last good-byes to Mac, who lies in his coffin in front of the pulpit. He was strong, but he had high blood pressure, like me, and he wasn't careful about taking his medicine, and two days ago, when he was rabbit hunting with his uncle and cousin, he had either a stroke or a heart attack in the woods, and died quickly, before they could get him some help. I have never been in a black church before, and of all the hundreds of people here in their best clothes, the faces of firemen in their uniforms and ties are the only white faces.

The church will not hold all the people who have come here. The church has no paint on the outside. I cannot believe that he is dead, but they open the coffin and there he lies, with his mustache, without the glasses he always wore, and a seventeen-year-old son bends over him with streaming eyes and kisses his cheek.

The preacher is standing at the pulpit, but the service is not going to begin until everybody is seated. All the pews are full and people are still coming in. The funeral procession looked miles long. Chairs are brought in and set down in the aisles and people sit in them, maybe forty or fifty more. We stand in silence, sweating in the heat, the women fanning themselves with little cardboard fans on a wooden stick, things I haven't seen or seen people use since I was a child in my own church and saw women do the same thing. The people stop coming in and somebody closes the door.

From a curtain behind the pulpit a line of old women come in wearing choir robes, maybe a dozen. They hold no hymnals in their hands and the organ sits dead and silent in the corner. The women sit down and put their hands in their laps and they begin singing. They begin singing like angels and they sing about Heaven and Jesus and the love of God and the hair wants to go up on my neck because it is unearthly and beautiful and my ears love it like no singing I've ever heard and the preacher stands tall in his black velvet robe with a face of stone and stares at the wall of the church. We sit enraptured and I look at the people in their fine clothes, some in work clothes, fresh from the job, their caps in their hands, all of us here for this wonderful music.

The singing ends. Then it begins again. I don't know how long it goes on. It stops again. It begins again. And finally it stops for good.

The preacher is a huge man. He looks like Alex Haley, only blacker. This man is as black as midnight. He begins his sermon in a gentle voice, talking of how we all must one day throw off this mortal coil, the way Mac already has, that his suffering is over, that God's got a better world waiting. He talks of how he remembers this boy in church as a child, how he saw him accept Jesus as his savior. He raises his voice a little and his words begin to assume a rhythm, and he starts to move, and we start to move a little with him. His voice gets louder and somebody says Amen. Somebody says Yes, Lord. His voice rises to a higher pitch and I can see people swaying a little. It's going to be something. They start to shout and talk back to him and we keep quiet. There's two things going on here at one time. It's looking like it's going to get out of hand. Pretty soon the preacher's moaning and his voice has gotten high and tight and he's caught up in it and the whole place is caught up in it and I'm caught up in it too and it's all I can do to keep from shouting something out at him myself because he's got me feeling something. The man's a great orator and he's got all these people right in the palm of his hand and he's making them jump and move and shout Yeah! Amen! Tell it brother! Sweet Jesus! I close my eyes and feel it and know that these people are some kind of strong. It goes on and on and it's hot in the church and the little walls reverberate with sound until the preacher winds back down slowly like a clock unwinding and by then just about everybody's crying, me too.

No more Mac.

I always feel guilty about going out and riding around at night. Just took off a while ago and went out and rode around for a while, drank some whisky, and now I'm feeling guilty. I ought to be in the bed in there sleeping, getting ready to go to a party tomorrow night, but as it often happens after that I feel the need to put some words down. So here are some.

There's a hell of a lot going on at night. If you think about it, the owls are out then, and the snakes, and the women. I rode around for about an hour and a half and did not meet another person. That suits me fine, and most people are at home asleep in the bed at the hours I usually keep. That's no bad strike against them or anything, it's just that they all have jobs they have to go to and they have to sleep to rest up for them. They probably don't drink like I do. They probably don't try to write fiction or cut down trees all day long as a means of soothing their souls. There's nothing finer than to make your angle cut on the side you want the tree to fall on, take you a big wedge out of there, one diagonal cut and one horizontal cut, knock that big wedge out of there, then cut on the back side slightly above the cut and go all the way through and start to see that big mother topple and keep the saw in there and running and cut all the way through and then draw the saw back and get out of the way and see the tree jump completely off the stump, limbs crashing, and crash to the ground.

I cut one down today that had a three-foot kingsnake coiled up inside it. The tree was rotten and nearly fell on me. I made a five-inch cut and it came down where I wasn't expecting it to, fell in the spot where I'd been standing a few seconds before. A girl with large breasts was walking down the road and she spoke to me and I became distracted when I spoke to her and suddenly the tree was falling. A man has to be careful of stuff like that, big trees and big titties at the same time.

I used to call myself a fireman but I probably wouldn't make a pimple on a real fireman's ass. Those guys in Chicago, in New York, in L.A., those guys are really firemen. I never rescued anybody from a burning building but I have entered burning buildings where people told me people were trapped inside and it turned out that nobody was trapped inside, just me and a few of my brothers confronted with bad walls of fire that we had to fight our way out of and nearly got trapped ourselves. That's a good way to get killed, people giving you bad information.

We're up on a bridge above Highway 7 overpass and the two men ahead of us in the decapitated car have been nearly decapitated and I'm reluctant to walk up there and see them in their death and blood. Some of the younger boys I work with don't feel like this, but I've seen it too many times already. I take the cops' word for it and go back and cancel the rescue unit. They'll send the meat wagon but we don't say "meat wagon" over the radio. The FCC likes for you to be careful about what you say over the radio. No cussing, no bullshitting, just report your business and then stay the hell off the air except for what's necessary.

Later I'll take this incident and put it into a novella called *92 Days* and act like I made it up, but here they both are, black, and drunk, and gasping for breath, one of them, anyway, and he'll die soon, even before the ambulance can get him to the hospital, and the driver is already dead. He hit a tractor-trailer that was crossing the road while he was doing about ninety and slid all the way under it and out the other side for 105 feet. The cops have the tape out and are measuring the skid marks. One brake shoe was working. We've got our pumpers parked in the middle of the road with all our lights working and we were probably eating something or watching something just before we were called out to witness this death and destruction. The cops need some chalk and they don't have any, so I get back in the van and ride back up to the station for the chalk. I keep thinking about the guy with his head cut off. The business I'm in, you can never tell where it will lead you. One day somebody wants you to get a cat out of a tree and the next day some kid may be burning up inside a house. The night we went into C. B. Webb, when three apartments were on fire and it was coming through the roof, the people standing out in the yard told us there were some kids trapped inside. We fought our way through hellish rooms of fire, knocking it down everywhere, fighting our way to the top floor, where there were only burned mattresses and charred walls and no bodies to be found. We found out later that one guy had jumped from the top floor, had hit a clothesline, had luckily only broken one leg. He had been standing in the window and the people on the ground told him to jump or die. As it turned out they gave him good advice. He wouldn't have survived what had gone on up there.

I never laid my life on the line. That day when those two little babies and their grandmother burned up, I was out at the elementary school giving a fire extinguisher class with the chief, and I had relinquished my pumper to another man. We got the call during the class and I rode with Uncle Chiefy out there and the house was going down. I was breaking in a new boy, Phil Cooper, and nobody had even told him to put his gloves on. He stood there in the yard and did all he could and blistered his hands badly while holding an inch-and-a-half hose. The house fell in and then we were told that there were people inside. It was late in the evening by then, winter. The ruins were smoking. The family was black. Cops tried to keep screaming family members back. The smoke shifted in the rubble and we all stood back, dreading what we had to do. The back door had been nailed shut for some reason. Only God knows why people do the things they do. We couldn't have saved that house unless we'd gotten there early, before it got so bad. Sometimes you can never stop them. We wetted it down and crying women were held back by the police. We entered the back side of the house and no words were said. I felt the reverence of the event that was happening. The police had brought out the body bags. It seemed like a hundred people were in the street, screaming and crying. The smoke shifted among the rubble and we had to find the things we were looking for. It was hard to tell, everything being so burned, everything looking so much alike. Only a fireman or a victim of fire can tell you what a terrible thing fire is.

There was silence among us as our people bent and lifted the bodies out. The children were so small. I thought of my own. No words were said. Maybe it was February or March. The women were still screaming in the street. I wondered what my life would ever come to. I knew that these children had suffered a terrible death. I blamed it on poverty, and ignorance, and me not being in my fire station when I needed to be, instead of out with the chief giving a lecture on fire extinguishers, although what we had been doing could prevent things like this. But I felt that if I had been in my place, maybe I could have made some difference. Maybe I could have broken down the front door and opened my nozzle and saved those little kids and their grandmother from dying. The lights blinked out in the street and even the cops seemed touched by this. I know they have a hard time. People mess with them and they have to mess with the drunks. But I'd rather be a fireman than a cop. I'd like to help people if I could.

A few days later, I saw the man who was the father of the dead children come into the fire station to try and get his hands on a copy of the fire report so he could turn it into his insurance company. A poker game was going on at our big table in the middle of the kitchen. This poor middle-aged black man had his cap in his hands. His clothes were ragged and some of the boys I worked with just kept on betting and never looked crossways at him. Maybe they didn't know who he was. Their voices got louder while the man stood there patiently, waiting for the chief to find the report in his files. The man looked humbled by what had happened to him. I knew that his children had probably been buried quickly. The poker game went on and on and the man kept standing there with his cap in his hands, until finally, mercifully, Uncle Chiefy found the report and took the man back to the office to make a copy of it. I wanted to tell them to stop the poker game at least until he left, but of course I never said anything. Sometimes there was a weird callousness about the work we did. We couldn't let it get too close to us because we didn't want to be touched by it. You never heard anybody talk about it later. When it happened, it happened, and we dealt with it. Then we went back and slept or ate or watched a movie or went on another call. We got through our shifts and then we went home and went fishing or hunting or made love to our wives or played with our children. We hoped that the bad things we saw would never claim us. We hoped that we wouldn't die in smoke and flames or torn steel like the people we couldn't save.

Spring 1992

The Most Human Sound

ROSANNE CASH

I EAT NO MORE THAN FOUR ORANGES A YEAR. They're either too tart or too bland. Definitely too watery. But in the winter of 1981–1982, in the months of December and January, I ate nearly a dozen oranges a day. I was heavily pregnant with my second child, and I lived in a big log house in the woods of Middle Tennessee with my then-husband Rodney, my two-year-old daughter, and my six-year-old stepdaughter. It was one of the coldest winters on record in the South. The house stayed warm until it got down to about fifteen degrees; below that the beautiful old virgin pine just could not hold the heat. For days on end, as the temperature hovered around zero, and below, we all stayed close to the stone fireplace in the great room. Rodney kept the fire going (a full-time job) and the little girls played quietly with their dolls on a green turn-of-the-century Chinese rug that had been rescued from an old brothel in Western Kentucky. I sat in a rocking chair next to them, profile to the fire, a little melancholy, with a bag of oranges on my lap. I ate my way through a new bag each day, tossing the peels in the flames as I rocked. The bitter, wild aroma of singed oranges cut the somber iciness of the room and soothed me. It was my personal statement against the chill. I spent many long days like this.

In the first few days of January, three weeks before my due date, my old friend Randy Scruggs called to ask Rodney and me to participate in a

113

project he was doing with his dad, Earl, and Tom T. Hall. They were making a record called *The Storyteller and the Banjoman*. He invited us to come to his studio and sing on a couple of songs. It was around Earl's birthday and there would be a lot of people there. I was past the point of maternal glow, way past being cooed at and patted, and lately inspired only expressions of shock and nervous retreat at this penultimate phase of gestation. But Randy was my dear friend, the record would be finished before I delivered my baby, and I really wanted to sing on it, so I decided to go. I didn't have a coat big enough to close around my belly, and that night turned out to be the coldest one yet of the relentless winter. The air was blue when we stepped outside. The thermometer in the carport registered eleven below zero, and sharp little ice crystals rose in gusts from the hard-packed snow in the driveway. I sulked as we started the long drive to the studio. Rodney, experienced with the ramifications of unintentionally provoking a woman near the end of her third trimester, gave me a lot of room. It was a very quiet trip.

But it was a wonderful evening. We sang on three songs: "Shackles and Chains," "Roll in My Sweet Baby's Arms," and "Song of the South." Instead of being a sideshow freak, I was treated as a ripe little goddess, and it brought out the best in me. The company of friends and the balm of playing music was liberating, and I was fatigued, but content, when we left. The silence on our return had a decidedly different texture.

We drove, as if in a dream—past the empty country roads at the borders of wide fields enclosed by Civil War–era stone fences, past big, dark, and looming old estates and grand, columned mansions that lonesomely adjoined lazy suburban tracts.

We had not seen another car for several miles when we made the turn onto the pike that began the final leg to our hidden house in its miniature valley surrounded by thick oaks and maples. Rodney drove very carefully as this road was used less than the others, and it was still swathed in ice. I was drowsily contemplating a few oranges by the fire before bed. Suddenly, flashing red lights appeared on the shoulder of the opposite side of the road about a hundred feet ahead. We slowed to a crawl and as we came upon the scene, we saw an ambulance, a car behind it, and, in between the two, a man stretched out on his back on the frozen ground. The few people standing over him seemed in no hurry to get him into the ambulance.

"Oh, my God," we both said softly when we realized the man was dead. Rodney quickly glanced at me. I turned away, profoundly conscious of the baby inside me, reacting to a fierce, primal impulse to protect it from unexpected surges of my adrenaline—the heady, dangerous mix of the hormones of hysteria and fear.

There was clearly no way we could help, so we drove on. A mile or so farther, we were astonished to see, striding toward us up the road, a sturdy-looking middle-aged woman with a tall walking stick. Her gait was so determined, and the stick planted so authoritatively with each step, I could practically hear the drumbeat behind her march. More astonishing still, she was dressed only in a skirt and sweater: no coat, scarf, or gloves, and she was bare-legged. On her feet were awful brown oxford-type discount-store shoes, shaped carelessly from thin, cheap leather. Only sandals would have been more inappropriate in this weather.

Rodney stopped and rolled down his window. "Ma'am? Can we give you a ride somewhere?"

In a tight, high-pitched voice she said, "Are you sure you don't mind?" and then got into the backseat. She was pale and fair, and though her demeanor was reserved, even stiff, her eyes were darting about, and she spoke quickly. "Oh, thank you so much! I'm just going back up the road a little bit. My neighbor there called and said someone had been hit by a car, and my husband was out takin' a walk, and now I'm a little worried about him."

I didn't dare look at Rodney, but I could feel that we had both stopped breathing. My heart began to pound, and a queasy feeling rose in my abdomen. Rodney eased the car forward to a little cross street where he could turn around. Fortunately, we didn't have to say anything because the woman was chattering nervously.

"I told him it was too cold to go out walking, but he's stubborn. Said he had to have his evening constitutional no matter how cold it was. Now, are y'all sure you don't mind takin' me back up there?"

"No, ma'am, not at all," I said. "We saw some kind of disturbance back there, but I'm not sure what it was."

"Oh my Lord," she trilled, pleading and panicked. "Now, I don't want y'all to get hurt, too!"

I was struck by that sentence as if by a two-by-four. It still reverberates now, fifteen years later: the pitch of her voice, her self-effacing Southern politeness, the tears building behind the contained panic, the uncontrolled sense that danger newly pervaded the entire world. My heart broke for her. In about thirty seconds her entire life was going to detonate and two strangers were sharing her last moments of peace. But it was not my place to tell her.

It was several years later that a friend gave me a tape of Irish keening, which is the sound of women wailing at the graves of their loved ones— long, sustained, unbearably plaintive cries elevated by the deepest sorrow to an art form; the most human sound of the genesis of music. It sent chills down my back and brought tears to my eyes when I first heard it, and the first thing I thought of was her.

She got out of the car that night and a woman came up to her and put her arm around her shoulder and began to talk softly to her. We waited for a moment, then drove slowly away.

Through the closed car windows I could hear her screams: long, deep, circular cries, rising from the roots of her body, like a train whistle disappearing into an endless series of tunnels, like the wrenching Gaelic echoes that hang in the graveyard, like the hiss that escapes from the permanently shattered heart.

I had to borrow from my future that night in protection of my unborn baby. I drew from an unknown reserve of circumspection. "I will feel this later," I thought. And I was unyielding, my hands over my ears, my head bent to my chest.

And I paid, with interest.

On January 25th of that year, I gave birth, after only six hours of labor, to a gorgeous, nearly nine-pound baby girl with enormous bright blue eyes. She was healthy and strong, and I felt proud that I had done my job so well. We named her Chelsea Jane, and I swaddled her warmly and took her home to the big log house. The girls welcomed their little sister and the temperature gradually eased back up into the thirties, where it belonged. My natural indifference to oranges returned abruptly, and the last few left in the bag shriveled and gathered mold before I finally threw them away. I kept the newspaper clipping: "Man Killed By Car On Icy Road," for a week or so longer, and then, that too, I threw away.

Summer 1997

Hussy in the Hood

TIM GAUTREAUX

IN 1958, WHEN I WAS ELEVEN YEARS OLD, a Hollywood production company came to my swampy little town in South Louisiana to shoot a feature. They set up their cameras outside the levee in an area known as "the Pit." No one seemed to know exactly what type of movie it would be, and once shooting started, some of the townspeople would come out and stand in the long, seedy grass of the levee north of town, watching the mysterious outlanders with West Coast accents and guessing at what they were doing. It was the '50s, and people were easily entertained. My father drove us along the clamshell road that skirted the levee, and we got out, fought the grass to the top, and sat down on the opposite slope. Fifty yards in front of us was the Pit, a chocolate-colored waterway bordered with a few shotgun houses on stilts, sunken trawlers, long-legged chicken coops, and camp boats. Across the water was an island carpeted with low willows, and beyond that the Intracoastal Waterway. The cameras and light stands were set up near a group of fishermen who were dunking their hoop nets into a vat of smoking tar. One net was hung high in a tree, open side down, and beneath it a pair of men dressed in clothes a little too new and clean began to fistfight and roll on the ground. Even then I could see it was a slow and silly fight; I'd seen much worse in my school yard. The men grappled until the hoop net fell out of the tree onto one of the combatants and the director yelled,

118

"Cut!" The cameraman pulled out a cigarette, and the light men began to walk back to their truck. They were ordinary-looking people doing a job. The only interesting thing about the scene was that we didn't know what the fight was about.

I spotted my great-uncle Leo standing barefoot on a drift log, his arms folded across his khaki shirt. My father walked over and began to speak to him in French, gesturing toward the cameras, and when I came up, he switched to English for my benefit. Leo, who'd trapped all his life, lived in a large camp boat at the entrance to the Pit, where it opened into the Atchafalaya River. In fact, the movie, he told us, was titled *The Pit* and, as best he could understand, was an adventure tale about competition between two brothers who were moss pickers. As to the scene we had just witnessed, Leo had no idea why the men were fighting. Any fool could see there was moss enough for anybody who wanted it.

On the way home I wondered why moviemakers would travel from California and come to the worst part of Morgan City, Louisiana, to film moss pickers. It made no sense. During the next few weeks I overheard people mention the film over coffee and on street corners. I began to wonder about this question that seemed stuck in the back of the town's mind, in the back of my own mind: How would Hollywood make us look? Eventually the movie crew disappeared from the Pit, set up for a few scenes at a plantation house five miles west, and then ebbed away toward California. Some months passed, and I don't think people in town thought about the movie very much, or if they did, it was the way they thought about a roll of film they'd dropped off at the drugstore and kept forgetting to pick up.

And then, I believe it was the middle of 1959, the news spread around town that the movie was coming back and would make its World Premiere at the Opera House downtown. When I heard this, I rode to the theater on my Schwinn and studied the marquee. I'm sure my mouth dropped open when I saw that someone had strung Spanish moss and nailed up big green hands of palmettos along the borders of the theater's sign, as though a population who lived in the middle of a billion cubic feet of moss and millions of palmettos didn't know what these plants were. What really hung my jaw was the movie's title, sliding out from behind like a blacksnake. Instead of *The Pit* the movie had been renamed *Louisiana Hussy*.

I had heard my mother use the word *hussy* in connection with certain local disreputable barmaids, and I linked the term with a species of train-wreck romance far beyond my interest. I was a Catholic-school kid, and the nuns had instilled some dim notion in me that I should not be interested in hussies, whatever they were. The whole town was basically Catholic, and I imagined that the priest planned to aim a few choice warnings the movie's way at eleven o'clock Sunday Mass. The effect the title had on me was that the film was some boring, cut-rate, Loretta Young-type thing, so I knocked back my kickstand and pedaled off into the rest of my youth.

Forty-one years later I was surfing an Internet auction site when I stumbled across a VHS copy of *Louisiana Hussy*. Seeing that title was like answering a knock at my front door and finding a superannuated, ugly second cousin coming for a semicentennial visit. Out of hospitality to the past, I bought the video and watched it in my living room, imagining that I was in the Opera House, part of that long-ago Morgan City audience. The movie appeared to be nothing more than a sleaze flick, as explicit as was legal in 1958. I think I can interpret how the audience felt about this one; people in little towns were of a singular mind then, all minnows in the same cozy puddle.

The movie is about a woman on the run, a cotton-mill cutie from the Carolinas described on the VHS box as a person of "bra-busting architecture." She is hired by a Louisiana plantation owner as a companion for his invalid wife. It is not long before her companionable traits are transferred intimately to the owner himself, and when the wife realizes that her husband has been seduced, she commits suicide. The grieving plantation owner runs off the Hussy, who then makes her escape on horseback. For some reason—perhaps her architecture—she falls off the horse after a few miles and is found by the somewhat cross-eyed leading man of the movie, Jacques Guillot, Cajun moss picker and brother of the feisty Pierre. It turns out that Pierre is getting married the next day, and somehow the injured Hussy winds up spending the night with the newlyweds in their brick-paper shack and seducing the bridegroom to boot. No sooner does she conquer Pierre than she beguiles the touchy Jacques and pits the brothers against each other. The sex scenes, though mostly clothed, are very racy for the late '50s. Several times, when the Hussy is at some pinnacle of delight, the camera rakes a corny close-up of one of her hands knotting the bedsheet. The script seems written by a slow-witted ninth-grader and ends with a foot chase through a swamp and a Hussy escape in an open jeep. When that vehicle runs out of gas in the mountains (mountains near Louisiana?), the Hussy seduces a portly old gent, obviously a student of her architecture, who has stopped his Cadillac to help her out. This final scene, which appears not to be a part of the same movie, is done with all the wit and subtlety of a Three Stooges short. The acting is that of a bad junior high play (here I recall the scene of Jacques and Hussy dancing the twist in his camp boat), and the South Louisiana accents are terrible, though Jacques has spent some time in Canada, I believe. The "gris-gris" woman named Callie, who speaks like a character out of a Charles Laughton movie, is just plain silly, a broad miss at a stereotype. The set consists of what was already there on the canal bank. Even the interior shots are made in somebody's camp boat borrowed for the afternoon. The only set expense I could detect was a square of poster board and a felt marking pen used to make Jacques's and Pierre's new moss pickers sign, a symbol of their reunion after the Hussy leaves town. In this movie the poor people are all stupid, the plantation owner is a lusty drunk, and the town doctor dresses like a crab fisherman. And the music! As one Cajun resident is paddling his pirogue up the slough, the soundtrack plays "Santa Lucia" as if the little Frenchman is supposed to be a gondolier. More lively sections of the film are backed by goofy, barn-dance tunes like "Skip to My Lou" and "Jimmy Crack Corn." No one in the movie seems to show a molecule of conventional moral scruple, hard to understand for a region so steeped in Catholicism that honky-tonk jukeboxes were always unplugged on Good Friday. The movie represents Louisiana's French heritage and music the way Chef Boyardee represents Italian cuisine.

The audience at the World Premiere included, I'm sure, some of the town's boosters, perhaps a councilman or two, maybe the librarian and the fire chief's wife, some teachers, and a raft of fishermen. I feel sorry for all of them because they were probably embarrassed and disappointed. Morgan City was a rough town, and there was enough tawdry behavior going on to make several salty movies, but by and large it was a pretty proper place, and I suspect that back then people hoped something better than the Hussy would represent where they lived.

So Hollywood got it wrong. No surprise. They generally know they're getting it wrong and plunge ahead anyway. The question that occurs to me now is, Why did they get it wrong in the South? The bad script could have been shot anywhere: poverty, ignorance, and people of bad character exist in every state in the union. Granted, a title like *Delaware Hussy* or *North Dakota Hussy* does not carry the same cachet, but how did the South get this cachet in the first place? Are we really so depraved, genetically challenged, and stupid that illogical scripts seem to work down here? Was this one of the worries in the minds of the audience members at the World Premiere, that Hollywood sees the South as a place where dumb scripts can go to be made into believable movies?

Maybe I'm looking too seriously at a lightweight film here, killing a garden slug with a shotgun, but the point is, an audience's reaction to a movie that touches on its culture is pretty damned significant. They can tell if the director got it right or if Hollywood continued its usual guessing game, relying on stereotypes and clichés that run all the way back to the first mint julep. Many years later I can pretend to be in that audience, and I can tell that when you get it wrong locally, you get it wrong universally as well. My advice to people shooting films in the South is to pretend they're in the Balkans or in some other complicated place about which they know nothing at all. Ask directions from the locals, for God's sake.

After my VCR rewound and clicked off I wondered if the company could have done better by us had it had a bigger budget. Then I thought of *The Big Easy*, which was entertaining but as inaccurate as they come, with its bungled accents and scenes of Cajun house dances that are unknown phenomena in Orleans Parish. No, a bigger budget only allows for more elaborate and expensive mistakes. I've also seen low-budget productions done by locals, such as the lobotomized *Terror in the Swamp* (which seemed to be filmed by a loup-garou high on cheap wine stumbling around in a palmetto thicket holding a Sears Super 8 camera), an unintentional self-parody.

If money's not the answer, then what about direction? I'm sure this was the biggest part of the problem with *Louisiana Hussy*, which was directed by Lee Sholem, who hailed from Paris, Illinois, and who had such notable productions as *Superman and the Mole Men* to his credit, not to mention *Ma and Pa Kettle at Waikiki*. When Lee and his crew descended into my swamp, it was like a polka band showing up in the projects to play hip-hop. Here was another West Coast group out to Californicate a culture because they didn't understand where they were. They certainly didn't understand that they had landed in the middle of a complex mini-culture (Cajun) that's one of dozens that make up the South.

Louisiana Hussy gives rise to the question, How does someone make a Southern film that is both good and good for you, i.e., culturally real? I would guess that one of two things is necessary: a genius director who does his research and finds good people from inside a culture to advise him, or a smart director from within the culture itself who understands the details (for example, that chicory coffee isn't popular outside of the New Orleans area and that diatonic accordion music was a thing unknown east of the Atchafalaya River until the 1980s). The director of the Great Southern Movie, or the Great Birmingham Steel Mill Movie, or the Great East Texas Bingo Hall Movie, will probably rise from a culture that he knows heart and soul. Once he makes his Great Film, it will be an archetype that can be extended and reproduced in the Great Amish Movie, the Great Norwegian-American Movie, and so on to the horizon.

Did *Louisiana Hussy* do any harm? Judging from a dozen phone calls I made to people who were around when the movie was made, nobody in town remembers it at all. Aside from the World Premiere audience, I'd say the effect was miniscule. (Not so with *The Big Easy*, which changed New Orleans' nickname forever. I'd never heard the soubriquet before the movie appeared. And because of this film, millions of Americans have come to New Orleans expecting it to be a Cajun town, causing some restaurants and bars to meet these expectations by hiring old-line French accordion bands and ratcheting up the menus with lots of pepper and roux-based dishes. It seems to me that New Orleans' tourist-oriented music stores sell more Cajun and zydeco CDs than they do in Lafayette, the heart of Cajun country). One casualty of the movie might have been the Hussy herself. Nan Peterson, who completely busted out of the movie business after this film was released. Pierre's bayou wife (by the way, I have never met anyone in Louisiana named Pierre, or Jacques, for that matter) eventually morphed into another cultural artifact, Barney Fife's girlfriend, Thelma Lou, on *The Andy Griffith Show*.

My flint-eyed great-uncle Leo, who lived on the set, never went to see the movie. He might have had the right idea. However, I keep thinking back to that first audience, and now I wish that I had been at the World Premiere. I'd have sat on the lumpy seats stuffed with steel coil springs and, yes, moss, watching the square screen, trying to see how we were, how much of us was in the accents and the lust, the weather-wracked cabins and the whitewashed boats listing into the tea-colored water, and understanding for the first time, maybe, how much of us was not up there on the screen, and holding on to that, instead.

Winter 2002

Horses and Boys

MARIANNE GINGHER

IN THE SPRING OF 1960 I BOARDED MY HORSE, CHEROKEE, at the Hill 'n' Dale Hack Shack. Burt LaMarr owned the Hack Shack and managed it as a boarding facility and riding school. He was probably in his late thirties, divorced (or getting there), and frequently you could smell liquor on his breath. His style of management was that he was everybody's pal.

A group of teenage girls, older than I was, hung out at the Hack Shack. A couple of them owned horses, which they boarded there, but the majority had a more ambiguous purpose. They mucked out stalls for Burt LaMarr and exercised his horses, and I don't think they got paid. They did the work because they were devoted to the place; my mother speculated that they did it because they were devoted to Burt.

They were lithe and fearless girls, the bravest riders I ever knew, utterly relaxed on horseback, their bones astutely floppy. Burt had taught them everything they knew about horses, and they rode with slit-eyed smugness, so confident that they looked sleepy. If a horse refused a jump and nearly threw them off, they sagged upon the horse's neck and laughed in its face. If they fell, they bounced up nimbly from the dust, like fallen acrobats springing from a safety net.

When the girls weren't riding or shoveling out stalls, they enthroned themselves on bales of straw, telling dirty jokes. Or they saddle-soaped tack. Or they leaned dreamily on fence posts and sucked in the daze-making air of the place. They satisfied themselves simply by being there.

I saw enthrallment in their faces when they talked to Burt. They competed for his attention the way pupils of a favored teacher might. But if any of them went slinking into the hayloft with him—as my mother suspected—nobody bragged or cried or whispered about it to me.

I viewed them all as girls foremost in love with horses. Burt was their means of access. That he was a cowboy and spoke their language, that he loved the horses, too, and was keen around animals, even when he was drinking, made him kindred. They thought of him, perhaps, as half-man and half-horse. It was a natural extension of their love for the horses if the girls admitted Burt into their hearts as well. They watched him stroke his ruddy man's hand down the neck of a troubled horse and listened raptly to his kindly, confidential voice, and they believed in the sort of man who probably does not exist except in lulls and snatches. His soft-spoken, placating manner earned their fantasies and crushes, unhealthy or not, but it was the girls themselves whom he seemed to shepherd away from trouble.

I never felt included in the camaraderie of the Hack Shack. I was wary around Burt LaMarr because of my mother's suspicions. I felt intimidated by the older girls, their daredevilry, their hotshot riding skills, the sensual drapery they made of themselves whenever they embraced a horse. When the weather turned steamy, they rode in their bathing suits and Burt squirted them with a hose.

The stable itself was a squat, grubby shelter; there were tree stumps in the yard that we used for mounting blocks. There were no riding trails close by, no streams or woods. The surrounding land had the exhausted, weedy look of lapsed maintenance. Above the barn and riding ring slanted one small, bleak, brier-stubbled field that always made me think of the fabled Wild West cemetery Boot Hill. But if you left the stable grounds and rode your horse along the narrow shoulders of either Lawndale Drive or Battleground Road, you contended with heavy traffic. The Hack Shack property, squeezed by development, had no rural context. It was more of a hangout than a genuine farm, my mother said. She didn't approve of Burt's loose supervision. The name Hack Shack sounded sleazy, she said.

I wasn't yet thirteen—a totally guileless, stringy-limbed, horse-crazy tomboy. My notion of paradise was spending a weekend with my girlfriend, who lived on a dairy farm, and rolling around in the silage. I had nothing in common with the Hack Shack girls, who were on the verge of giving up their horses for boys, who lit their cigarettes with big wooden kitchen matches that, now and again, they struck against one leg of Burt LaMarr's tight jeans.

Yet my parents feared for my innocence. There was too much fecundity adrift at the Hack Shack: too much animal breath, cats birthing kittens in straw, the feverish copulation of green flies in dung. High up in the barn rafters cobwebs floated as silkily as tossed-off lingerie. And so my parents made arrangements to board Cherokee elsewhere.

Normally docile, Cherokee was a stocky, compact, easily managed horse. The white blaze on his forehead, as bright and friendly as a search beam, gave him a bedazzled look. His shaggy fetlocks fringed tough, platter-shaped hooves that went unshod. Heavyset, molasses-colored, with a blond mane and tail, he gave evidence of having Belgian work-horse in his mixed-up blood. He was considered a pleasure horse because he never said no, but there he stood on moving day, a massive block of rootedness, telling Burt LaMarr no. As Burt tried to tug him toward the horse trailer, Cherokee snorted and balked. He turned into a monument of resistance—magnificently large and unruly. No, he would not clomp onto that strange little stall on wheels—and go where?

I interpreted Cherokee's fear as some awareness, similar to a wave of encroaching homesickness, that he was about to be parted from familiar ground. I imagined that tears glimmered in his eyes. When I stepped forward to comfort him, Burt briskly directed me out of the way and produced from his pocket the dreadful twitch.

It was a simple tool: a blunt wooden paddle with a cord of thick rope looped through one end. The rope lassoed an animal's top lip and, when twisted, cinched it. I watched as Burt applied the twitch while the dispassionate Hack Shack girls smacked Cherokee's flanks with sticks. "Get into the damn trailer, you son of a bitch," one of them snarled—and in front of my father.

I was nearly crying. I was years from experiencing an inkling of what the Hack Shack girls knew about timely assertions against brute force. They were not, these girls, in as much danger as my parents supposed; a precocious toughness carapaced their hearts, a toughness that would elude me for decades and arrive only in miserly increments. Perhaps this is what my parents knew about me: that I needed time to love my horse in my own sprawling and unprotected way. And they were moving us to a place where I could do just that—be a softhearted child for as long as I could, love my horse on my own silly terms, not anybody else's, humanize him, let him break my heart, make a fool of me with his orneriness. I was an eager, sacrificial kind of young girl. I could only learn to be master by first offering myself as slave. I would not be ready to move past my idolatrous love of a horse into other phases of rapturous preoccupation—writing poetry, painting, searching for a boyfriend—until, like the Hack Shack girls, I could view Cherokee as an obstacle and bully him out of my way with a stick.

Mr. Tom Lambeth, the retired owner of a Greensboro, North Carolina, construction company, lived just outside the city limits on nearly fifteen acres of unspoiled countryside wedged between Westridge and Jefferson roads. His vista included lawns as pampered as golf greens, sloping pastures, a scrubby field or two fringed by woods, flower and vegetable gardens, an arbor of scuppernong grapes, and down a sandy lane that led from his house and through a gate, a tidy red-and-white-painted Dutch Colonial barn with a corral. His farm was one of the last well-kept expanses of verdure between Greensboro and Guilford College.

Mr. Lambeth's own house, set back from Westridge among a huddle of shade trees, was an unaffected but spacious ranch with the assertive, modern look of crank-style windows. The house had yellow shutters—a woman's sunny touch, I always thought, probably because Mr. Lambeth was so hard-boiled. But I do not recall meeting his wife and seem to remember that she was an invalid. The household was well tended by people in uniform: a cook, a maid, perhaps nurses, bustled in and out. On occasion, when I needed to use the telephone and entered the back door as I'd been instructed to do, I observed a meticulous order. A spotless kitchen was always redolent of someone's supper preparations. Sometimes I spied a pie, set on a trivet to cool. Deep within the mahogany shadows of the house I could hear a mantel clock ticking.

A young, neatly dressed handyman named Willie—polite in a simmering way, like Sidney Poitier—mowed the yard and fields, repaired fences, tended the garden, stacked firewood, and generally did whatever Mr. Lambeth required to ensure the farm's upkeep. Mr. Lambeth himself had ceased laboring. I suppose I believed he was a taskmaster, adept at barking orders and keeping his help busy. I never observed Willie lounging on a bale of straw, daydreaming like the Hack Shack girls.

Mr. Lambeth was a small, taut man with a flushed and veiny face. He had a full head of whitening hair that reared stiffly back from his tall forehead. He was slight enough to have been a jockey and gave the impression of having sat atop many a horse in the winner's circle. His stance, slightly bowlegged and sporty, made him look like he was wearing jodhpurs. I never saw him ride a horse, nor did he own any animals. He smoked cigars, ventured not a syllable of small talk, carried a walking stick, and possessed a skeweringly judgmental blue-eyed gaze. I was, of course, afraid of him. As a landlord, he loomed over the pleasure we took from his property as a kind of gentrified Oz.

I don't know why he opened his farm to us. He didn't need rental money. He could have kept its pastoral serenity intact. Perhaps he missed the commotion of his long-grown children. He had been a family man.

My father, a doctor, had found out about Mr. Lambeth's barn through a patient whose daughter boarded her horse there. Stall and pasture rental was fifteen dollars a month. We were required to order and pay for our grain and hay and to share feeding duties with the other boarders.

My father and I drove together into Mr. Lambeth's kingdom on the morning we moved Cherokee. Burt LaMarr's truck, towing the trailer on which Cherokee had bravely borne his journey across town, rumbled close behind. Mr. Lambeth was waiting at the pasture gate. Beyond him unfurled acres of shining pastureland bordered by woods and swamps of shade. A froth of wildflowers drifted atop the tall grass, and all manner of insects and birds swooped in giddy trajectory, as if carrying love notes from one end of the land to the other. My impulse was to leap out of the car before it stopped, rush for the gate, and slip into that wild, green world, unimpeded by the nice skirt my mother had insisted that I wear and the protocol of introductions. My mother had wanted me to make a good impression on Mr. Lambeth, not to appear to be too much of a ruffian.

A girl emerged from the woods as if she were a dream of my freed self. She was my age, brown as cider, with a cap of ginger-colored sunlit hair. She wore shorts, a t-shirt, and holey sneakers without socks. She was leading a plump black-and-white spotted mare by a halter, and she arced her free arm in a broad and friendly wave.

"That's Sunny," Mr. Lambeth said.

Burt LaMarr had parked his truck, preparing to unload Cherokee. I watched Mr. Lambeth sizing *him* up as a ruffian—I was glad I had worn my skirt—then I moseyed over to the gate to talk with Sunny.

"It's a beautiful place you've got here, Mr. Lambeth," my father said.

"Yes indeed," said Mr. Lambeth, puffing his cigar.

"Horse heaven," my father said, grinning at me.

"Girl and horse heaven," amended Sunny.

"That's right," said Mr. Lambeth. "Girl and horse heaven." He swept the land with a proprietary gaze. He studied Sunny and me, too, as if searching for proof that we had not misrepresented our intentions. We were a couple of good, trustworthy innocents, weren't we? He seemed to peer into our very hearts as if into arenas where fences might need mending or reinforcement.

"There's one rule here," he said. "No boys allowed."

Time spent at the barn in the company of horses and dogs and field mice and blacksnakes and spiders who strung webs the size of hammocks and wanton stray cats who furtively dropped their litters in the hayloft introduced me to the gorgeous righteousness of the small, the brutal, the ugly, and the forgotten. In the flare of a horse's nostril I glimpsed something as private and visceral as the pulsing of a heart. My little piano-practicing palms grew calloused. I could poke a dead bird with a stick and not wince at the maggots stitching in and out. Time spent breathing the pungent air above fermenting piles of dung steeping in warm grass—a scent not unlike the fragrance of my father's whiskey sours—and time spent showboating, riding backward, sidesaddle, provoking Cherokee to buck me off, daring him, goading him without mercy, clanging against earth, landing in thorns and mud and jumping back on, crazy time in such diversions transformed me into some dusty creature midway between child and pest: part girl, part crust, more spit than dewdrop. I turned tawny, shucked off my pearly indoors skin, and tanned the colors of Cherokee himself, the better to fuse with him and disappear. When I was at the barn, I did not want to separate myself from a single mote or splinter of it.

We rode rowdily, without helmets, cowgirls in English saddles (mine was actually an old cavalry saddle that a relative had given me). Sometimes we mounted our horses from the rear, at a run, then whooped across the big pasture as startled birds flapped out of the weeds. We were still young enough to play gypsies or Indian girls. We made costumes and painted our horses and braided their tails with feathers. When it snowed—a phenomenon in our part of North Carolina—and schools closed, we'd head for the barn with our sleds. Attaching them to our saddles with long swags of rope, we'd journey into the suburbs to sell horse-drawn sled rides to the kids.

Each summer morning, before the day grew hot, we took trail rides. Beyond Mr. Lambeth's fences, woods and fields were plentiful. We discovered an old logging path that twisted through vacant land between Jefferson Road and Guilford College. We knew where there was a ravaged apple orchard, never harvested, and we took advantage of the fruit that by midsummer bowed the tree limbs. Our horses grazed on what had fallen on the ground while we lolled on their backs in the buzzing shade, eating apples so tart they made our teeth chime. We took the horses swimming in the Guilford College lake. The movement of a horse in deep water is the distinctly lilting up-and-down rhythm of a carousel animal. Up and down they pumped, with astonishment on their faces, snorting at the water, tricked into it but trembling with the thrill of buoyancy and cool. Their dung rose and bobbed plumply on the water's surface.

We investigated all open and wooded land, posted or unposted, within a five-mile radius of Mr. Lambeth's barn. Of course we weren't foolish enough to jump our horses over barbed wire fences, but where we found breaks in the wire, we trespassed, possessed by a pioneer's sense of entitlement.

The terrain that we crossed on horseback seemed as varied as continents, and we named each parcel for its distinctive traits, like explorers would have done. We called a sun-blasted barren field "Wester." A lush acreage bordered by tall black cedars that floated above the land like unbottled genies we named "Greenfields," after a popular wistful song by the Kingston Trio. The fact that we were smitten by the nearly holy loveliness of these places—so much so that we were compelled to lavish them with lyrical titles—suggests to me that at twelve or thirteen we not only cherished but feared losing them. Naming the fields and woods that we traversed gave them permanence. How could a young, reckless girl, cometing her horse across a meadow, foresee the end of such completely healthy wildness, bring her horse to a halt, and for an instant, grieve for the delicacy of her joy and what might become of it? But I say that more than once this happened to us. We were nostalgic for our girlhoods even before we began to lose them. It was 1960. Ours may have been the last uncynical girlhoods possible in America.

We took risks, imperiled ourselves in a thousand ways, might have killed ourselves a time or two but for luck or good timing. Daring had nothing to do with our boldness; freedom did. We ordered and dispensed all our own grain and hay; we phoned the vets and farriers. Sometimes the horses broke out of their fences and we chased them down Westridge Road, stopping traffic, racing through people's yards, ducking clotheslines, sweet-talking to lure them back. Once, in a runaway, somebody was nearly beheaded when her horse dashed under the grape arbor. Once, we found newborn kittens that had been cannibalized by wasps.

At the barn, we entered a world more harrowing and unsparing in its lessons in brutality and coarseness than our parents ever suspected. We saturated ourselves with it, yielded entirely to its roughness, its flashes of grace.

At school I felt like the Clark Kent version of my Superman self. My hands looked awkward in repose, scratched and bruised, the insides of my palms and fingers waxy and tough from tugging off baling wire and jerking reins. I clunked around gawkily, tall and flat-chested. I wore powder blue harlequin glasses and fat biscuit-looking tie-shoes for arch support because I had pronated ankles. Everybody else scooted around the hallways on slim loafers. On rare occasions I was invited to a make-out party by some loser boy who had mysteriously deemed me worth a try; but I was not interested in making out. I seemed to be permanently encased in a protective aura of barnness. If there had been a boy who looked like Cherokee, I might have been tempted. Young teenage boys are only physically dissimilar from horses: They are human versions, behaving with the same plodding indifference and erratic civility toward a young girl's worshipfulness.

I turned thirteen, fourteen, and I entered eighth grade. Some afternoons after school I rode a different bus—not home but to the barn. I didn't know many of the kids I sat with. One cocky, older high school boy named Kenny rode the Westridge Road bus, and he began to pay attention to me. His stop was farther down the road, but he frequently threatened to disembark at mine and follow me up to the barn. He had a lank flag of oaky blond hair and wet, pouty, rock-singer lips. He wore dark glasses, but whenever he slid them down the bridge of his nose to peer more closely at me, I saw that his eyes were the icy blue of breath mints. He carried a rabbit's foot on a chain for good luck, and he was always taking it out and trying to swing it in front of some girl's face to hypnotize her.

"Where's it at?" he said, craning his neck to try to see the barn through the trees. "I don't see no barn."

"It's way back behind Mr. Lambeth's house. You can't see it from the road," I told him, hastily gathering up my books.

"Is there a hayloft? I sure do love a hayloft."

"It's private property," I told him sternly. His lackeys, toad-shaped younger boys, laughed.

"I want to see the hayloft, Blondie."

"I already told you it's private property, no boys allowed."

"Well, maybe I forgot you told me that," Kenny said, grinning. "Or maybe I just happened to be out for a walk one day and got lost and accidentally wandered into the private property that I forgot you told me about. Next I found the hayloft, and you were up inside it. What would you do then?"

I couldn't judge his intentions or the narrow distance between flirtation and meanness. I didn't know what I would do if he surprised me in the hayloft. I only hoped he was teasing.

"I'd scream if I was her," said one of the toad boys, and everybody laughed, including me.

"Hey, Blondie!" they shouted out the windows as I scurried off the bus and down Mr. Lambeth's driveway. "Invite Kenny to go riding with you some day. Hey, girl!"

By twilight on such an afternoon, if I was the only girl up at the barn, every muted creak as the barn shifted and settled in the evening cool, every wind-jittered pane spooked me. I jumped if a horse snorted or pawed. I imagined Kenny's loose, oily shadow spilling down the stairs from the loft into the feed and tack room where I worked, and my heart pounded with the dread of reckoning.

He never came, but I listened for him, and I tried to determine what I would say when he finally detached himself from the shadows. If by his teasing he had diminished the haven I'd always believed the barn provided, then I owed him anger, although he was big and merciless. Yet a part of me was made restive by his threats of invasion, tantalized. I even thought I understood his bluster. It was similar to our charging our horses at fences too high to jump or entering posted land, snarly with vines, and daring something perilous.

I began to think of Kenny when I brushed and curried Cherokee. I had too much time to think. I imagined him slipping up on me and fastening his hand over my mouth like a gag. I imagined myself screaming. But Sunny and I were always screaming and laughing and hollering over something, and who might distinguish one sort of scream from another? I imagined myself going limp, perhaps fainting, and Kenny leading or carrying me into the loft and kissing me there. I imagined that his lips would be warm and soft, not brutal. I imagined Mr. Lambeth, who couldn't hear the scream, hearing the kiss and rushing up to the barn, bursting in on us, furious at my betrayal. I pictured my unstoppable leakage of tears as I tried to explain myself, knowing full well that what I had done was irrevocable. Whatever was happening to me felt dire and skulking, panicky and profuse.

In the months that followed, I was not unhappy, not bored. I felt vaguely uneasy, as if I had mislaid something vital. The barn felt vacuous, my chores mechanical. The windows at sundown flashed unbearably luminous; the moon seemed too full and Cherokee, too simple. I could not stop thinking about the benefits of being elsewhere.

Was it boys I gave up my girlhood for—or was it ambition? Was it mistaking one for the other? Soon I would sell Cherokee to a cowboy who wanted to show him Western Pleasure. I had misgivings. To an English rider, like I was, the thought of dressing a horse in the heavy, ornate gear of Western tack seemed the clodhopper equivalent to outfitting him for the Grand Ole Opry. I felt as if I were selling Cherokee to another country, betraying our manners and our style. But the day the man led him away, my heart didn't lurch. He was, after all, just a horse.

November/December 2000

The Faulkner Thing

JOHN GRISHAM

IT WAS DALLAS, OR SOME OTHER CITY. They all look the same at the end of a book tour so it makes no difference where you are, really, you just keep telling yourself that this city, whatever it is, is one step closer to home. I was sitting on a small, creaky, makeshift throne in a corner of a quaint little bookshop. The throne was between the fishing and erotica shelves; my back was to the poetry. Before me was a table stacked with copies of *The Firm,* and beyond it a line of people waited patiently as I scribbled my name and made impossible small talk.

I heard a commotion at the front door, then saw her as she surveyed the place and headed for me. Behind her was a burly cameraman, and he followed her with great discipline as she elbowed past the others and approached me. She had plastic hair and an orange face, and I knew immediately she was another of those busy TV beat reporters scouring the streets looking for holdups and house fires. Evidently, it was a slow day for Dallas (?), so she dropped by the bookstore to gather a few gems from the guy who wrote *The Firm.*

On this day, I had already suffered through three interviews, all properly arranged through my publisher, and I was in no mood for another, especially one that materialized from nowhere. I scrawled my name, thanked the person, and tried to ignore the reporter. But there she was, suddenly standing near me with a microphone.

"Are you John Grisham?" she asked loudly, waving the mike.

I did not look up but began inscribing the next book. I wrote very slowly. She was the first interviewer to ask that question.

"Of course he is," said a man waiting in line. I, too, thought it was rather obvious who I was.

"Is it true you live in Oxford, Mississippi?" she asked, even louder. Why would I lie about something like this? My picture is on the dust jacket, and under it is a sentence that plainly states where I live.

"Yes," I said abruptly, without looking into the orange face.

This inspired her. She came closer and stabbed the mike to within inches of my head. The bouncer with the camera hit a switch, and suddenly there was bright light everywhere.

"How do you compare yourself with William Faulkner?" she asked.

A handful of morons have asked me this question, and nothing irritates me more. Those who ask it have read neither Faulkner nor Grisham but are sharp enough to know Oxford is home for both of us.

"Faulkner's dead," I said, glancing in her general direction but being careful not to look at the camera.

I'm sure she knew he was dead, but she seemed a bit surprised. Undaunted, she pressed ahead. "It must be difficult to write in Oxford," she said.

It's difficult to write anywhere. I have found nothing in life more boring than staring at an empty sheet of paper and praying that something happens. But, truthfully, if you're going to write for a living, there's no better place than Oxford.

"Why?" I asked.

"Well, you know, the Faulkner thing."

There are least a half a dozen published novelists in Oxford. I know them, some better than others, and I see them occasionally at Square Books or Smitty's or at parties, and we talk about books and editors and agents and deadlines and other writers, but I have yet to hear any of them discuss "the Faulkner thing." He was a literary artist of immense proportions, a genius, a writer thoroughly dedicated to his craft, the greatest American novelist of this century. He won the Nobel. He was peerless, but, bless his heart, he's dead. Life goes on for the rest of us.

I decided not to be ugly. "Do you read Faulkner?" I asked with a smile as I signed another book.

She hesitated. "Some." I knew she was lying.

"What's your favorite Faulkner novel?" I asked.

Hesitation. Everyone in line waited. Painful hesitation. I slowly signed another book as the mike stopped waving and everything was silent.

"Uh, let's see, I guess, *The Reivers*," she said in desperation.

They made a movie out of *The Reivers* and it starred Steve McQueen, who at the time was much more famous than William Faulkner. Nothing against the novel—it's a fun story—but it's not exactly his masterpiece. I figured she had seen the movie but had not read the book.

I was about to nail her and ask the titles of her second and third favorite Faulkner novels when she seized the moment and said, "I've been to Oxford, you know."

"What for?" I asked.

"I was a cheerleader, and we competed there."

Of course. I said, "It's a lovely town, isn't it?"

She slinked forward, the microphone now centimeters from my nose. "It's beautiful. I went to Rowan Oak, you know, Faulkner's place," she said. "I could almost feel his presence."

I almost asked what she had been drinking when she went to Rowan Oak and felt his presence, but again, I decided not to be ugly. She was just trying to do her job. The philistine with the Minicam stepped on a woman's foot, and the woman snapped at him, and for a second things were almost out of hand. He apologized without removing his face from the camera. The owner of the bookstore appeared at the end of the line to see what was happening.

The orange face was even closer. "Surely, it must be intimidating writing under the shadow of Faulkner."

This did it.

"I swear he's dead. I've seen his grave. Died thirty years ago when I was in the second grade."

I was clearly irritated, and this, of course, was exactly what she wanted. The camera moved closer.

"But what about the legend, the aura, the magic of Faulkner? I read somewhere that all Southern writers labor in the shadow of Faulkner."

I had read this somewhere, too. "I'm not a Southern writer," I said slowly without looking at her. She thought about this for a second.

"Then what are you?" she asked, definitely puzzled.

"I'm a commercial writer who lives in the South. I try to write commercial fiction of a high quality—no attempt at literature here—just good books that people enjoy reading. The libraries are already filled with great literature. There's no room for me."

"That's interesting," she said.

"Is that a question?" I asked.

She ignored this. "So you write for money?"

"Yes. At one time I was a lawyer, and I worked for money. When I served in the state legislature, I got paid for it. When I mowed grass as a kid I did so for money. You wouldn't be holding that microphone if you weren't getting paid for it."

"What about writers who say they don't care if their books sell?"

"They're lying." I handed a book back to its purchaser. The line was growing longer. The proprietor was now standing nearby.

"What about Faulkner? Did he write for money."

I honestly don't know why Faulkner wrote. His best books were written when he couldn't give them away. He spent many agonizing years in Hollywood cranking out screenplays so his family could eat. He was not well off, financially speaking, until late in life.

The owner stepped forward. "Mr. Grisham, your plane leaves in an hour."

"Thank you," I said. It was a welcome lie. My flight was three hours away. I ignored the reporter.

But she was not to be ignored. "Do you think Faulkner wrote for money?"

"Why don't you ask Faulkner?" I snapped as I took another book and scribbled in earnest. The light went off. The microphone was withdrawn. She mumbled something that sounded like "thanks" as they made a noisy retreat and left the store.

Book tours attract nosy little reporters who are completely uninhibited and will ask for all sorts of details such as, Do you write for money? How much money will you make off this book? How much money did you make off your last book? How much did you pay for your house? What kind of car do you drive? Does your wife work? Where do you vacation? What'd you sell the film rights for?

Nothing is private. They'll ask anything. Faulkner didn't like them either, and I'll bet he was never quizzed about legends or shadows.

Spring 1992

Willie Morris, 1934–1999

DONNA TARTT

THINKING ABOUT WILLIE IN THESE DAYS SINCE HIS DEATH, this honorific comes again and again to mind: "the greatest of the Boys." It was said, originally, of Stephen Crane, but it could be as easily said of Willie. Often I had the hilarious incredulous sense, being with Willie, of being with Huckleberry Finn all grown up—for who knew, really, what happened to Huck after he lighted out for the Indian territories? One can easily imagine Huck grown up (and out) into a big old tender-hearted man much like Willie: a practical jokester, a foe of injustice, a friend to all dogs; a man who loved taverns, and old cemeteries, who poured big old slugs of bourbon into his coffee to warm himself up on chilly autumn nights. Like Huck, too, his happy carelessness for material comforts bordered on the vagabond—his raggedy sweaters, his torn tennis shoes, his modest little bachelor home back in the Oxford days before he married JoAnne, a house that was (except for an unframed photograph of his terrier Skip, then twenty years dead) wholly unadorned. When we met, I was seventeen and he was in his late forties, but what I think struck me most about him was this great open-hearted quality of boyishness that he had, for he was far more boyish than most of the actual boys I knew at Ole Miss, passionless frat boys whose hearts had already narrowed and tightened (even at seventeen, eighteen, nineteen) into the hearts of the burghers and businessmen they would someday become.

Willie, on the other hand, was a boy in all the very best ways: quick to make friends, quick to take sides, quick to laughter and outrage and tears and mischief. Because of his unsuspicious good nature, he was not always so quick to defend himself, or to look out for his own best interests, but no one leapt more rapidly to the aid of a friend, and he mourned the disappointments of others as if they were his own. He had the boy's romantic way of thinking always about death, even in the raucous wholehearted tumble of life. Moreover, he had the boy's heroic refusal to accept some of life's more petty brutalities. The bonds of affection were not lessened for him—as they are for most people—by the fact of physical death. For him, the wounds were always fresh. In the midst of life, he continued to grieve for, and honor, his dead—everyone, all the little ones, down to the very dogs, in a way that calls to mind the Bodhisattva's vow: "However numberless sentient beings are, I vow to save them." If it were up to Willie, he would have saved them all, kept the doors of Heaven open until all Creation was safe inside: every hobo, every stray, every last june bug. (One of the lines he loved most, from *King Lear*: "The little dogs and all, / Tray, Blanch, and Sweetheart, see, they bark at me." To me, he said: "See now, darling, this is what makes Shakespeare a great poet. He remembers the little dogs, he calls them by their names." Then, glancing down at Pete the Labrador retriever, his constant companion of those days: "Shakespeare would have loved old Pete here, wouldn't he though? If old Pete was there, Shakespeare would have called Pete's name too, don't you think?")

Back when I was introduced to Willie, when I was just a kid myself, he was a great, mythical Mr. Micawber of a figure, walking the streets of Oxford in the late afternoons with his toes pointed out and his Ray-Ban sunglasses on. He grabbed me by the hand and pulled me down the street, so that I had to run to keep up with him, and it was as if we had known each other always. He was like that, I think, with all his friends: he knew them when he saw them, fell in step right alongside them, and loved them forever. "Would you like a Coca-Cola, young lady?" he asked me on that first night, interrupting himself in the middle of a story, when his old pal Clyde the bartender came around to take our order at the bar of the Holiday Inn.

"No, sir, I believe I'll have what you're drinking."

Terrific roar of laughter. "Why," he shouted, staggering back as if dazed by my prodigy, rolling his rich old eye round at the assembled company, "this girl is a WRITER!" When the bourbons arrived, he insisted that we clink glasses: "A toast."

"To what?"

"To you! To us! This is a historic night! Someday you'll be famous, you'll write about this very meeting, you'll remember it forever. . . ."

I was a little overwhelmed, with this big drunk famous person towering over me at the bar, proclaiming blood brothership, offering eternal friendship, thundering outlandish prophecies. But—God bless you, Willie!—you were right, because here I sit at the typewriter nearly twenty years later, recalling all this.

I lived right down the street from Willie that year, when I was seventeen and then eighteen, and I was lucky to get the chance then to know him so well and spend as much time with him as I did. We loved and hated a lot of the same things. Never will I forget my naïve astonishment at discovering that there existed another person who loved words in much the same sputtering and agonized way that I did, who fought them and cursed them and cried over them and stood back dazzled and agog in admiration of them. After all those years isolated in my hometown, shut up in my bedroom reading books, I had thought I was the only person in the world so afflicted.

"Oh, no, honey. There's a lot of us out there. You'll meet them."

And I did. But he was the first, and the one I loved the best, and—

when I look back through the years, at all the things I ended up doing that I never dreamed were possible, if I look back far enough I always see Willie, with his shirt untucked, standing at the very back of the room and blowing me a kiss.

Willie had his light moments, no doubt about it; he was a great phone prankster, chatting away straight-faced and unconcerned to one of his unsuspecting colleagues in the character of "Mae Helen Biggs" or "Clinton Roy Peel" or some such: "Yas suh!" he would cry. "I sho did see it! Yo car rolling down the street just now and an ole black dog sitting right up at the wheel. . . ." Afterward, he would hang up quite soberly— as if he'd just phoned to check on his bank balance—and not until some moments later (returning from the kitchen, fresh drink in hand) would he convulse with laughter, stricken all at once by the genius of the joke that he'd so brilliantly pulled off.

Rich companion that he was, Willie also suffered terribly. It was a commonplace among those who knew him—those who didn't love him, but also some who did—to attribute Willie's operatic range of emotion to drink. The truth was more complicated, and had to do with that raw, gigantic, intensely tender heart of his about which we've heard so much in the last weeks, that heart which he seldom guarded or protected in any way but left right on the surface for the world to scratch at. What drink could palliate those ancient, chilling sorrows that settled over him? "How are your spirits, darling?" That is the first question, or among the first, he always asked—for, when he wanted to bend forward and look close, he could see into other people's hearts with a rather terrifying clarity. The word spirit was chosen quite carefully: for when Willie asked this question he was inquiring about your spirit in the sense of your mood, but also the state of your immortal spirit, your soul; about your spirits in the old, high-colored French sense (wit, sparkle, intelligence), and the spirits in your glass (did you need a refill?), and even your spirits in the sense of your ghosts, as in memories and people of the past (the recent past, a hundred or two hundred years past) which might be haunting you. All these things he was checking up on when he bent his head low and tried to catch your eye, like a waggish doctor, and asked his perennial question.

Further: he really wanted to know. And he wanted to do something about it. "Let's go get a steak. Let's drive over to Rowan Oak. Let's call up old George Plimpton in New York and talk to him on the telephone." If Willie thought you were sad, he'd stand on his head if he thought it might cheer you up. (I think of how I once saw him following his housekeeper around his Oxford home, in and out of rooms, ruthless as a bird dog, because he thought something was bothering her and he had, absolutely had, to know what it was.) But in spite of his solicitude for others, Willie's own grief harrowed him continually; in many respects he was simply not at home here and by here I mean the world, with all its callousness and cruelties and forgetfulness; he was inconsolable, too haunted by the inferno of loss, by time, and change, and mutability. "Brightness falls from the air; / Queens have died, young and fair." Sometimes he would stop dead—in the middle of a sentence, in the middle of a room—as if sensing subterranean tremors. You could see it in his eyes then, that sickening awareness he had of the lurching, inescapable grind of time: time like sand, time sliding under our feet, time inescapable and relentless, time rolling forward—on all we love, and would like to save—with a sickle and a grin. And this too was a part of his genius. He was exquisitely calibrated to sense these dreadful underground rivers of sorrow, constantly quaking beneath the surface of everyday life; everybody senses them at one time or another, but Willie was so constituted that he was shaken by them constantly, and it is to this vertiginous but quite accurate awareness that he had, of time collapsing about us moment by moment, and shifting beneath us, that I attribute his occasional unsteadiness on his feet—a sort of motion sickness of the soul. Though it's there all the time, this knowledge of the hourglass running out, time slipping away, most people don't feel it the way he did (at least not so constantly—else they couldn't get out of bed in the morning). But Willie—like a dog driven crazy by a whistle too high-pitched for the human ear—was constantly stricken by this inexorable motion that others, less sensitive, were unable to detect and because of it he could never quite recover his equilibrium, his balance. No wonder he liked to slosh a little bourbon in his coffee from time to time.

In some sense, Willie's preoccupations were those of the Chinese poets. Fallen blossoms, dewy stairs, and lost youth. The sorrow of leavetakings, farewell to friends, soldiers on the march, and geese flying south. His sense of history pained him, and so did his sense of beauty. I can easily imagine him—like the great Li Po—toppling drunken into the river while trying to embrace the moon. He was tremendously moved by things like fallen sports idols, aging movie stars, dead animals on the road. Forlorn or desecrated monuments in the cemetery. Rain and autumn bonfires. (Some neighbor hammering in a garage, on a foggy gray day in the winter: "Sounds like they're making somebody's coffin over there, darling.") When he was sad, sometimes he would ask me to recite poetry to him—poems I had learned in high school—which I didn't quite see the point of as they only seemed to make him sadder. Of my small repertoire, he especially liked Housman's "To an Athlete Dying Young"; "Annabel Lee"; and Gerard Manley Hopkins: "Margaret, are you grieving/Over Goldengrove unleaving?"

> It is the blight man was born for,
> It is Margaret you mourn for.

He also liked to read aloud. Thomas Wolfe. The last page of *The Great Gatsby*. "So we beat on, boats against the current, borne back ceaselessly into the past." And he would lean back in his shabby chair and close his eyes with the relief of hearing someone else describe, so well, the rhythms that beat so ceaselessly against his own poor heart.

After I left Mississippi, at Willie's urging, to go to college in New England ("You've learned what you need to know here," he said to me, and he was right), we didn't see nearly so much of each other, though we certainly had our laughing glorious reunions in the years to come: after he'd married JoAnne and moved to Jackson, after I'd published my first book. (Perhaps my very happiest memory of Willie is a comparatively recent one of being in a hotel room in New Orleans, on tour for my first book, hearing a knock on the door and thinking it was housekeeping but no, it was Willie, with JoAnne right behind him, Willie who grabbed me up and practically threw me in the air for joy. Still up to his old tricks: he'd deceived me with that timid little casual rap at the door, and neither of us could stop laughing about it. So many people were happy for me when I published my first novel, but apart from my mother, I don't think that anybody in the world was happier or more proud than he was.)

But it is much farther back—to that distant time when he and I were neighbors, and saw each other almost daily—to which my thoughts return again and again now that Willie has died. I've been thinking about his frequent visits to Faulkner's grave, and his scratchy old record of the song "Moon River"; he played it over and over when he was sad, and upon at least one occasion he played it so incessantly that I—and several other guests—were driven from his home. I think, too, how the movie *Casablanca* always made him cry—especially the scene where everyone stands up in Rick's Café and sings the "Marseillaise" in defiance of the Nazis. This episode was so important for Willie that it became a sort of shorthand, a code, a way for him to explain why he loved the people he did. "They'd sing the 'Marseillaise,'" he'd say, nodding across the room at someone he loved: Ron Shapiro, say, or Deanie Faulkner (how he loved Deanie!) or Masaru or David Sansing. "And Pete. Pete'd be right up there in the front, leading the band, wouldn't you, boy?"

Something else that comes to mind—I don't know why, but it does—is an evening I walked from my dormitory over to his chilly little bare house. That house, with its lawn never raked, deep in dead leaves, was sunk all the year round in a perpetual autumn. (There's a word, in French, for that particular still, sad quality that Willie's house had, in the early '80s, with the forlorn little picture of Skip the dead terrier propped up on the bare mantelpiece: *fadeur*. When I first came upon it, in Verlaine, I told Willie about it and he got all excited, too. "Oh, that's a marvelous word. Nothing like it in English at all, is there? Pete, can you think of anything? Pete?")

I found Willie there, in the twilight, in his little *fadeur* house, sitting with his face in his hands without the lamp on, crying in the most desolate and brokenhearted way, so that I could not immediately understand what he was saying: "That girl," he cried, "that poor girl," and it was a while before I realized that he was crying for the movie star Natalie Wood, who (it was in all the papers that day) had fallen off a yacht, and drowned.

I was stricken, sympathetic. Had she been a great friend of his?

"No," he cried, rolling his head back, "no, of course not, she was just so beautiful. . . ."

This recollection surfaced, from apparent void, two or three days after Willie's death, and it was so sharp and sudden that I flinched from it a little bit without quite knowing why: why had this odd fragment bobbed up so perfect and whole (I can still see the smoke spiraling from his cigarette) from the past? Why this memory? Why now? Because, of course, it is Willie, not Natalie Wood but Willie whom they are reading about in the papers, Willie himself whom the strangers are crying for this time.

How his great lying-in-state would have pleased him! If the dead are in any way allowed to return and witness such things, Willie was there and eavesdropping on his mourners, reveling in the event, like Huckleberry Finn at his own funeral. I am so confident of the ability of that dear great soul of his to continue after death (for if Willie doesn't rise again, no one will) that—now that the flowers are browning on his grave—what I strangely find myself worrying about most are the whereabouts of Skip and Pete. (This, too, was a concern of Willie's; his friends will remember his insistence upon giving Pete a proper burial in the Oxford cemetery.) Buddhist theology gives hope upon this question, as does the theology of my own Roman Catholic faith, but still I return night after night to my heaviest books in an attempt to reassure myself on this point. I don't care how nice Heaven is, really I don't: he's not going to be happy if those dogs aren't there.

And, as I read over these pages (written hastily, as the magazine goes to press), I wonder if I ought to tone down the emotion of these recollections but no: I absolutely refuse. Willie flung around words like great and noble and brave and genius wherever he went—great profligate showers of outdated coin, moidores, guineas, pieces of eight, stamped with all the crowns and statesmen of history. And this is the very coin that I wish to heap up in heavy glittering masses on his grave: "Now cracks a noble heart." He deserves all the glory we are able to give him—the flights of angels singing him to his rest, all of it—for he felt this way about the people and the things that he loved, and it is only natural that we who loved him should wish to bring him the same tribute now that he is gone.

September/October 1999

The Chess King of Decatur Street

MATTHEW TEAGUE

JUDE ACERS, CHESS PLAYER EXTRAORDINAIRE, was to wait somewhere in the French Quarter, wearing a red beret. According to his instructions, I was to approach him holding a printout of his online manifesto, *ChessFlash News*, and greet him by asking about "the small black boy in the laundromat."

After half an hour roaming around the Quarter, I saw a man with a wine-colored beret walking in Jackson Square, pacing back and forth along a row of painters and palm readers. I had not expected Acers to be such a large man—circular face, bulbous nose, wrecking-ball belly— but the beret was in place, and he had glanced at me twice, obviously impatient for my introduction. So I stepped up and—with a flourish of the manifesto—delivered my line about the boy. He recoiled from me, gripping a box under his arm and stumbling a little on the gray-slab sidewalk. Right then, a heavyset woman emerged from a porcelain doll shop and joined the man, and together they hustled off across the Square.

Crap, I thought. Maybe I had muttered, or overlooked some mincing piece of deal-breaker protocol. I followed the couple, rehearsing my opener, and when I caught up, I shoved the manifesto close to his face and sprang my line on him, this time with special emphasis on the boy's smallness and blackness. But he just glared at me, hooked an arm around the woman, and burst away again, the unbelievable jerk. I chased after

152

them and this time grabbing at his arm: *"Are you Jude Acers?"* He seemed to shrink a little, still gripping his box. Then, in a thick, vaguely Swedish accent he said, "Leave us alone. We have nothing for you, please." A tourist, I realized.

I eventually found another red beret outside a café on Decatur Street, attached to a man sitting behind two chess sets on a cafeteria-style table. He wore thick glasses, and silver hair poked from beneath the beret. His face looked like a Mardi Gras mask, with the long chin and nose comically downturned. Behind him, a handwritten sign announced that a game with "JUDE ACERS—CHESS MASTER!!!!!" could be had for five bucks, and a four-hour lesson cost two hundred dollars. He was once heralded by the chess world as a genius and has appeared six times in the *Guinness Book of World Records* for playing the most simultaneous chess games. Although the seat across from him was empty, he leaned far over the chessboards, face down, ignoring me. He seemed to be napping.

"Um," I said. "There's a small black boy—"

"Stop!" he yelled, jumping to his feet. He slapped his hands down on the chess sets, scattering the pieces across the sidewalk. People stopped to watch. His face went red, and he shouted, "I MUST TELL YOU THAT I AM THE GREATEST CHESS PLAYER OF ALL TIME!"

He whipped around and bounded off across the street, narrowly missing the front bumper of a fast-moving city bus. As the bus passed, I saw the tail of Acers's blue sportcoat disappear into the door of a restaurant.

By the time I caught up, he was standing in the center of the place, arms out and palms up, oscillating slightly. "This is where I feast," he said. "This is my daylight palace. My palate palace, where I please my palate because the food is good. Good, but not as good as the coffee. Because coffee is what makes the world go around when it is free. Like our great country. America. Land of the free. . . ."

He went on like this, loudly, for a couple of minutes, until a burly guy in an apron emerged from the back of the restaurant. I slinked away, sure that the cook was going to throttle Acers, but instead the guy handed him a gigantic cup of coffee. With a nod, the chess player marched past the cash register and out across the street, toward his chessboards. His boots thunked against the asphalt as he walked, and his monologue flowed from subject to subject, slipping and sliding along the path of least resistance.

"Comfortable boots," he said. "I must dress smart head to toe, toe to head. Boots on my feet, beret on my head. The beret is red. Red in traffic means stop, so people walk past my boards and stop to play. And red is just a beautiful color. Nobody used color like Van Gogh. Now there was a genius. He knew nobody was going to buy his paintings. He was going a little crazy, but he knew it. Knew it perfectly well. Knew nobody was going to understand him, and knew he would die poor. But he was the boss of his world. . . ."

Acers was four years old when police in New Bern, North Carolina, found him and his sister digging through garbage. He remembers that. Most of his early childhood is blurry, but a few things do stand out: dirty dishes pouring out of a closet, crashing to the floor, because his paranoid mother hid one too many there; his mother falling to the floor when his father put his fist in her face too many times; news that his mother's plane had gone down on the way to the asylum. He remembers that his father, a marine, was away at war most of the time, so when Jude was young, he spent most of his childhood in orphanages. When he was five years old, he came across a book about chess, and his obsession began. He used soda bottle tops to make chess sets, but the nuns at the orphanage took them away. So he made more.

When Jude was an adolescent, his father returned from war, fetched him from the North Carolina orphanage, and took him to New Orleans. The elder Acers became a raging alcoholic who abused Jude with flair.

Sometimes that meant forcing him to shave his head or wear shorts to school in the winter or spend the night kneeling on linoleum. He recalls those tortures as "small stuff." Small, at least, compared with what came later.

The sun had just set, and the woman was wasted, in the worst way. She was dressed up, except for her left shoe, which was missing. She careened around Acers's table and crashed down hard on a chair opposite him. She put her fist against her face, with the back of her hand smashing her nose, then uncoiled her index finger, drawing an invisible line from her left eyeball to Acers's. "Plaaay," she said. "Meeeee." Acers put his *New York Times* aside and mated her twice, quickly, at five bucks a pop.

She drew herself up and wiggled the index finger toward Decatur's darker end. "My apartment is down the shhtreet," she said. "I've been walking past here eight years, wanting to play you. Now I did." And she strode off, listing a little to port. As he did after every game, Acers whipped an envelope out of his fanny pack, stuffed in his cash, jumped up, and shot off around the corner.

When he returned, he said, "I send my fees straight to the bank. I never keep money on my person. It's too dangerous." He picked up his newspaper. "I have made a lot of money on this sidewalk. Two hundred thousand, easy." To the casual observer, Acers appears to have scraped by for twenty-three years on fewer than ten grand a year, winning an endless stream of five-dollar bills off drunks and tourists. But to him, the money is a fortune, compiled and invested in twenty-three years of coffee and beignets. Each time a new opponent pays to play, he sees it as validation, as proof that he is a global treasure, and that pilgrims from as far away as Alaska and Italy travel to sit at his little table and bask in the light of his genius.

"Hey, chess man," a guy yelled from his silver 4Runner, sitting still in the Decatur Street traffic. He smiled at Acers, but nudged his buddy in the passenger's seat: *Hey man, get a load of this guy.* "What do I get if I win?"

Acers pushed his plastic chair back, stood, and made a grand bow, sweeping his arm from high above his head to down around his ankles. "Dear sir," he cried, "we shall not speak of things that cannot come to pass."

Traffic moved on, and the guy dismissively waved off Acers, who strutted back to his table, pulled a handkerchief from his jacket, and swiped it across the seat of his chair. "A little civility is nectar for the gentleman," he said, winking. "And poison for the barbarian." Having defeated the aggressor, he sat down, picked up his paper, and waited for his next challenger.

Hours passed. Acers finished the *New York Times*, the *Times-Picayune*, and *USA Today*, all of which are brought to his table each morning by an old man whose name Acers doesn't know. As time passed, Acers's constant stream-of-consciousness soliloquy careened from international politics to the value of the Internet, from the personal cleanliness of New Orleans mayor Marc Morial to the genius of Henry Ford. "People today still don't grasp the possibilities of the simple motorcar," he said. "So many levels of utility, such variety. You want to take your wife for a night of dancing, you don't take her in a dump truck, do you? No, of course not. You take a limo. Not a bus, not a cab. A limo. There's no other way to do it, for a lady. I have seen some ladies at this table, I'll tell you that. Outstanding women of all shapes and colors. I don't distinguish. I think black women are absolutely stunning. . . ."

When Jude was fourteen, his father suddenly stopped beating him and delivered the hardest blow. He committed the teen to Louisiana's state mental institution in Mandeville, where loneliness only fueled his drive to study chess. By the time he was seventeen, the U.S. Chess Federation had rated him a master—a status reserved for only the most brilliant players. The state paid his way through Louisiana State University, where he studied Russian so he could pore over obscure chess texts. After graduation he hopped on a Greyhound bus and crossed the country, searching for better chess players and free meals. In 1968 his ride ended in San Francisco's Haight-Ashbury district, where he found a vigorous chess culture and earned a snippet of fame. He picked up an agent. He played blindfolded against multiple opponents in legendary West Coast auditoriums. He stood at a urinal next to John Fogarty and played basketball with the Doors between sound checks. And, for a while, he roomed with Janis Joplin.

"She was not a pretty lady," he said. "She was always insecure about that. That's the reason for the drugs. I never did the drugs. One day during a party I was in the bathtub, where it was quiet, reading, and she came in, naked, and sat down on the toilet. She looked at me and said, 'Funny, funny Jude. You play with your little pieces all day long, and you know what? You'll live to be an old, old man someday.' And here I am."

In 1977, broke and hungry, he returned to New Orleans with a chessboard under his arm. He set it up on the Decatur Street sidewalk, and waited for the world to find him.

"How have you been?" Acers said, nodding to a middle-aged couple as they approached the table. He turned to their daughter. "You've grown quite a bit." The people stopped instantly, as though Acers had just publicly announced the color of their underwear.

"Good God," mumbled the father, a tall, handsome guy with a graying beard. "It's been thirteen years."

Acers folded his hands under his chin and smirked a little. "Twelve," he said, as the dumbstruck father sat down in the challenger's seat. The man lost in fewer than a dozen moves, then stood up, shook Acers's outthrust hand, and walked away with his wife and daughter following.

"I remember him because he gave me a good run last time," Acers said once they were out of earshot. "He's actually quite a good player. I just rattled him. Excellent. Excellent." Again, he pulled out an envelope, stuffed it, and dashed off around the corner. By the time he came back it was almost midnight. "Time to close up shop," he announced. "The workday is over. We have an appointment for entertainment."

Acers wouldn't tell me where we were going, except that it was "high quality," and that I would be "paralyzed by the beauty of it all." We left Decatur Street, and Acers struck off down a set of dark railroad tracks that run along the river. Drifters stumbled by, and inky figures swayed in the shadows, but Acers plowed ahead like a locomotive on the rails. "This is the no-traffic way," he said. "I can't walk anywhere in this city without people recognizing me and wanting to talk, so I have devised no-traffic routes to all my destinations. Desti-desti-destinations. Destiny. Direct routes to destiny. Just keep moving or they'll cut your throat."

After a while we left the tracks and dodged down several alarming alleys before stepping onto a well-lit street. Acers suddenly stopped. "Look at those two lamps over that door," he said. "I played Bobby Fischer in that building many years ago. It is the site of my proudest day."

"You won?"

"No, of course not. The man is a god. Or he was a god. Now he's just insane, completely lost his mind. A pity."

He ducked into a corner drugstore, where a lone clerk watched nervously from behind the register. Acers turned to me. "Are you hungry?"

I was starving. Neither of us had eaten in seventeen hours. "Yeah," I said. "A little." He grabbed a turnover pie from a shelf and weighed it in his hand. "Sweet potato," he said. "Excellent. I'm partial to the sweet potato." Then, standing in the middle of the store, he unwrapped the pie and stuffed half of it into his mouth. "Delicious," he said, spraying flecks of potato on the other pies. "Try the chocolate." The clerk, who looked about nineteen years old, gawked at us. Acers raffled through the pies again. "The world revolves around the cherry ones," he said. The clerk picked up a phone. "There's no cherry here," Acers announced, facing the clerk, who stood transfixed with the phone in his hand. "This is a blight on your otherwise fine establishment, sir." Acers hooked his thumbs behind the breast of his jacket and stepped briskly toward the door. "My gentleman friend here has an expense account, and he will kindly pick up the tab."

"This is perhaps the greatest feat of architecture in the modern world. And look at the waitresses."

Acers's "appointment for entertainment" was at the new Harrah's casino, a sprawling, orangish building recently erected near the Quarter. He strolled in and surveyed the premises with the critical regard of a high roller. "Excellent. Excellent."

It was astonishing: rows of slot machines fading into the distance; roulette, baccarat, blackjack tables, all attended by buxom waitresses in spangled outfits; lights blinking, music pounding, women laughing, and men with cigars puffing like smokestacks. Acers wove in and out of the tables and machines like a pro, sweeping his arms left and right for my benefit: *On the right we see the cashiers' booth, and on the left you'll find the high-stakes salon.*

"First we need to get drinks," he said. We roamed the floor of the casino for almost an hour until we found a dark-haired waitress with smooth skin and deep-set eyes. When she caught sight of Acers homing in, panic skittered across her face, then pity. Acers sidled up with a dollar fluttering at his fingertips, then he sneaked the dollar onto her drink tray. I felt the scrutiny of a hundred security cameras training in on that dollar, then the red beret, then the dollar. Then the beret.

"Hey there," he said, quite the cool cat.

"Hey, Jude," she said.

We had apparently found his appointment. He leaned in close to her face and said, "How about a coffee? And a Coke for my friend." She delivered an admirable smile and walked away. Acers flattened out his right hand, palm down, at his waist, as though pushing away the nose of a curious dog. The gesture seemed to signify, Stay cool. He said, "There won't be a charge. I know her. You keep the ladies happy, and they'll take care of you. Did you see her smile? I am surrounded by beautiful women. Exotic women of all kinds. . . ."

After she returned with our drinks, Acers continued his tour of the casino, which seemed to be roughly diamond shaped. "Look over here," he said. "This is the finest restaurant you'll find for the money." It was a buffet, a mammoth one, and most of the food looked bland, perfectly suited for the wary tastebuds of vacationing Midwesterners. "Look at this," he said, sashaying down the buffet with his fingers trailing lightly on the glass sneeze guard. "Pork, chicken, every kind of fish you could ever want. Look at the salad section. Did you ever see anything like it? Fresh, everything fresh. I don't see turkey, though. That's a blight. I'm sure they'll have it out next Thursday. I'll be coming by for that. I'm going to fill up on turkey and dressing and a big piece of pumpkin pie. That's the only way to do Thanksgiving dinner. The only way. . . ."

A fat bass beat rolled through the restaurant area, followed by the growls of an ersatz Aretha Franklin. "It's show time!" Acers said, moving toward the source like a child to the Pied Piper, elbows out, bony knees pumping up with each step. We pinballed through the casino, moving toward the center, where the show was under way. A tremendously large woman was belting out a soul medley, while a tiny woman in a dollar-sign-covered cat suit danced around her. A shockingly tall man—he may have been on stilts—marched back and forth across the stage in a sequined Uncle Sam outfit, complete with long coattails and top hat. Lights flashed, confetti glittered, horns blew; more girls streamed onstage, with feathers trailing; liquored-up businessmen in the crowd loosened their ties and danced with the girls; the purple and gold of Mardi Gras swirled with patriotic colors, Christmas colors, every hue of cummerbund. We had found the lowest point in the city, where the runoff from a thousand gaudy celebrations had pooled and fermented, a hundred-proof concoction guaranteed to sicken all but the hardiest drinkers. Acers swayed to the music, beret in hand, and silently moved his lips: "Excellent, excellent."

We were approaching Acers's home in the Quarter. He is secretive about its location—I was the first person in twenty-three years to be invited over, he said—and to get there we took a confusing, circling route through alleys and courtyards that were increasingly narrow and cramped. "I'd say almost everybody in this section is gay!" Acers said. He seemed to be yelling. His voice bounced along the cobblestones and rang off the wrought iron, seeking ears to fill. "They don't bother me. I stay to myself, and they leave me alone. But I have seen some oddities!"

The last passage we wound through was so narrow that we had to walk sideways, and Acers whacked his shoulder on a mailbox. We emerged into a tiny courtyard that had one palm tree in the middle. Acers started up a spiral staircase. "This is my stairway to the sky," he said. "People ask where I live. I tell them I live in the sky. The other day a little bird flew in the window while I was taking a shower, and it sang to me. I knew then that I had been accepted as a citizen of the sky. . . ."

At the top of the stairs he threw open the door to his apartment, and the smell that poured out drove me back a step. It was a mixture of old clothes, coffee, and mildew. The entire apartment was about eight feet by four feet. There was a closet at one end, and at the other end a toilet and shower, where Acers washes his clothes. Newspaper clips featuring Acers—including one that described his relationship with roomie Janis Joplin—were randomly tacked to the walls. On the floor there was a pile of towels and blankets used as a bed, and stacks of books: hundreds, maybe thousands of books, some in Russian and Chinese, all about chess.

"Look at this," he said, grabbing up one of the books and flipping to an opaquely notated chess game. "It's brilliant." Before my eyes could focus, he tossed the book aside and tried to illustrate the game physically, rushing around the room and issuing a stream of chess moves: "You've got to get your pawns forking down the middle, like this, see, just like this, forking like a snake." He stabbed his index and middle fingers toward my eyes to demonstrate, which was startling, and I stumbled backward onto one of the piles of books. Acers didn't seem to notice. "And then down the side come the rooks," he continued. "Options, always options. Keep the options open so you can dance without fear." He pranced around the room, bringing his knees up high to his chest, flailing his arms, sucking in the room's poor supply of oxygen and expelling it in a stream of suddenly Russian commentary, shouting and weeping and raging and laughing.

He had left me behind long ago and gone somewhere else. A place where the food is delicious, the women are beautiful, and the entertainment is endless and free. He was a little off, but he knew it. Knew it perfectly well. Knew nobody was going to understand him, and knew he would die poor. But he was the boss of his world.

March/April 2000

I'm Not Leaving Until I Eat This Thing

JOHN T. EDGE

IT'S JUST PAST FOUR ON A THURSDAY AFTERNOON IN JUNE AT JESSE'S PLACE, a country juke joint seventeen miles south of the Mississippi line and three miles west of Amite, Louisiana. The air conditioner hacks and spits forth torrents of arctic air, but the heat of summer can't be kept at bay. It seeps around the splintered doorjambs and settles in, transforming the squat, particleboard-plastered roadhouse into a sauna. Slowly, the dank barroom fills with grease-smeared mechanics from the truck stop up the road and farmers straight from the fields, the soles of their brogans thick with dirt clods. A few weary souls make their way over from the nearby sawmill, the kind of place where more than one worker has muscled a log into the chipper and drawn back a nub. I sit alone at the bar, one empty bottle of Bud in front of me, a second bottle in my hand. I drain the beer, order a third, and stare down at the pink juice spreading outward from a crumpled foil pouch and onto the dull, black vinyl bar. *I'm not leaving until I eat this thing,* I tell myself.

Half a mile down the road, behind a fence coiled with razor wire, Lionel Dufour, proprietor of Farm Fresh Food Supplier, is loading up the last truck of the day, wheeling case after case of pickled pork offal out of his cinder-block processing plant and into a semitrailer bound for Hattiesburg, Mississippi.

His crew packed lips today. Yesterday, it was pickled sausage; the day before that, pig feet. Tomorrow, it's pickled pig lips again. And today, like every other weekday, Lionel has been on the job since a quarter of three in the morning, when he came in to light the boilers. Damon Landry, chief cook and maintenance man, came in at four-thirty. By seven-thirty, the production line was at full tilt: six women in white smocks and blue bouffant caps, slicing ragged white fat from the lips, tossing the good parts in glass jars, the bad parts in barrels bound for the rendering plant. Across the aisle, filled jars clatter by on a conveyor belt as a worker tops them off with a Kool-Aid-red slurry of hot sauce, vinegar, salt, and food coloring. Around the corner, the jars are capped, affixed with a label, and stored in pasteboard boxes to await shipping.

Unlike most offal—euphemistically called "variety meats"—lips belie their provenance. Brains, milky white and globular, look like brains. Feet, the ghosts of their cloven hoofs protruding, look like feet. Testicles look like, well, testicles. But lips are different. Loosed from the snout, trimmed of their fat, and dyed a preternatural pink, they look more like candy than carrion.

At Farm Fresh, no swine root in an adjacent feedlot. No viscera-strewn killing floor lurks just out of sight, down a darkened hallway. These pigs died long ago at some Midwestern abattoir. By the time the lips arrive in Amite, they are, in essence, pig Popsicles, fifty-pound blocks of offal and ice.

"Lips are all meat," Lionel told me earlier in the day. "No gristle, no bone, no nothing. They're bar food, hot and vinegary, great with a beer. Used to be the lips ended up in sausages, headcheese, those sorts of things. A lot of them still do."

Lionel, a fifty-year-old father of three with quick, intelligent eyes set deep in a face the color of cordovan, is a veteran of nearly forty years in the pickled pig lips business. "I started out with my daddy when I wasn't much more than ten," Lionel told me, his shy smile framed by a coarse black mustache flecked with whispers of gray. "The meat-packing business he owned had gone broke back when I was six, and he was peddling out of the back of his car, selling dried shrimp, BC powders, napkins, straws, tubes of plastic cups, pig feet, pig lips, whatever the bar owners needed. He sold to black bars, white bars, sweet shops, snow-ball stands, you name it. We made the rounds together after I got out of school, sometimes staying out till two or three in the morning. I remember bringing my toy cars to this one joint and racing them around the floor with the bar owner's son while my daddy and his father did business."

For years after the demise of that first meatpacking company, the Dufour family sold someone else's product, someone else's lips. "We used to buy lips from Dennis Di Salvo's company down in Belle Chasse," recalled Lionel. "As far as I can tell, his mother was the one who came up with the idea to pickle and pack lips back in the '50s, back when she was working for a company called Three Little Pigs over in Houma. But pretty soon, we were selling so many lips that we had to almost beg Di Salvo's for product. That's when we started cooking up our own," he told me, gesturing toward the cast-iron kettle that hangs from the rafters by the front door of the plant. "My daddy started cooking lips in that very pot."

Lionel now cooks his lips in eleven retrofitted milk tanks, dull stain-less-steel cauldrons shaped like oversized cradles. But little else has changed about the business. Though Lionel's father has passed away, Farm Fresh remains a family-focused company. His wife, Kathy, keeps the books. His daughter, Dana, a button-cute college student who has won numerous beauty titles, takes to the road in the summer, selling lips to convenience stores and wholesalers. Soon, after he graduates from business school, Lionel's youngest son, Matt, will take over oper-ations at the plant. And his oldest son, a veterinarian, lent his name to one of Farm Fresh's top sellers, Jason's Pickled Pig Lips.

"We do our best to corner the market on lips," Lionel told me, his voice tinged with not a little bravado. "Sometimes they're hard to get from the packing houses. You gotta kill a lot of pigs to get enough lips to keep us going. I've got new customers calling every day; it's all I can do to keep up with demand, but I bust my ass to keep up. I do what I can for my family—and for my customers.

"When my customers tell me something," he continued, "just like when my daddy told me something, I listen. If my customers wanted me to dye the lips green, I'd ask, 'What shade?' As it is, every few years we'll do some red and some blue for the Fourth of July. This year we did jars full of Mardi Gras lips—half purple, half gold," Lionel recalled with a chuckle. "I guess we'd had a few beers when we came up with that one."

Meanwhile, back at Jesse's place, I finish my third Bud, order my fourth. Now, I tell myself, my courage bolstered by booze, *I'm ready to eat a lip.*

They may have looked like candy in the plant, but in the barroom they're carrion once again. I poke and prod the six-inch arc of pink flesh, peering up from my reverie just in time to catch the barkeep's wife, Audrey, staring straight at me. She fixes me with a look just this side of pity and, as I continue to toy with the lip, wonders aloud, "You gonna eat that thing or make love to it?"

Her nephew, Jerry, sidles up to a barstool on my left. "A lot of people like 'em with chips," he says with a nod of the head toward the pink juice pooling on the bar in front of me. I offer to buy him a lip, and Audrey fishes one from a jar behind the counter, wraps it in tinfoil, and places the whole affair on a paper towel in front of him.

I take stock of my own cowardice, and, following Jerry's lead, reach for a bag of potato chips, tear open the top with my teeth, and toss the quivering hunk of hog flesh into the shiny interior of the bag, slick with grease and dusted with salt. Vinegar vapors tickle my nostrils. I stifle a gag that seems to roll from the back of my throat, swallow hard, and pray that the urge to vomit passes.

With a smash of my hand, the potato chips are reduced to a pulp, and I feel the cold lump of the lip beneath my fist. I clasp the bag shut and shake it hard in an effort to ensure chip coverage in all the nooks and crannies of the lip. The technique that Jerry uses—and I mimic—is not unlike that employed by home cooks mixing up a mess of Shake 'n Bake chicken.

I pull the lip from the bag, a coral crescent of meat now crusted with blond bits of potato chips. When I chomp down, the soft flesh dissolves between my teeth. It tastes like a flaccid cracklin', unmistakably porcine, and not altogether bad. The chips help, providing texture where there was none. My brow unfurrows, my stomach ceases its fluttering.

Sensing my relief, Jerry leans over and peers into my bag. "Kind of look like Frosted Flakes, don't they?" he says, by way of describing the chips rapidly turning to mush upon contact with the pickling juice. I offer the bag to Jerry, order yet another beer, and turn to eye the pig feet floating in a murky jar by the cash register, their blunt tips bobbing up through a pasty white film.

Farm Fresh Pickled Pig Lips are sold in convenience stores and bars throughout southern Louisiana, Mississippi, and Alabama. If you live outside those areas, well, you're out of luck.

September/October 1999

Forbidden Fruit

JOHN SIMPKINS

EVERY TIME WE WERE SERVED WATERMELON AS A TREAT in grade school, I noticed the snickers of the white kids. As one of only two or three black kids in my class, I realized it was a "race thing," but wasn't sure which one it was. I had yet to reach the age where I would be intimately familiar with the baggage that goes along with skin color.

Soon enough, though, I'd hear the black-man-caught-up-in-the-watermelon-patch jokes and the overt remarks about how much black people love watermelon. Although it was never completely clear, these insults apparently were supposed to illustrate how black people suffered from animalistic, uncontrollable urges, lusting for everything from white women to watermelon to respect.

I would also learn that use of the n-word and watermelon consumption occupy a similar space in black America. Both are condoned only in certain social contexts. As comedians like Chris Rock continue to demonstrate (all too clearly), the n-word is tolerated when one black person speaks it to another. It can even be a term of endearment (though I've yet to figure out how). Other times it signifies distinctions: blacks are a quiet, agreeable people, averse to the twin evils of fried chicken and watermelon; "niggers," on the other hand, are a dangerous mix of uppity and stupid, with a steadfast loyalty to all the "badges and indicia of slavery," which I guess includes fried chicken and watermelon.

Interestingly, just as we refrain from using the n-word in mixed company, so too have we relegated watermelon to an "us" activity. We black folk continue to eat and enjoy watermelon when socializing among ourselves, but we refuse it in the company of whites. Because of America's perverse national pastime of making race count in even the most ridiculous of circumstances, a simple pleasure like eating watermelon is denied us. As a result, we cut ourselves off from the little kids we once were, the little kids who grew up liking watermelon.

There were so many different kinds of fruit growing in our Lexington, South Carolina, neighborhood that my friends and I thought we could live off the land.

The spring rains and hot June sun would push the wild plums in our neighborhood to the edible side of half-ripe. They were best eaten with salt, and despite maternal warnings of stomach aches and diarrhea, we devoured them. The blackberries that grew beside my Aunt Ruby's and Aunt Mae's house did not come with such warnings. In fact, we found in grandmothers and great aunts willing accomplices who were eager to turn our berry bounty into cobbler or wine.

But watermelon was king, and its first appearance always signaled the true beginning of summer. When I was growing up, I wasn't just one of those kids who liked watermelon, I loved it. Other foolish little boys wasted their love on bikes, dogs, or maybe even little girls, but not me. If anything was created for summer, this was it. Eating watermelon captured the freedom of summer vacation. Each piece melted into cool liquid. Not having to worry about looking nice for school, I could let the juice run down my arm and all over my shirt. All a grown-up had to do was ask, "Y'all want some watermelon—" and kids would be at the table before they could get to the question mark. Like Kool-Aid, watermelon had the power to make kids come running. More important, it was a communal food. And it was economical, too: one or two watermelons could feed half a neighborhood of kids. That in itself was a boon, as most Southerners use eating as an excuse to get together, or getting together as an excuse to eat. But watermelon brought out a special kind of fellowship. The old folks didn't seem to think it was right that watermelon be eaten in solitude. It was meant to be shared, carved up to feed all and sundry during summer cookouts and Sunday dinners. The bigger the gathering of children, the better reason to make it a watermelon moment. (Secretly, I came to judge relatives by the generosity of their watermelon portions.)

Caring for watermelon the way I did, it was jarring to learn that this was something I was not supposed to take pleasure in. The stigma became clearer as I grew older. Besides the comments I heard at school from white kids, TV shows like *All in the Family* and *Good Times* provided the occasional watermelon joke.

If there was any doubt about what these comments meant, childhood vacations to Charleston cleared up the confusion. Arts and crafts were on vivid display at the market in the city's tourist district, including countless coal-black porcelain Mammies and Sambos holding up watermelon slices while smiling in idiotic delight. These grotesque, buffoonish figurines had the effect of turning watermelon into a weapon. The aim of this weapon was to force me to think I was sub-human. This sort of attack bred in black folk the kind of twisted guilt that would have fascinated Freud had he spent any time in South Carolina.

Several of my friends refuse to eat watermelon in public because they don't want to perpetuate the stereotype. When I ask them if they like watermelon, they aren't even sure anymore. What puzzles me most about "watermelon guilt" is how a particular food can actually change a group's eating habits. Italians don't refrain from eating garlic in the company of non-Italians. Jews don't pass on the matzo balls when goyim are around. No other food seems to have the same perverse effect on any other group in the U.S. as watermelon has on us.

The legal scholar Patricia J. Williams indicates just how perverse in a recent essay in *Transition* magazine. Williams talks about how when she was a child her mother would "dress up" watermelon by scooping it out in tiny balls and serving it in crystal goblets, like sorbet. Williams describes those times as "guilty, even shameful moments, never unburdened by the thought of what might happen if our white neighbors saw us enjoying the primeval fruit."

While black people are feeling so uptight about eating watermelon in public, everyone else is enjoying it wherever and whenever they like. Whites may joke with black people about eating watermelon, but they enjoy it just as much.

My friend John Rashford, an ethnobotanist at the College of Charleston, tells me that watermelon is enjoyed all over the world. Furthermore, it originated in Africa. In a botany book called *The World in Your Garden,* watermelon is described as "Africa's greatest contribution to the joy of eating."

I am reminded of a joke my mother once told me. A white man noticed that a black man had a bug on his shoulder and brushed it away. "Put it back!" yelled the black man. "Every time we get something, y'all try to take it away." Somehow, probably with the emergence of Mammy and Sambo, black people lost watermelon. Well, I've decided to reclaim my old joy. Unlike the pejorative n-word, which did not originate with black people, watermelon was ours. It was not introduced by someone from the outside, but instead hailed from the same place so many black people call home. Yet while Afro-centrists have busily combed the annals of history to find inspiring personages and symbols, they've overlooked one of Africa's greatest gifts. What better symbol of cultural pride than an object that has for so long been a source of ridicule? If we can salvage something as unpalatable as the n-word, then surely we can reclaim watermelon. Once we do, we should share it freely.

After all, that's what watermelon is really about.

September/October 1999

The Beautiful Bowel Movement

JOHN UPDIKE

Though most of them aren't much to write about—
mere squibs and nubs, like half-smoked pale cigars,
the tint and stink recalling Tuesday's meal,
the texture loose and soon dissolved—this one,
struck off in solitude one afternoon
(that prairie stretch before the late light fails)
with no distinct sensation, sweet or pained,
of special inspiration or release,
was yet a masterpiece: a flawless coil,
unbroken, in the bowl, as if a potter
who worked in this most frail, least grateful clay
had set himself to shape a topaz vase.
O spiral perfection, not seashell nor
stardust, how can I keep you? With this poem.

Spring 1992

Grandma's Table

STEVE YARBROUGH

AT ONE TIME MY GRANDMOTHER WAS A LEGENDARY COOK. She excelled at a kind of country cooking that you will no longer find much of in the Mississippi Delta, where I grew up. You will no longer find much of it because these days, more often than not, Deltans cook out of boxes. They make cakes the way everyone else does, from Duncan Hines containers, and they make their corn bread from prepackaged mixes. If they remain resistant to canned biscuits, they have come to terms with Bisquick. Frozen vegetables, they have learned, cook nicely in microwave ovens. So does bacon. Soup does, too.

But when I was growing up, in the late fifties and early sixties, country people made their cakes and breads and biscuits from scratch. They created their own sauces and gravies, seasoning them to taste, and the vegetables they ate came from their gardens. They made their own sausage. The chickens they fried had, until lately, been their neighbors.

Grandma scrambled eggs for me for breakfast, then she tore a couple of fluffy biscuits into bite-size bits and mixed them in with the eggs. If I asked her to, she would fry me up three or four slices of bacon—and the bacon, by the way, had come from our hogs. Sometimes, for a change, she gave me biscuits with a jar of her homemade molasses. The molasses was dark brown, and it was so thick that when you stuck a spoon into it you had a hard time getting it back out, almost as if it were trapped in a pool of quicksand.

Grandma was, at that time, an energetic, hardworking woman. Though blind in one eye from a childhood accident, she was the one who jumped in the pickup truck in the middle of the night to pull cotton trailers to the gin. When the farmhands chopped cotton in June and July, she was out in the field with them, leading the way. She worked her own garden, cleaned the house, and cooked, and for a few years, in the late fifties, took care of her bedridden mother.

If she was troubled by the harshness of the life she'd known, she seldom let on. Yet she had raised my mother during the Great Depression, and I knew from my grandfather, who talked about such things, that the family had almost starved. The WPA saved them. He got a job helping to build the Yazoo County Courthouse. Between the small amount he made there, and Grandma's ability to create meals out of vegetables and fatback, the family survived.

By the time I came along, Grandma and Grandpa were living in a house on sixteenth-section land. They owned a television, an old car, and a truck. The house was equipped with running water. There was always plenty to eat—neighbors liked to joke that at mealtime, the table sagged from all the good food Grandma laid on it. Considering where they had been, she and Grandpa must have felt like they had come a long way. I don't think it's an exaggeration to say that they were both fairly proud of themselves.

At least both of them were until Mike Seaver came to stay at their place, at which time Grandma's feelings about food and family, house and hearth, underwent certain changes.

Mike Seaver was from Texas. He was from Texarkana, Texas, but if you pointed out that the city of Texarkana was only half Texan, he would puff himself up and tell you, "A little bit of Texas is still one hell of a lot." He pronounced the word *Texas* just like Ernest Tubb did. *Tex-Us.*

Mike had married my second cousin Anne, who I had always thought was the most beautiful girl I'd ever seen. I remembered going down to Jackson when I was two or three to watch her being crowned homecoming queen at her high school. She had worn a long white gown that night, with sequins on it that sparkled under the stadium lights. Her blond hair seemed to sparkle as well. On the way home that evening I had told Grandma that I hoped to marry Anne. Naturally enough, I was disappointed when I found out about Mike.

She had met him at a dance in Texarkana. She had moved there in 1960 with her mother—my Aunt Lena, who was Grandma's sister—and her father and two grown brothers. At the time it seemed normal enough to me that they would all leave Mississippi at once. I did not learn until many years later that Aunt Lena's husband and my two male cousins had been threatened by the man who owned the automotive repair shop where they worked. Apparently, the man believed they had been stealing from him for several years. As it turned out, he was right, but that's another story.

Mike came to stay at Grandma's house one weekend in the summer of 1963. Anne wanted to show him off to all her relatives, so they planned several stops. Because she lived so close to Highway 82, Grandma was the first.

It's been more than thirty years since the afternoon I stood on the porch of my grandparents' house and watched, with the special kind of eagerness that I'm convinced only country kids feel, as Mike and Anne drove into the yard. They were riding in a long, silver Cadillac. The Cadillac sported Texas license plates. A sticker on the front bumper announced Mike's allegiance to the Dallas Cowboys. He'd played football in college, Grandma had told me, but she was uncertain exactly where.

Chickens scattered, squawking, when the Cadillac pulled in. Mike parked beneath the chinaberry tree, next to the rusty pitcher pump where, for many years, Grandma and Grandpa had drawn their drinking water.

Mike did not cut the engine right away. For a minute or more, the Cadillac idled. Through the windshield I could see my new cousin. He had wavy black hair that looked as if he'd applied Brylcreme to it, and his chin was big and square. He stared at me, at the porch I was standing on, and at Grandma, who had just walked out the screen door. Then he looked around the yard—at the chickens, at the old section harrow that stood near the road, overgrown by Johnson grass, at the tractor tire in which Grandma had planted a bed of azaleas.

Then he looked at Anne. He said something to her, and her face, which seconds before had worn a big smile as she waved at me and mouthed the word *hi*, suddenly went slack. It was as if she'd suffered some massive muscle failure.

"Y'all get out and come in," Grandma hollered. "I just about got supper on the table."

It would help to say a thing or two about the house that Grandma lived in.

The house had a tin roof and tar-paper siding. Because it was very close to Beaverdam Creek, it flooded from time to time. Grandpa had killed a water moccasin in their bedroom once, and they were always finding snakeskins in the chest of drawers and the closet.

It wasn't that the house wasn't clean; it was as clean as any house could be, given the fact that it occasionally flooded, that it had the kind of roof which was bound to leak. It was clean, given the fact that it had been built two feet off the ground so that chickens could walk around beneath it and do their business there, as could Grandpa's dog Buster, who was beset by ticks and fleas. But if you lived in a modern ranch-style house in the suburbs, and if you had a maid who came twice a week to clean, Grandma's house left something to be desired.

The room Grandma put Mike and Anne in was next to the kitchen— between it and Grandma's own bedroom. You had to walk through that room to get from one end of the house to the other. It was the room

I slept in when I spent the night with my grandparents—and most nights in the summer I stayed at their house. I remember the room now as the place in which I spent many of my happiest times. I recall the shape of the water stains on the ceiling—one of the stains, Grandpa had told me, was shaped exactly like Lake Michigan, and he'd shown me a map of the Great Lakes to prove it. I remember the way the floor creaked when you put your foot on one particular floorboard in the middle of the room, and I remember how you could hear Buster whimpering beneath you at night when he had a bad dream.

I also remember the conversation that took place between Mike and Anne in that room the day they arrived. Grandma had led them in there and closed the door so that they could get out of their traveling clothes before supper.

Mike's voice was resonant. He was trying to whisper, but he didn't succeed. "I can't do this," he said.

I was in the kitchen helping Grandma. She'd fried up a huge mess of catfish that Grandpa and my father had caught that morning in the Sunflower River. There were homemade hushpuppies and a tangy slaw she'd made of shredded cabbage, chopped celery, sweet pickles, and mayonnaise, with a dab of French's mustard thrown in to enhance the flavor.

The kitchen was full of good food, and getting it all on the table, along with the plates and the knives and forks and the big Mason jars we drank tea from, was going to take a while. But Grandma had stopped moving. She stood there next to the sink, listening, and so did I.

"I can't sleep in this bed," Mike said. "I can't shit in that toilet, I can't eat at that table. Hell, I'd be scared of the food."

We couldn't hear what Anne said, but in some form or fashion she must have asked him why.

"Because," he said, "I haven't ever done it before."

I did not, at that time, understand that a fair amount of what is wrong with the world on any particular day, in any particular century, is apt to be the result of somebody's unwillingness to experience something he's never experienced before. I did not, at that time, even understand what a person like Mike would find wrong with the bed I'd so often slept in or the toilet I'd relieved myself in almost every day of my life.

But there was one thing I knew for sure: If he sat down at Grandma's table and ate this meal, he would be very happy to sleep in the bed in the next room and attend to nature on the toilet. If he ate this meal, he might very well want to spend the remainder of his life in this house.

Of that there could be no doubt.

Many years later, after I moved to California to teach at a university, my cousin Anne came to visit my wife and my daughters and me. She still lived in Texarkana, but she and Mike had been divorced for almost ten years. She was in her mid-fifties, a tall silver-haired woman with a deeply tanned face. She came to Fresno in a new Mercedes. It was one of the V-12s, a car that cost more than our house.

She said the Mercedes belonged to the man she was seeing. He lived in Orange County. He was a developer, she said. She'd met him the previous summer on the beach in Key West.

In the backyard, while I cooked burgers on my gas grill, I asked her if things between her and the developer were serious.

"When you're my age," she said, "everything's serious."

She had called me a few days earlier and said she was on the West Coast and would like to visit. She had read both my books, she said, and she was proud to have an author in the family.

"And you're a college professor, too," she said. "That's wonderful."

I believed she meant it, but as I stood there flipping burgers, it crossed my mind that maybe she'd learned her lesson. Our English Tudor might have looked as lowly to her Orange County magnate as Grandma's house had looked to Mike. Maybe that was why she'd come to see us by herself.

At dinner that night she asked my daughters lots of questions about their school and their hobbies, and she asked my wife Eva, who is Polish, lots of questions about Poland. Anne said she and the developer had talked about visiting Eastern Europe next spring. They were mostly interested in seeing Prague and Budapest, but she said they might put Krakow on their list, too.

Then she leaned back, surveyed the four of us, and said, "It's nice to see two people from such different backgrounds make such a wonderful family."

That seemed as good a time as any to raise the specter of Mike. Where was he now, I asked her, what was he doing?

She said he managed a country club in Bryan, Texas. She never saw him anymore, and neither did her sons. The last few years they were all together, she said, had been pretty awful.

"But you know what?" she said, brightening. "He never did quit talking about that meal your grandma cooked him. You remember that night we stayed there?"

I said I did.

"He always wanted me to cook catfish that way and hushpuppies, too, but I never could do it to satisfy him. He said that meal your grandma cooked him was the best he ever ate in his life,"

"Do you remember the pictures?" I asked.

"What pictures?"

"The ones Grandma sent you after y'all had been to see us."

Anne frowned. "I'd forgotten those," she said. "Hey, what was that all about anyway?"

All of us sat at the table in the dining room. Mike and Anne, Mother and Dad and I, Grandpa and Grandma. Mike was accorded a place of honor at the end of the table.

He had changed clothes. He was wearing white pants and a short-sleeved Hawaiian shirt. It looked like he'd rubbed another layer of Brylcreme on his hair. It was stiff now and shiny.

He sat there with his arms crossed, staring at his plate, steeling himself for the worst. *The Beverly Hillbillies* had entered the American consciousness the year before, and you could tell he was preparing himself for the kinds of concoctions Granny Clampett might serve. Possum fried in lard, owl cutlets, stewed groundhog—that sort of thing.

Grandma and I had heard Anne pleading with him. "She's my favorite aunt. She helped Momma raise me. Please, just bear it tonight, and we'll leave in the morning. They can't help it if they're poor."

"I knew they were poor," we heard him say. "I was ready for that. It's unsanitary here. That's what worries me. Who knows whether or not the food's safe to eat?"

"It's safe. They've been eating it all their lives. I used to eat it, too."

"If I get sick," he grumbled, "you better haul me to a hospital quick."

The catfish and the hushpuppies had been dumped onto a huge green platter, which rested in the middle of the table. The cole slaw was in a big brown bowl. A bottle of Hunt's ketchup stood near the fish. The plates that we would eat from were of three different varieties. There were four heavy brown plates, a couple of white plates with Christmas designs around the rims, and one off-white plate that had no design at all on it, though if you turned it upside down you would find an inscription on the bottom. The inscription read, *Property of South Sunflower County Hospital.*

"Mike," Grandpa said, "you want to say grace?"

It was customary to ask the guest to say the blessing. No one had ever refused. But Mike Seaver did. "I'm not the church-going type," he said.

"We got married in church," Anne blurted out.

"Yeah, we did," Mike said. "But it was mostly just a social occasion."

For the last half hour, ever since we'd overheard the argument between Mike and Anne, Grandma had been silent. She had replied to every question I'd asked her about setting the table with a shake of her head. Now she said, "Ain't this a social occasion?"

As I've said, we didn't know much about Mike, except that he'd played football in college. We also knew that he worked for a company of some sort, that he was an executive, a man who wore a suit to work and gave orders and fired people. He didn't own the company, though, so he must have taken orders, too. He must, at some time, have found himself in a position in which his word was questioned. Knowing what I do now about people like Mike Seaver, I will risk a guess and say that when his word was questioned by a superior, he behaved in a very obliging, perhaps apologetic, manner.

But Grandma was not his superior. He uncrossed his arms, laid his palms down flat on the table, and spread his fingers out as if he were getting ready for action.

"Well, now," he said, "ain't this a social occasion? Yes, by doggie, it sure enough is."

While the rest of us sat there stunned, Mike Seaver bowed his head and shut his eyes. "Jesus," he said, doing his best to sound like Billy Graham. "Yes, *Jeez Us*. Bless these fish. Bless these hushpuppies. Bless this house and them that's in it. Bless the dogs and the cows and the chickens and the pigs. Bless all their leavings in the yard outside. Bless the hay and the cotton and the soybeans and John Deere. Bless this cole, cole slaw as you bless our hard, hard hearts."

And then Mike Seaver raised his head and opened his eyes and lifted up his fork. "Let's eat," he said.

He stabbed a piece of fish and laid it on his plate, then he picked up a hushpuppy and popped it in his mouth, and when he started to chew, I swear you could see a light enter his eyes. Slowly, while he and he alone ate, while the rest of us sat there and watched as he swallowed one hushpuppy after another, as he ate piece after piece of catfish, and pile upon pile of cole slaw, as stains appeared on his Hawaiian shirt, and his hands became so greasy he wiped them on his thighs, the snobbery drained out of his face.

I didn't know that day what it was that had left him, and I didn't know that it would leave him for only a little while and then come surging back, but I knew in my heart that his heart had softened. And I knew what had brought on the change: not the prayer he had spoken, but the meal he had eaten.

At Grandma's table, the food was a blessing in itself. But having said that, I am saddened to have to say this.

Just as the blessing wore off Mike Seaver, so that a few years down the road, after *Deliverance* hit the screens, he would disrupt cocktail parties by suggesting certain familial links between Anne and the mountain men who raped Ned Beatty, the blessing wore off the food on Grandma's table.

The change, unlike the change which had come over Mike that night in 1963, was not sudden. It came about gradually. It came along with many other changes that, at first glance, would seem to have little or nothing to do with food. Grandma began to look at new cars. You would sometimes see her walking around the lot at the Pontiac dealership or, at other times, down the road at the Ford dealership. Finally, she found the one she wanted, a new cream-colored Tempest. I remember the day she drove it home. She parked it in the front yard, near the chinaberry tree, in almost the exact same spot where Mike Seaver had parked the silver Cadillac. Grandpa's pickup truck had never looked strange there, but the Tempest, so shiny and new, seemed out of place. And so, a few days later, Grandma told Grandpa she wanted him to build a carport.

She bought a new refrigerator with an ice maker in it, and she bought a color TV. She visited Lott's Furniture Company and bought linoleum rugs for each room in the house. She bought a stereo, though she almost never turned it on, and she bought several standing lamps and a new bathtub and toilet. She re-papered the walls in every room.

She quit raising chickens. When Grandpa's dog Buster showed the first signs of illness, she insisted Grandpa shoot him, and they never had a dog again. She made Grandpa nail tin siding around the bottom of the house so that animals could not get under it.

She began to buy canned or frozen vegetables, and these were what we ate for supper. She discovered Swanson's frozen roast beef and gravy. It came in a pouch, and all you had to do was drop the pouch in boiling water for three or four minutes, and you had yourself a main dish. She bought apple pies frozen. She bought pecan pies that came in a box with a clear layer of plastic on top, so that you could see the pie, which had been baked in Cincinnati or St. Louis within the last two weeks. She developed a preference for Wonder bread. Any suggestion that it was made of styrofoam would turn her livid.

"I've got better things to do," she would say, "than stand in the kitchen half the day making pies and corn bread. This ain't the days of covered wagons. This is the modern world, and I for one refuse to regret it."

One night, two or three years after Mike and Anne came to visit, she brought a Polaroid camera into the dining room where Grandpa and I sat, resigned to a supper of Oscar Mayer weenies chopped into links and buried in a casserole dish full of Kraft macaroni and cheese. Alongside that, on one of Grandma's new plates, from the set of chinaware she'd bought at United Dollar Store, was half a loaf of Wonder bread, all the slices stacked neatly on top of one another. A blueberry pie, still in the box, was next to the bread.

"What are you doing?" Grandpa said.

He thought she planned to take a picture of him and me. I thought so, too. But when she aimed the camera, she aimed at the food. The flash clicked once, then twice, and she was gone.

1997

At the Young Composers' Concert

DONALD JUSTICE

Sewanee, Tennessee, Summer, 1996

The melancholy of these young composers
Impresses me. There will be time for joy.

Meanwhile, one can't help noticing the boy
Who bends down to his violin as if

To comfort it in its too early grief.
It is his composition, confused and sad,

Made out of feelings he has not yet had
But only caught somehow the rumor of

In the old scores—and that has not been enough.
Merely mechanical, sure, all artifice—

But can that matter when it sounds like this?
What matters is the beauty of the attempt,

The world for him being so far mostly dreamt.
Not that a lot, to tell the truth, has passed,

Nothing to change our lives or that will last.
And not that we are awed exactly; still,

There is something to this beyond mere adult skill.
And if it moves but haltingly down its scales,

It is the more moving just because it fails;
And is the lovelier because we know

It has gone beyond itself, as great things go.

July/August 2000

First Tell Me What Kind of Reader You Are

ROY BLOUNT JR.

WHEN PEOPLE OF THE NORTHEAST ASK WHAT I DO, I long for one of those professions that would qualify me to respond as follows:

"Before I answer that question, I am ethically obliged to inform you that as soon as I do answer, our conversation will be billable at two hundred dollars per hour or portion thereof—and the answering of the question itself shall constitute such a portion, as will what I am telling you now, retroactively."

That would dispense with a lot of the idle conversation in which I find myself bogged down, in the Northeast.

"What do you do?" people ask.

I say, "I'm a writer."

And people of the Northeast don't respond the way you'd think people would. They don't say, "I knew a writer once. He could never sit still in a boat," or, "Yeah, that's about all you *look* like being, too. What do you do, make it all up, or do the medias tell you what to say?" or, "Uh-huh, well I breed ostriches." I could roll with any one of those responses. One reason there are so many Southern writers is that people of the South either tell a writer things he can use, or they disapprove of him enough to keep his loins girded, or they just nod and shake their heads and leave him to it. But people of the Northeast act like being a writer is *normal*.

185

"Oh," they say with a certain gracious almost twinkle in their eye, "what kind?"

What am I supposed to say to that? "Living"? "Recovering"? They'll just respond, "Oh, should I have heard of some of your books?" I don't know how to answer that question. And I'm damned if I'm going to stand there and start naming off the titles. That's *personal!* Can you imagine Flannery O'Connor standing there munching brie on a rye crisp and saying, "Well, there's *The Violent Bear It Away. . . .*"

People of the Northeast don't seem to think it *is* all that personal. They seem to think that you can find out about books by having a schmooze with the writer, in the same way they might think you find out about whiskey by chatting up someone in personnel down at the distillery.

What I want to do, when somebody asks me what kind of writer I am, is sull up for several long seconds until I am blue in the face and then, from somewhere way further back and deeper down than the bottom of my throat, I want to vouchsafe this person an utterance such that the closest thing you could compare it to would be the screech of a freshly damned soul shot through with cricket-song and, intermittently, all but drowned out by the crashing of surf. But I was brought up to be polite.

I was also brought up Methodist and went to graduate school, so I can't honestly say what I want to say: "Self-taught annunciatory. I received a vision out of this corner, of this eye, at about 7:45 P.M. on January 11, 1949, and since that moment in earthly time I have been an inspired revelational writer from the crown of my hat to the soles of my shoes. And do you want to know the nature of that vision?

"The nature of that vision was a footprint in the side of an edifice, and the heel of it was cloven and the toes of it was twelve. And how could a footprint be in the side of an edifice, you wonder? Especially since I stood alone at the time, stark naked and daubed with orange clay, in a stand of tulip poplar trees some eleven miles outside of Half Dog, Alabama, way off a great ways from the closest man-made structure in any literal sub-annunciatory sense. That footprint could be in the side of an edifice for one reason and one reason only: because—"

But then they'd just say, "Oh, a *Southern* writer. What *are* grits?"

I don't live in the South anymore. I maintain you can't live in the South and be a deep-dyed Southern writer. If you live in the South you are just writing about folks, so far as you can tell, and it just comes out Southern. For all we know, if you moved West, you'd be a Western writer. Whereas, if you live outside the South, you are being a Southern writer either (a) on purpose or (b) because you can't help it. Which comes to the same thing in the end: You are deep-dyed.

Whether or nor anybody in the South thinks you are a Southern writer is not a problem. Englishmen think of Alistair Cooke as an American. Americans think of him as English. So he's in good shape, as I see it: Nobody keeps track of whether he goes to church.

One thing to be said for being in the Northeast, and you being Southern, is that it provokes you to keep an edge on your Southernness. Sometimes I'll bring up obscure examples of anti-Southern prejudice— "You ever think about the fact that in the book, the good witch is the Witch of the South, but when they made the movie they changed her to the Witch of the North?"

Also I make a point of taking no interest whatsoever in what passes in the North for college sports. When I was a boy in Georgia, college sports was Bobby Dodd versus Bear Bryant immemorial. Compared with that the Harvard-Yale game is a panel discussion. When all the college sports you can follow in the local media are Nehi or Lehigh, or whatever, against Hofstra or Colgate, or somebody, why bother? You know what they call the teams at Williams College? The Ephs. Let me repeat that: The Ephs. Pronounced *eefs*. Do you think that anybody who is willing to be called an Eef is capable of playing any sport at a level anywhere near root-hog-or-die? Caring about college sports in the Northeast is like caring about French food in South Carolina.

A good thing about being Southern is that it often involves getting to a point where you don't know what to think. People of the Northeast act like they have never been to that point before. Certainly they think they know what to think about Southern things. Whenever such people try to prove they are down with Southern culture by professing love for, say, Garth Brooks, I look at them with a certain expression on my face and ask whether they haven't heard of the real cutting-edge genre, Faded Country—songs like "I Guess Fishin' Is Sufficient, But I'd Like a Little Love" and "I'm So Lonesome I Could Go Out and Ride Around on I-285." Or if people start telling me how deeply they respond to B. B. King, I'll say, "You know they've isolated the blues gene."

I let that sink in, and then I add, "Now. *What do we do with that knowledge?*"

I bring up awkward racial questions whenever possible. For some years now, drastically bad race relations have been cropping up mostly outside the South, and I want to see some Northern white people sweat. I don't accuse them of being racist, because they know they aren't *that kind of person.* What I will do is say that anybody who claims to be "colorblind" or not to have "a racist bone" in his or her body is at best pre-racist and has a longer way to go than the rest of us. I also spoil scintillating dinner parties by bringing up the O. J. verdict. A lot of enlightened-feeling Northern white people, who have never even suspected themselves of what we might call ethnocentric assumptions, are completely unself-conscious about blaming the whole thing on the jury.

The reason O. J. got off, people of the Northeast feel fine about asserting, is that the jury was (a) too black to have any sympathy for the victims and (b) too dumb to get out of serving on the jury.

My response to (a) is to wonder aloud whether, if we stay humble long enough, *Southern* white people will ever be qualified to get away with bald-faced color-coded mind reading. My response to (b) is that it sounds to me like the sort of assumption that enabled noncombatants to feel cozy about blaming Vietnam on American draftees.

I won't hear a word against the O. J. jury until I hear several thousand words against the L.A. cops and the prosecutors. I point to all manner of bungling on the part of these professionals, and I observe that the DNA doesn't prove anything if the specimens were planted.

"Oh," people of the Northeast say, as if they've got me now. "Was the investigation-prosecution a conspiracy, or was it incompetent? You can't have it both ways."

"The hell I can't," I counter. "Y'all never heard of an incompetent conspiracy?"

"But O. J. did it!" they say.

"Most likely. Chances are, so did some of the people who—as has not been forgotten down where I come from—used to get lynched."

And whatever else you think about Johnnie Cochran, whether his client was the devil or not, the son of a bitch can *preach!* Alive in his words—without *needing* impeccable high ground. I will presume to put myself in the mind of a given black juror to this extent: I believe if I were such a juror listening to Johnnie Cochran represent a black defendant, I'd be thinking, "Let's remake *To Kill a Mockingbird* with this brother here as Atticus Finch!"

I don't throw lynching at people of the Northeast lightly, but I do freely say *y'all*. The language needs a second-person plural, and *y'all* is manifestly more precise, more mannerly and friendlier than *you people* or *y'uns*. When Northerners tell me they have heard Southerners use *y'all* in the singular, I tell them *they* lack structural linguistic understanding. And when they ask me to explain grits, I look at them like an Irishman who's been asked to explain potatoes.

All too often in the Northeast, *writers themselves* seem to regard being a writer as normal. When people ask a Northeastern writer what kind he or she is, instead of expostulating, "What do you mean what *kind?* Getting-by-the-best-I-can kind! Trying-to-make-some-kind-of-semi-intelligible-sense-out-of-the-god-damn-cosmos kind! If you're interested, see if you can't find a way to read something I wrote! If I knew it by heart I would recite the scene in *Marry and Burn* where the fire ants drive the one-legged boy insane (which I'll admit I think almost comes up to what it might have been, but it's not *simple* enough, there are too many *of*'s in it, I couldn't get enough *of*'s out of it to save my life!); but I don't carry it around in my head—I was trying to get it out of my head; and even if I did, reciting it wouldn't do it justice! You have to read it"—a Northeastern writer will natter away about being poststructuralist or something. And everybody's happy. Writers fitting into the social scheme of things—it don't seem right to me.

Grits is normal.

June/July 1996

Rose of Lebanon

WILLIAM FAULKNER

I.

DR BLOUNT STOPPED HIS COUPE BEFORE A TWO-ACRE SPRAWL of scrolled and gabled house. It had a great amount of plate glass and fanlights, set among neat big trees on a neat, big lawn; the street itself was neat and broad and quiet. The trees on the lawn were mostly oaks and maples, the oaks still bare, though the maples were already swelling into feathery russet against the late February sky. It was a gusty, chilly, thick day across which came as from a great distance, rather of time than space, the faint sound of the city, of Memphis.

The coupe was of a popular make sold on the instalment plan, though Blount's widowed grandmother and the maiden sister of his father, with whom he lived in a house a little like the one which he was now approaching, owned two clumsy limousines of esoteric make that used to be advertised by the inch in the magazines twenty-five years ago.

He went up the concrete walk and rang the bell. An old negro man, in a white serving jacket which looked as though he had borrowed it for the emergency when the bell rang, opened the door. "How you, Mr Gavin?" he said.

"I'm fine, Ned," Blount said. The negro had a slick, saddle-colored head fringed with gray hair. "How are you?"

"Aint so good," the negro said. "We thought maybe you wasn't coming this evening." Blount took off his overcoat. He was slight and dapper, in a dark suit that might have cost twenty-five dollars or a hundred and twenty-five. He was dark, with a long, impractical face, thirty-seven years old and a bachelor. He lived in the house in which his grandfather had been born. It was in the country then, though it now sat on a street named after an inferior flower, surrounded by subdivisions of spurious Georgian houses bought and sold among themselves by Main Street and Madison Avenue Jews. He lived there with his grandmother and his aunt and three negro servants. The grandmother was a fat woman who lived in a wheel chair, though she had a good appetite, coming to the table in the wheel chair, where she would unfold her napkin, refold it and smooth it along the table edge and lay neatly upon it her small, plump, soft, ringed, useless hands. "You may commence now, Gavin," she would say.

Blount left the negro in the hall, and mounted the stair. The stair was broad, heavy, and gloomy, the hall broad and heavy and gloomy too, and a little too warm to be healthy. The upper hall was identical, faced with doors of dark and gloomy wood. He entered a room where a woman lay on a day-bed drawn across the hearth, with a small table and one chair drawn up beside it. The woman was wrapped in a steamer rug. Her hair on a white pillow was perfectly white.

"I had begun to think you were not coming today," she said.

"Yessum," Blount said. "I was late. I met Ran Gordon this afternoon at the Battery." He sat down, on the chair beside the table. "And you'll never guess it."

"He's made another million," the woman said.

"Yes," Blount said. He spoke in an eager, oblivious tone, leaning a little forward. "I reckon so. You'll never guess it, not in a year." He talked, rapidly, leaning forward, in that eager, diffuse tone. "It was the men that got whipped in that war; if they'd just got out of the way and let the women, the women like—" The door opened. The negro in the white jacket entered, without knocking, carrying a tray bearing a coffee pot, a cup, a decanter, a flared, heavy wineglass almost as big as a goblet. He set the tray on the table.

"Cherry Bounce done give out," he said. "This here's Yankee's Head, but it'll bounce you, too." He filled the coffee cup at the woman's hand, and the wineglass from the decanter at Blount's, and went and stood beside the fire. "Aint seed your Grammaw in some time," he said to Blount.

"She was here not six weeks ago," the woman said to the negro. "You brought the coffee up, yourself."

"You thinking about Miss Levinia," the negro told her. Miss Levinia was Blount's aunt. She was a thin, indefatigable woman. She was president of the Confédération Française, a woman's club which exchanged volumes of the *Mercure de France,* of Paul Fort and Mallarmé and Henri Becque. They met on stated afternoons at the Country Club (the oldest one, the Country Club; the others all had designations, names or locations) where they drank coffee and talked in English of their sons and daughters, nieces and nephews, of the Junior League and the Nonconnah Guards. "It was Miss Levinia that come to see us," the negro said. "About Christmas time. But you aint seed Mrs Blount outen that house since last summer. And you aint going to see um till summer come again." He watched Blount sip from the glass. "How you like that Yankee's Head?"

"It's fine," Blount said.

"Aint as good as that Bounce was. But Bounce all gone now. We didn't make no more this winter. I told um it was getting low."

"No you didn't," the woman said. "You didn't tell me until about two days ago."

"Just listen at her," the negro said. "I told her long before Christmas. But you cant do nothing with um. I done found that out long time ago."

He went toward the door. "I reckon I better get on down and see about them kitchen niggers."

"I wish you would," the woman said. "I wish you would stay out of here."

"Yessum," the negro said. He went out; again he opened the door and looked in. "When you get home, Mr Gavin, you tell your Grammaw I inquired for her kind health and say for um to come and see us."

"I will," Blount said. The door closed again. He turned back to the woman, his mouth already open for speech, but she spoke first.

"How much did Ran Gordon make?"

"Make what?" Blount said. Then he said: "It's better than that. Lewis Randolph is coming back to town."

"Lewis—?" The woman's voice ceased. She looked at him. Her hair was quite white, her face waxy, flaccid, shapeless, the eyes like the coals of two cigars which might at a single breath be drawn into life.

"Yessum. She's coming back to town; it's only been sixty-five years." He talked rapidly, the half-empty glass in his hand, leaning a little forward. The woman watched him with that dark, arrested, intent expression about her eyes.

"How much money have you made this year?" she said.

"—what? What did you—"

"How much money did you ever make?"

"I buy my own clothes, and pay for the car."

"Which car? The twenty-one dollars a month on that little one of your own?"

"How did you know it is twenty-one dollars?" They stared at one another. She had seen him within a week of his birth. Her eyes were inscrutable, speculative. She watched the astonishment fade from his face, but before it was gone, he was talking again. "Not since sixty-five years; not since she came up from Mississippi, sixty miles in a muddy carriage in December, to the Guards' Ball in '61."

"I know that," the woman said. "I was there." Her voice was impatient, a little testy. "Those balls used to be full of Mississippi and Arkansas country belles. I've heard they still are."

"Yes," Blount said; "all right." Then he was talking again, leaning a little forward into the firelight, the half-empty glass in his hand.

II.

Almost every afternoon he walked North along the levee, from the same point to the same point. He descended the levee, the steep pitch of worn cobbles, at the Beale Street landing, and followed it and mounted the bluff, to the Battery. This was a small park, with tended grass and walks and flower beds, with a low rock revetment along the bluff studded with bronze tablets bearing serried names, and through the apertures of which rusting iron cannons with spiked touch-holes gloomed down upon the river below. Here he would stand for a time, among the quiet and rusting guns and the careful pyramids of ammunition, the austere (yet florid too) bronze tablets, on one of which he could read the name which he now bore. Beneath the bluff lay the railroad tracks, the cobbled slant of the levee, the shabby and infrequent steamboats warped into shabby landings, taking on shabby and meagre cargoes bound for inaccessible destinations which scarcely scarred any landscape, whose names were on no maps. The boats lay along the levee, with scaling and rust-streaked sides, with grandiloquent names in fading four-foot letters across counter and wheel-box, derided by shrieking apparitions of locomotives and pullman cars fleeing back and forth, to Chicago in twenty hours, New Orleans in ten. From the parapet where he would stand, the river was now almost invisible, bidden by what was, thirty years ago, a shoal, and then a scarce-broached sand-bar, and what was now an island bearing a virgin growth of willow trees among which nomad squatters lived in houseboats hauled or floated ashore and in actual houses built on piles above the sand. But almost invisible was the stream itself, up and down which in '62 and '63 the Federal gallipots steamed, firing into the bluff with Parrott howitzers until the city fell; whereupon the Rebels captured the gallipots and steamed up and down in turn and fired in turn with the same Parrotts, into the grim and abiding and oblivious bluff named after a vanished race.

He had inherited his practice, as a lawyer inherits his; a practice which took him on regular and leisurely rounds to smug, well-to-do houses, where old women overtaken at last by indolence and rich food, who had outlived his father and some of whom would outlive him, received him in close bedrooms where the elegant heavy walnut of the seventies gleamed in the pulsing firelight, and where, like another old woman himself, they would talk also of sons and daughters and the Junior League and the Nonconnah Guards. This was a semi-military organization with a skeleton staff of regular army officers and a hierarchate of elective social officers with semi-military designations, the highest of which was that of Flag-Corporal, an office which Blount had held for fourteen years. In 1859 it had been organised by fifty-one young men, bachelors. They gave the first ball that December. In 1860 it had become a National Guard unit; at the ball of that year the men wore blue dress uniforms, with the yellow stripe of cavalry. The membership had grown to one hundred and four. In 1861, at the third ball, the men were in gray, their new kits stacked in a dressing-room, a train at the station ready to leave for Virginia at midnight. The armory was filled that night, not only with dancers, but with older guests, parents and relatives. At the end of the hall, above the band platform, mute nails still shaped the ripped-down Federal flag, while in its place was fixed the new flag which was not quite yet familiar; beneath it the figures, the gray uniforms and the flared crinoline and fans and scarves, formed and turned. At half past eleven the music—three fiddles, two guitars, a clarinet played by negroes—stopped. The major, the late major in the United States Army, cleared the floor. The men fell in in single file against the wall, the major in front, facing across the empty floor the older guests. The major's uniform was no different from the ones of the men, without insignia save for a crimson sash and a cavalry sabre upon which he now leaned. At the far end of the ball the girls, the late partners, had gathered into still another distinct group. The room was high, a little chilly, looming, the walls lined with improvised candelabra and oil lamps. The major began to speak.

"A lot of you all have already gone. I'm not talking to them. A lot of you all will have made your plans to go. I'm not talking to them. But there are some that can go, that believe it will be over by summer. I'm talking to them." His voice was not loud, yet it carried distinct and sonorous in the cavernous room. Outside, it had begun to snow, though as fast as they fell, the flakes died into the deep, churned, icy mud. "You've heard of Virginia, but some of you haven't seen it. Washington. New York. But haven't seen it." In the cavernous silence, the tenseness, the expectancy, his voice had a profound, sonorous, meaningless quality like the sound of a bee trapped in a tin bucket. ". . . empowered by the President of the Confederate States of America. . . ."

They shouted, the guests, the older men, the voices of the women shrill; that same shout without words that was to be gaunted and worn thin and shrill by many battlefields, to outlast the war itself and be carried westward across the Mississippi by veterans and the sons of veterans and of the slain, to rush, punctuated by galloping hooves and pistol shots, across the dusty plazas of frontier towns. Before it had ceased the music was playing again, a shrill tune too fast for dancing, as though composed for highland pipes. The spectators saw the girls, who had been clumped at the end of the room, moving now toward the gray line in a sort of order, looking in their flaring, delicate dresses like a series of inverted vases as they advanced, blotting the gray line from sight, kissing the men in turn, moving on, so that when the gray line began to come into sight again, against each tunic there was a red rose like a pistol wound. For a little while longer there was order, then gray and crinoline became commingled, inextricable, from which came the shrieks of girls, shrieks of terror not so much feigned and not so very feared, and from all parts of the room voices began to sing with the swift fiddles, the guitars, the shrill clarinet:

> Wish I was in the land of cotton,
> Simmon seed and sandy bottom,
> Look awayyyyyyyyy,
> Look awayyyy
> Look awayyy, Dixie Land.

The major had not moved. He leaned on the sabre, looking at the guests, the civilians, the young men in formal black. "Now, boys," he said, "who wants to spit into the Potomac river before Christmas?"

III.

"Lewis Randolph was one of the girls there that night," Blount said. "She was one of the girls that kissed a hundred and four men. Coming all the way up from Mississippi in a muddy carriage paved with hot bricks—they'd have to stop now and then and build a fire with the pine wood they brought with them, the niggers, I mean, and heat the bricks again—to kiss a hundred and four men, so she could give a red rose to Charley Gordon. I dont remember Grandfather very well, but I have heard Granny tell about Lewis Randolph. Maybe it's because Granny was a toast of the town herself. Maybe it's because, even when they get to be ninety, they do not realise that a woman fills and empties the objective shape of a toast just as people fill and empty a telephone booth in a busy railroad station, engendering with the same motion the same sound of the same bell. Anyway, when they have been toasts themselves, they are tolerant, almost unselfish about other women. She told me about how Grandfather told about how Charley Gordon would come to town two days before she was due, from down in Mississippi too, bringing with him a negro boy and a mule. On the day the carriage was due, from daylight on, I hope from daylight on; it must have been from daylight on,—that nigger boy squatting and shivering in the December rain, beside the mule at the roadside, with wrapped in an oilcloth cape a bouquet as large as a yard-broom, cut and borrowed and bribed out of private pits; and Charley Gordon himself a little further along the road, beyond a thicket, in the rain too, waiting from maybe daybreak too, to ride out bareheaded when the carriage came up, in sopping linen and a sopping coat."

"I always said that he was a fool," the woman on the bed said.

"Was it to her you said that?" Blount said. The woman watched him, the face on the propped pillows, in the steady firelight, bloated and waxlike. "Would you say it now, to either of them, if he was still alive? You couldn't say it to him or to his kind, anyhow. Maybe because it would be true. But it's too late to tell them that, now. They all galloped bareheaded with brandished sabres when they had them, but anyway galloping, off the stage altogether, into a lot more rain than a December drizzle; maybe into somewhere else where they could bang themselves to pieces again, like puppets banging themselves to pieces against the painted board-and-plaster, the furious illusions of gardens and woods and dells; maybe to meet brighter faces than Lewis Randolph looking out a carriage window halted in a muddy road. Maybe to him she wasn't anything, anyway, but the sound of the words, Lewis Randolph, above the glasses at Gaston's. Had you ever thought of that?"

"I have told her that they were both fools," the woman on the bed said.

Blount ceased. He looked at her, the flaccid face wakened somehow, the eyes intent on his face, her body backthrust a little, as though he had offered to strike her; her eyes, coming alive for the moment like the two cigars drawn into life, not courageous but invincible, not victorious yet undefeated. "Your name might have gone around above those same glasses too. Dont tell me you have ever forgotten that you ever believed that." Her face died while he looked at it, the eyes died; again on the propped pillows was the face of an old woman, tired with overlong looking and seeing. "I know that men and women are different. It's a deliberate provision. Through no fault nor control of their own, women produce men children, who ennoble them. Not the maternity: that's an attribute, both crown and chastisement, of any female. A girl-child is mothered and fathered and grandsired by her contemporary genera-tion; a man-child by all time that preceeded him."

"I don't see what this has to do with Lewis Randolph."

Blount finished the drink, set the glass down and reached for the decanter. But he began to talk again before he uncapped the decanter. "You were there, that night. You kissed a hundred and four men that night, too. That night when she and Charley Gordon found they could not live without one another. You were probably at the station and heard the noise when the train moved and she on it, with Charley Gordon's cape above her ball dress, and she went to Knoxville in that day coach full of soldiers and heated by a wood-stove stoked by a negro bodyser-vant, and the next day they were married by a minister who happened to be a private in a regiment waiting there to entrain, just in time for her to take the next train south, back to Mississippi, with a letter from Charley Gordon to his mother written on the back of a bill-of-fare from the station eating-room."

The eyes of the woman on the bed were closed. "There were other girls at that ball prettier than Lewis Randolph," she said in a tired tone.

"And (I'll say it for you) saw that train leave without them on it, with a soldier's cloak above a hooped ball gown." He was smoking a cig-arette now. "She went back to Mississippi, to her new home. It was a big, square house twenty-five miles from any town. It had flower beds, a rose garden. When she got there, with the letter on the bill-of-fare, her father-in-law was organising a regiment. She and her mother-in-law embroidered the colors, with negro girls to pick and iron the bright, fragmentary silk. From the high, quiet room where they worked they could hear thick boots in the hall all day long, and voices from the diningroom around the punchbowl. The lot was full of strange horses; the lawn, the park, spotted with tents and littered with refuse. In the evenings there would be a bonfire on the lawn, its glare red and fierce upon the orators; up to the porch where the women sat or stood the voices came, orotund and sonorous and endless. On the shadowy porch the two women would stand then, their arms about one another, in the darkness lighted by the remote glare darkly too, touching but not speaking, not even looking at one another. Then the regiment went away; the talk, the boots in the hall; the rubbish and litter on the lawn was healed by the first November rains, leaving only the scarred earth, the trampled and broken walks and flower beds. Then the house was quiet again with only the two women in it and the voices of the negroes, the mellow shouts, the laughter, the sounds of chopping wood, coming peacefully up from the quarters on the monotonous twilight.

"She was an only child. She was born in a house like the one she now lived in. They might have been interchangeable: the planks, the flower beds, the negroes. Her own father wore the same broadcloth, the same hats and boots. When she was fifteen he took her in the heavy carriage, the one with the removable brick floor, to a seminary for young ladies in Oxford, where she spent three years. When she was eighteen, they took her to Memphis, to her first ball. They stayed at Gaston's Hotel, and on the night of the first Guards' Ball in 1859 she saw Charley Gordon for the first time. Two years later she got off that troop train in Knoxville and was married in the station, surrounded by soldiers in new gray, by bright, not yet familiar regimental flags. She had not slept in thirty hours, yet she stood there in her ball gown, with not a hair turned and not a bow misplaced. She looked like something made in an expensive shop, of lace and bright frosting, and turned upside down in the center of a hollow square of troops all young and none of whom had ever heard a bullet; by strange faces which, for all their youth and inexperience and perhaps foreboding, wore none the less of doubt for that. I imagine she was the only calm one there. Because women have lived so long when they begin to breathe. While men have to be born anew each hour. Each second."

He reached the decanter again. This time he filled the glass. The woman on the pillow had not moved or opened her eyes. The firelight pulsed quietly upon her face. The windows were fading with dusk, the wet, thick February twilight. "So the two of them lived in that big house. In the late fall of '62 a carriage came, the first one to enter the gates in almost six months. She did not recognise it until it reached the house, then she recognised the driver. It was from her old home, three days away. She had not seen her parents since the previous spring, and she would not see her father again. 'Pappy is dead,' she told her mother-in-law. 'I'll have to go home for a while.'

"When she got home, she found her mother in bed. The mother had fever. 'The silver,' the mother said. 'We've got to get it buried.'

"'All right. We will. We will.'

"'They killed your father. Now they'll come down here. We must bury it.' It rained that night. The daughter went to bed in her old room, hearing the rain. After midnight she was wakened by a negro woman.

"'It's Mistis,' the negress said. She found her mother in the kitchen, a cloak over her nightgown, wet and muddy, her hair draggled across her flushed face. She was unconscious. The negroes had found her in the garden, trying to dig a hole, beside her was a silver coffee service wrapped in a quilt. Three nights later she died of pneumonia. The rain had not ceased; they buried her in it, in the family burying-ground.

"It rained all that winter. I remember how Granny used to tell about that winter, with the sound of the guns from the river batteries, a thick slow sound, and then the Yankee troops in the city and the patrols riding the streets at night. Mississippi must have been full of them; that was when she began to carry the derringer in the pocket of her calico dress. She was back with her mother-in-law then. Then it was almost summer again. One evening a riding horse and a spring wagon came in the gates. Her father-in-law was on the horse. Her husband was in the wagon, on a shuck mattress. He was weak, but mending; but it was six months before he left again to join Van Dorn's cavalry. The father-in-law was already gone, into Bragg's army, captured, and was now in the Rock Island prison. Again the two women were alone in the house, with fewer negro voices from the quarters and the kitchen now. The negroes left one by one, stealing away at night, going to the cities; men and women hanging around the Federal army kitchens and the barracks of the troops, the men waiting for the forty acres and the mule; the women, their desires and needs more simple and more immediate, not having to wait.

"The next year, Ran was born. There was no doctor, but they got along without one, only that night the mother-in-law fell down the stairs while on her way to the kitchen to heat water, and from that night till her death she did not leave her bed. There was still one old negro man and two women. The father-in-law was still in the Rock Island prison, as far as they knew, but one night in the meantime Van Dorn rode into Holly Springs and burned Grant's stores, and Charley Gordon was killed. Shot off his horse. Something about a chicken roost. Ran told me. Anyway, it was dark and close and hurried, with the red sky behind them and a close yard full of surging, excited horses and hurried men; I reckon they were robbing the chicken roost. Then someone fired point blank into them with a shot gun.

"Ran was big enough to remark things, to remember things. Or so he claims. But they are probably things the negroes told him afterward. He said that his mother didn't tell him any of them. He said he didn't talk to her much, because he was afraid of her, afraid to ask her. Like the negroes were afraid of her, the three negroes who were still there when he was big enough to remember. It was them, not his mother, who told him about his grandfather, the Rock Island prisoner. It was almost a year after the surrender, and almost a year since the grand-mother had died in the room which she had not left since she fell down the stairs on the night Ran was born. One day his grandfather came home. He came on foot. The negroes said he looked like a hant, wasted, with no hair and no teeth, and he wouldn't talk at all, and the negroes would have to clean the floors and rugs after him like a puppy or a kitten or a child. He stayed there two years, not talking to anyone, not telling anyone where he had been during that year after the war stopped, refusing to take off his clothes to go to bed. One morning one of the negroes came into the kitchen, where Ran's mother was preparing some infant mess for him out of whatever it was they had to make it with. 'Marster's gone,' the negress said.

"'You mean, dead?' his mother said; the negroes told him she did not even stop stirring the dish.

"'Nome. Just gone. Unk Awce been looking for him since early. But cant nobody find him.'

"That was the sort of thing that Ran meant by remembering. Like when he told me of lying in the shady corner of a fence while his mother, in the calico dress with the pocket where the derringer stayed, and a calico sunbonnet, stood with folded arms, not touching the fence, watching a negro plow. 'And he plowed fast, too, while she was there,' Ran said. Or, about lying, wrapped in a quilt on the frozen ground on the lee side of a boiling iron kettle, his mother stirring the kettle while the three negroes flayed and dressed a hog. Then one day—he could have taken no cognizance of war or peace, or of any actual and definite date—he knew that, not only was the derringer missing from his mother's pocket, but that it had been missing for some time. 'It was just gone,' he told me. 'Like there wasn't any further use for it. I knew that Yankees had been there once, but even the negroes would not tell me what had happened. "Ask her to tell you herself when you man enough to hear it," they told me. But they knew that I knew that I would never be that man. So I dont know what happened. Maybe she shot him or them and the negroes buried them in the pasture. I just knew that the derringer was gone, without knowing when I had missed it. As if the need was gone at last.'

"Which it obviously had," Blount said. He drank. The woman on the bed had not stirred nor opened her eyes. "Though what had happened when the Yankee patrol, or maybe a single scout, came there and found a white woman and an infant and three frightened negroes. . . . I hope she didn't shoot him. Think of it: a Yankee, *a Yankee,* to get shot by Lewis Randolph. By a hand in honor of which men, *men,* had drunk glasses of fine whiskey; that until four years ago, had never laid a stick on a fire.

"When Ran left home he was fifteen. She (she was still thin; hard as nails, probably, and sunburned, in the same calico, with the same eyes which he had remembered watching the plowing negro across the fence) had taught him to read and to write, and that was all. He left home in a cart made out of the front end of a collapsed buggy, drawn by a mule and driven by a negro woman, the old man having died at last, which carried him to a crossroads store. From there he went on afoot, bumming rides when he could, to the county town and the railroad. He had a homewoven shirt and a black gum toothbrush and a baking powder can of homemade soap tied in a handkerchief. He had never seen a town before, or a railroad. He came to Memphis in a box car, sixteen hours without food, light, anything much; he didn't even dare to ask if the car was going to Memphis. Twelve months later he wrote his mother that he had saved two hundred dollars and that she could now come on to him. She wrote back that she was not coming. Two years after he left he went back home on a visit. He had a thousand dollars then. The place had not changed: the big, scaling house, the faint traces of flower beds on what had been a formal lawn; the two negro women; his mother (she had apparently not aged a day) in the same calico, watching a negro boy plowing the same mule beyond a fence, the plow moving at a good pace, too. He did not see her again for seven years. He was married then, cashier in the bank, owned his own house. He found her as he had left her. Again she refused to come to Memphis, even on a visit. 'I dont like cities,' she said. After that he saw her perhaps each two or three years, because he was getting to be president of the bank and such, with a son and a daughter and his wife with her eye already on the Junior League and maybe the Guards. She changed very little when he would see her: the same calico, though the house was falling down. She let him repair it a little, though not much, even when he was a millionaire.

"One day (he was fifty himself, with a grown family) he got a letter. It was written on a jagged piece of wrapping paper, in pencil, in a crabbed, terrific hand like a palsied schoolboy's. He went home (he went home by car then) and found the neighbor in the house and his mother in bed. She had had a mild stroke, yet on the pillow her face was still indomitable, cold, a little coldly outraged at the failure of her own flesh. He moved her anyway then, though he could not get her to make the trip in his car. He had to get a carriage for her, had to buy it. And, even though she was still helpless, he could not get her nearer to Memphis than that bungalow out there on the Pigeon Roost road. He bought that, too, the carriage halted in the road in front of it. She has been there twelve years, in that ten acres of orchard and garden and chicken runs. She has never seen Memphis since she left it that night sixty-five years ago on a Rebel troop train.

"So this afternoon I met Ran. 'She's coming in to dinner tomorrow night,' he told me. 'I have persuaded her at last. But early; six o'clock;

she insisted on six, because she believes that she must get back home by eight-thirty. But I had a time finding a carriage for her. There is an Italian truck-farmer that owed me a note. He let me have one, but it had to be repaired and painted.' And that's where I have been," Blount said. "I have been with Ran, seeing how the carriage was getting along, watching them stripe the wheels." He held the glass in his hand. He had not touched it since he refilled it. The windows were completely dark. The woman in the bed had not moved. On the pillow her face was still, the eyes closed, the motion of the intermittent firelight giving it more than ever an appearance of immobility. "As it will look when she is dead," Blount said to himself. "Like the faces of women in this country, in the South, have looked and will look after they have died, and will die for a little longer yet but not much longer, for a lot of years." Then he said aloud: "I had believed . . . feared—I was afraid that I would never have sent flowers to Lewis Randolph. Could never have. That's a summing, a totality, of breath."

IV.
She sat at her son's right at the long, heavy table lined by two rows of formal black-and-white and gleaming and flashing bosoms, in the long, heavy diningroom: a small woman in black that was not silk, without any ornament, not even a wedding ring. On her head was a frilled cap of coarse, clean white stuff that negro women wear. Her face was not an old face, in the sense of slackened muscles and flesh; it was old in the sense that wood or stone becomes old, as though scoured down upon itself by the sheer impact of long weather, the passing of sheer days and hours of time. Her eyes were dark; her hands a little stiff, with gnarled knuckles; from the instant when she entered the room and took her place beside her big, broad iron-gray son, in the almost furtive gesture with which her hand came out and touched the ranked silver and with-

drew again while her covert glance took in the other faces to remark if anyone noticed the action, there was about her that alertness, that watchful, sidelong stiffness of a woman born and bred in a hill cabin.

At first they made much of her, the women especially urgent, smooth, deferent, and she still sitting beside her son, her soup untasted before her, answering now and then in a cold final voice, in a single word when possible. Then her son intervened and they took the cue, the talk becoming general, and presently she began to eat. She took up the soup spoon and looked at it and put it down and took up a teaspoon and began to eat, putting the whole spoon in her mouth. She did it, discarded the proper spoon and took the other, not as though by mistake or indecision, but as though by prompt and deliberate design.

Dr Blount was opposite her across the table. He had been given his choice of places. "I'd rather be where I can see her face," he said. Most of the guests were young people. "She wont want to meet a lot of fogies, be bothered about Yankees and the war," the son said. "Besides, they wouldn't be any novelty, change, for her. Next to her though was a contemporary, a man who remembered the Yankees in the city; presently Blount saw that they were talking, and about the war. "Conditions were different in the country, I suppose," the man said. "Worse than here."

"The trouble is," Blount said. He leaned a little above the table. "The trouble is, we could never keep them in the right proportions. Like a cook with too much material. If we could have just kept the proportion around ten or twenty Yankees to one of us, we could have handled them. It was when they got to be a thousand to one, or ten or twelve Yankees to a woman and maybe a child and a handful of scared niggers—" He leaned a little forward, his soup too untasted yet. From across the table she watched him. She was chewing a piece of bread. She continued to chew with that careful, deliberate motion of the toothless. Gordon looked at Blount, then at his mother. Blount leaned forward, his face eager, diffuse. "When just a few of them came around to houses away back in the country, where the folks should even have been safe from Yankees; slipping around back doors because they knew the men were gone, the scarecrows without shoes and without ammunition charging the other hundred thousand of them without even wanting less odds—"

She was looking at Blount, still chewing. She ceased to chew and glanced swiftly both ways along the table, her face composed, granite-like. She put her hands on the table and thrust her chair back a little. "Mother—" Gordon said, rising a little also. "Here, Blount—You folks—"

But she was not leaving the table. She was talking. "It was just five of them that I ever saw. Mymie said there were some more in front, still on their horses, but it was just five of them that came around the house, walking. They came to the kitchen door and walked in. Walked right into my kitchen, without even knocking. Mymie had just come back through the house, running and hollering, saying the yard was full of Yankees, and I was just turning from the stove, where I was heating some milk for him—" without moving, with a pause in her speech or a change of inflection she indicated her son—"for his bottle. I had just said, 'Hush that yelling and take that child up off the floor,' when those five tramps came into my kitchen, without knocking."

"You, Mother," Gordon said, half risen, leaning forward too.

She was sitting well back from the table now, her hands on the edge of the table. She was looking at Blount, at the face leaning opposite hers across the table, the two of them: the one cold, controlled; the other wild, eager, like something poised that was fine and bright and of no particular value, that when it fell, it would break all to pieces. "The pan of boiling milk was on the stove, like this. I took it up just like this—" She and Blount rose at the same instant, rigid, erect, like on the same wire. She took up her bowl of soup and threw it at Blount's head. "And I said—" They faced one another with that furious rigidity of puppets, oblivious of the very stage, the miniature boards and tinsel wings within which they created their furious illusion; for the moment the whole huge, ugly, rich room was reduced to the dimensions of a Punch and Judy stage. In her hand she now held a fruit knife, not clutched by the handle like a dagger, but buried somehow in her forward-thrust fist so that the small bright blade protruded level and rigid like the barrel of a small pistol. Standing so, facing Blount above a silence too sudden to yet be consternation or even astonishment, she said to him what she had said to the five Yankees sixty-five years ago, in the same language, in the strong, prompt, gross obscenity of a steamboat mate.

V.

From a window ten minutes later Blount and Gordon watched the car drive away, taking her back home. She wouldn't stay, even to finish her dinner. For maybe a full minute she stood there beside the table, clutching the fruit knife in her fist, with on her face that expression which people say that sleepwalkers wear when suddenly wakened, facing Dr Blount's still rigid and erect and dripping head and shoulders, while the silence became astonishment and then became a single shout of laughter, hysterical, relieved, and exultant; for maybe another half minute she stood there, looking from one roaring or shrieking face to another, then she turned and left the room. Dr Blount followed along his side of the table, running, but she passed him at the door. Gordon followed her, and found her in the room where they had gathered before dinner. She had sat down on the first chair she came to. She looked up at him, her face unmoved. Her voice was level. "I want to go home."

"Yes," he said. "All right. But Blount—"

"I didn't," she said. "I don't—"

"He knows you didn't mean it. He is to blame. He knows that. He wants to apologise." She was not looking at him now. She sat, quiet and small, in the chair, her face turned aside but not lowered.

"I want to go home," she said again, in the same tone. Then he heard her draw a long breath. "I reckon I might ride in the car."

"Sure," Gordon said. He believed that it was because she was ashamed, as a child is ashamed when it has been tricked by grown people into an unwitting violation of its own sense of dignity. "The car will get you home quicker. You dont want to see Blount? He can come in here; you wont have—"

"I want to go home," she said.

"All right. You wait here. I'll have the car sent up."

He left her. When he returned, she had her hat and coat on, sitting as before, in the same straight, hard chair. "We can go out the side door," he said. "You wont have to meet anybody that way. But I wouldn't worry about that. There are words like that in all the books nowadays. Without half the reason you had. But where you ever—" he stopped, holding his face smooth. But she did not look up.

When the car moved on and he returned to the house, he could hear the voices in the diningroom, the hysterical laughter which was abating slowly in recurrent surges and gusts. Blount met him at the door. "She asked me to—" Gordon said,

"You're lying," Blount said. "She didn't ask you to tell me any such thing. By heaven, I am the same kind of folks she is; you're the one that's an interloper. I'm nearer Charley Gordon's son than you are." Through the window they watched the tail-lamp of the car pass down the drive. "I know why she wanted to go back in the car; you dont know that. I know about that derringer too, now. It wasn't that she found she didn't need it anymore; it was because she found she didn't deserve to be protected by a clean bullet, the clean bullet which Charley Gordon would have approved. She learned that she could be tricked and surprised into language which she didn't know she knew, that Charley Gordon didn't know that she knew, and that niggers and Yankees had heard it. She believed that now the whole Yankee army would pass the house and they would say, 'That's where that hill-billy woman lives that cussed Jim and Joe and them.' By heaven," he said, looking out the dark window, where the ruby light had disappeared. "She kissed a hundred and four men in one night once, and she gave Charley Gordon a son. But, by heaven, it was Gavin Blount she threw a soup plate at."

VI.

In the car, she sat in the exact middle of the seat. She had never travelled so fast before, and the swift glimpses of passing lights, the high, half-seen back-sweep of trees against the lighter darkness of sky added to her feeling of exhilaration, of triumph, of speed. "Maybe he rode this fast," she said to herself. "Except for the sound of the horses, the galloping. And with the glare yonder, it might be the fire of the warehouses." The car went steadily, swift, almost noiseless. "And smooth," she said. "Than a horse. And warm. And I aint going to sleep tonight. I know I aint."

When she reached her home and got out of the car and was admitted out of the quiet, chill darkness by the negro girl who lived with her, she would not go to bed, though it was already a good hour after the time when she usually lay down. "I want to see about the chickens," she said.

"You come on to bed," the girl said. "What you want to wake the chickens up for?"

"Get me a cup of feed," she said.

"At this time of night? You come on to bed, now, Miss Lewis—"

"Let me alone. Get me a cup of feed."

There was an enclosed passage from the back porch to the chicken house. She turned a light switch beside the kitchen door, whereupon a light came on inside the chicken house, the house itself coming into squat, rectilinear view. She carried the cup of cracked corn and entered the chicken house, into stale warmth, a sudden shifting of white huddled shapes on the roosting poles, and cries of raucous protest. She scattered the corn and with a stick she prodded the chickens down from the roosts, where they huddled again with cries disconsolate and cacophonous, pecking now and then at the corn with blundering, half-hearted thrusts. "Go on," she said; "eat." But they wouldn't eat. She stood among them for a while longer, until they turned and began to blunder back onto the poles again, flapping and leaving the corn untouched. She went out and closed [the door] and returned up the passage, to the porch, and turned [off] the light. It was chilly on the porch, and dark save for a light in the kitchen. This also was worked by a switch near the door and she turned it out and stood on the porch again, still in her coat and hat. Then there was no light anywhere; on all sides the countryside lay quiet and dark under the sky. She couldn't even see the hen house. She found the switch again; again the chicken house squatted into pale relief, the flat, neat, whitewashed walls, the good windows, the patent doors. "Maybe if there had just been a light in that one, that night in Holly Springs," she said, not loud. "So he could have seen. . . . And I aint going to sleep tonight. I know that." She snapped the switch again; again the darkness came down, like a black blanket coming down for an instant before she began to see a little in the dark, since the sky was a little lighter. It lay thick and close above the dark earth, holding between them the gusty rushing of damp wind among the trees, invisible too. But the sound was there, the long rushing surges dying away like a sudden rush of horsemen, so that, inextricable from the feeling of exultation which she knew was not going to let her sleep, she could almost hear the clash of scabbards and the swift dying thunder of hooves.

Written in 1930; published first in The Oxford American, *May/June 1995*

Black Death

ZORA NEALE HURSTON

THE NEGROES IN EATONVILLE KNOW A NUMBER OF THINGS that the hustling, bustling white man never dreams of. He is a materialist with little ears for overtones.

For instance, if a white person were halted on the streets of Orlando and told that Old Man Morgan, the excessively black Negro hoodoo man, can kill any person indicated and paid for, without ever leaving his house or even seeing his victim, he'd laugh in your face and walk away, wondering how long the Negro will continue to wallow in ignorance and superstition. But no black person in a radius of twenty miles will smile, not much. They *know*.

His achievements are far too numerous to mention singly. Besides many of his curses or "conjures" are kept secret. But everybody knows that he put the loveless curse on Della Lewis. She has been married seven times but none of her husbands have ever remained with her longer than the twenty-eight days that Morgan had prescribed as the limit.

Hiram Lester's left track was brought to him with five dollars and when the new moon came again, Lester was stricken with paralysis while working in his orange grove.

There was the bloody-flux that he put on Lucy Potts; he caused Emma Taylor's teeth to drop out; he put the shed skin of a black snake in Horace Brown's shoes and made him as the Wandering Jew; he put a sprig of

214

Lena Merchant's hair in a bottle, corked it and threw it into a running stream with the neck pointing upstream, and she went crazy; he buried Lillie Wilcox's finger-nails with lizard's feet and dried up her blood.

All of these things and more can easily be proved by the testimony of the villagers. They ought to know.

He lives alone in a two-room hut down by Lake Blue Sink, the bottomless. His eyes are reddish and the large gold hoop ear-rings jangling on either side of his shrunken black face make the children shrink in terror whenever they meet him on the street or in the woods where he goes to dig roots for his medicines.

But the doctor does not spend his time merely making folks ill. He has sold himself to the devil over the powerful black cat's bone that alone will float upstream, and many do what he wills. Life and death are in his hands—he sometimes kills.

He sent Old Lady Grooms to her death in the Lake. She was a rival hoodoo doctor and laid claims to equal power. She came to her death one night. That very morning Morgan had told several that he was tired of her pretenses—he would put an end to it and prove his powers.

That very afternoon near sundown, she went down to the Lake to fish, telling her daughter, however, that she did not wish to go, but something seemed to be forcing her. About dusk someone heard her scream and rushed to the Lake. She had fallen in and drowned. The white coroner from Orlando said she met her death by falling into the water during an epileptic fit. But the villagers *knew*. White folks are very stupid about some things. They can think mightily but cannot *feel*.

But the undoing of Beau Diddely is his masterpiece. He had come to Eatonville from up North somewhere. He was a waiter at the Park House Hotel over in Maitland where Docia Boger was a chamber-maid. She had a very pretty brown body and face, sang alto in the Methodist Choir and played the blues on her guitar. Soon Beau Diddely was with her every moment he could spare from his work. He was stuck on her all right, for a time.

They would linger in the shrubbery about Park Lane or go for long walks in the woods on Sunday afternoon to pick violets. They are abundant in the Florida woods in winter.

The Park House always closed in April and Beau was planning to go North with the white tourists. It was then Docia's mother discovered that Beau should have married her daughter weeks before.

"Mist' Diddely," said Mrs. Boger, "Ah'm a widder 'oman an' Deshy's all Ah got, an' Ah know youse gointer do what you orter." She hesitated a moment and studied his face. "'Thout no trouble. Ah doan wanta make no talk 'round town."

In a split second the vivacious, smiling Beau had vanished. A very hard vitriolic stranger occupied his chair.

"Looka heah, Mis' Boger. I'm a man that's travelled a lot— been most everywhere. Don't try to come that stuff over me— What I got to marry Docia for?"

"'Cause—'Cause—"the surprise of his answer threw the old woman into a panic. "Youse the cause of her condition, aintcher?"

Docia, embarrassed, mortified, began to cry.

"Oh, I see the little plot now!" He glanced maliciously toward the girl and back again to her mother.

"But I'm none of your down-South-country-suckers. Go try that on some of these clodhoppers. Don't try to lie on me—I got money to fight."

"Beau," Docia sobbed, "you ain't callin' me a liah, is you?" And in her misery she started toward the man who through four months' constant association and assurance she had learned to love and trust.

"Yes! You're lying—you sneaking little—oh you're not even good sawdust! Me marry you! Why I could pick up a better woman out of the gutter than you! I'm a married man anyway, so you might as well forget your little scheme!"

Docia fell back stunned.

"But, but Beau, you said you wasn't," Docia wailed.

"Oh," Beau replied with a gesture of dismissal of the whole affair. "What difference does it make? A man will say anything at times. There are certain kinds of women that men always lie to."

In her mind's eye Docia saw things for the first time without her tinted glasses and real terror seized her. She fell upon her knees and clasped the nattily clad legs of her seducer.

"Oh Beau," she went, struggling to hold him, as he, fearing for the creases in his trousers, struggled to free himself. "You made—you—you promised—"

"Oh, well, you ought not to have believed me—you ought to have known I didn't mean it. Anyway I'm not going to marry you, so what're you going to do? Do whatever you feel big enough to try—my shoulders are broad."

He left the house hating the two women bitterly, as we only hate those we have injured.

At the hotel, omitting mention of his shows of affection, his pleas, his solemn promises to Docia, he told the other waiters how that piece of earth's refuse had tried to inveigle, to coerce him into a marriage. He enlarged upon his theme and told them all, in strict confidence, how she had been pursuing him all winter; how she had waited in a bush time and again and dragged him down by the Lake, and well, he was only human. It couldn't have happened with the *right* kind of girl, and he thought too much of himself to marry any other than the country's best.

So the next day Eatonville knew; and the scourge of tongues was added to Docia's woes.

Mrs. Boger and her daughter kept strictly indoors, suffering, weeping growing bitter.

"Mommer, if he jus' hadn't tried to make me out a bad girl, I could look over the rest in time, Mommer, but—but he tried to make out—ah—"

She broke down weeping again.

Drip, drip, drip, went her daughter's tears on the old woman's heart, each drop calcifying a little the fibers till at the end of four days the petrifying process was complete. Where once had been warm, pulsing flesh was now cold heavy stone that pulled down pressing out normal life and bowing the head of her. The woman died, and in that heavy cold stone a tiger, a female tiger, was born.

She was ready to answer the questions Beau had flung so scornfully at her old head: "Well, what are you going to do?"

Docia slept, huddled on the bed. A hot salt tear rose to Mrs. Boger's eyes and rolled heavily down the quivering nose. Must Docia awake always to that awful desolation? Robbed of *everything*, even faith. She knew then that the world's greatest crime is not murder—its most terrible punishment is meted to her of too much faith—too great a love.

She turned down the light and stepped into the street.

It was near midnight and the village slept. But she knew of one house where there would be light; one pair of eyes still awake.

As she approached Blue Sink she all but turned back. It was a dark night but the Lake shimmered and glowed like phosphorous near the shore. It seemed that figures moved about on the quiet surface. She remembered that folks said Blue Sink the bottomless was Morgan's graveyard and all Africa awoke in her blood.

A cold prickly feeling stole over her and stood her hair on end. Her feet grew heavy and her tongue dry and stiff.

In the swamp at the head of the Lake, she saw Jack-O-Lantern darting here and there and three hundred years of America passed like the mist of morning. Africa reached out its dark hand and claimed its own. Drums, tom, tom, tom, tom, tom, beat her ears. Strange demons seized her. Witch doctors danced before her, laid hands upon her alternately freezing and burning her flesh, until she found herself within the house of Morgan.

She was not permitted to tell her story. She opened her mouth but the old man chewed a camphor leaf or two, spat into a small pail of sand and asked:

"How do yuh wants kill 'im? By water, by sharp edge, or a bullet?"

The old woman almost fell off the chair in amazement that he knew her mind. He merely chuckled a bit and handed her a drinking gourd.

"Dip up a teeny bit of water an' po' hit on the flo',—by dat time you'll know."

She dipped the water out of a wooden pail and poured it upon the rough floor.

"Ah wanta shoot him, but how kin ah' 'thout. . . ?"—

"Looka heah." Morgan directed and pointed to a huge mirror scarred and dusty. He dusted its face carefully. "Look in dis glass 'thout turning' yo' head an' when he comes, you shoot tuh kill. Take a good aim!"

Both faced about and gazed hard into the mirror that reached from floor to ceiling. Morgan turned once to spit into the pail of sand. The mirror grew misty, darker, near the center, then Mrs. Boger saw Beau walk to the center of the mirror and stand looking at her, glaring and sneering. She all but fainted in superstitious terror.

Morgan thrust the gun into her hand. She saw the expression on Beau Diddely's face change from scorn to fear and she laughed.

"Take good aim," Morgan cautioned. "You cain't shoot but once."

She leveled the gun at the heart of the apparition in the glass and fired. It collapsed; the mirror grew misty again, then cleared.

In horror she flung her money at the old man who seized it greedily, and she fled into the darkness, dreading nothing, thinking only of putting distance between her and the house of Morgan.

The next day Eatonville was treated to another thrill.

It seemed that Beau Diddely, the darling of the ladies, was in the hotel yard making love to another chamber-maid. In order that she might fully appreciate what a great victory was here, he was reciting the Conquest of Docia, how she loved him, pursued him, knelt down and kissed his feet, begging him to marry her,—when suddenly he stood up very straight, clasped his hand over his heart, grew rigid, and fell dead.

The coroner's verdict was death from natural causes—heart failure. But they were mystified by what looked like a powder burn directly over the heart.

But the Negroes knew instantly when they saw that mark, but everyone agreed that he got justice. Mrs. Boger and Docia moved to Jacksonville where she married well.

And the white folks never knew and would have laughed had anyone told them,—so why mention it?

Begun in 1931, completion date unknown;
published first in The Oxford American, *March/April 1995*

Young Nuclear Physicist

WALKER PERCY

RALPH MOVED TOWARD THE STERN OF THE FERRY. He had seen Miss Terhune, the mesotron technician, and one of his instructors talking together. Perhaps he would join the conversation. They would not know him by name, but as one of the new students, he should be welcome. They were staring at the retreating bank. Ralph looked in the same direction, but there was nothing to see except a large sewer which gaped above the water line.

"It must be very largely digested by bacterial action," the instructor was saying.

"Or perhaps it simply dissolves. Toilet paper is not very substantial," Miss Terhune said.

They continued to stare at the sewer as though the answer were about to emerge any moment. Ralph looked closely at Miss Terhune to see if she were carrying off an elaborate joke. But she was neither amused nor concerned nor revolted. She didn't seem to care whether the East River fairly swam with toilet paper, only interested in the explanation of why it didn't. After all, Ralph admitted to himself, it was an acute observation that one never saw gross pieces of toilet paper floating so close to a Manhattan sewer.

They began talking about the suicides. Sooner or later every conversation on the Island got around to them. It was a bad start for the Institute, especially since the tabloids had made a big thing of it. The front page of one had carried a full-page picture of the men's dormitory with a superimposed trajectory of dashes starting from a window near the top, rising jauntily like a springboard diver, and plunging to a Maltese cross on the gravel path, and a caption below: "Atom Student Takes Dive." That was the Tennessee boy. Ralph had not known him: he jumped the day after school started.

The other was a young Jew from Queens named Tepper, a graduate of Columbia. He had stolen some potassium hydroxide from the chemistry lab and late one night had munched the better part of two sticks, holding them between thumb and forefinger, as the destruction of these tissues clearly showed. The motive in his case was more obscure. An acute attack of homesickness in an unstable person might conceivably induce such an act, but Tepper could hardly have been homesick, since he died within a mile of home.

"It's a psychiatric problem," said the instructor. "There should be an integration of personality studies with matriculation."

"That would do it," agreed Miss Terhune.

"But all in all, it's not too surprising. In any vast new undertaking like the Institute, it's a question of getting the bugs out of it."

Ralph, who was standing next to the rail half-facing them, nodded seriously as the instructor spoke. But by now the ferry had docked at the Island, and they left without noticing him.

He sat at his desk in the dormitory room and made a few calculations on the slide rule. It was the most expensive one that he had been able to find. But how could one waste money on a slide rule? The semester was new enough so that he still felt some of the exuberance of the first day. It had always been the best time of the year for him—ever since the first time with the new satchel, pencils, pencil sharpener, crayons, tin of watercolors, compass, ruler, and the books: the stiff primers with the new smell and the limp, slick textbook pages. It was the time for putting on the New Man, for casting off all the old bad habits. Life became simple again. The way was straight then as now. All he had to do, then as now, was to start on page one and keep going, take it all in from the first page of the first primer with the big black A and little a, each covering a whole page.

This fall the renewal was total: a new man, a new school, a new city. The books were bigger than ever, so big that each included a slip of directions on how to open it without damaging the binding. It was easy to fancy that a new textbook was a perfect thing. It was perfectly manufactured, and so its text must be a perfect revelation of the subject. Surely there could be no typographical errors, misspellings, bad sentences, or gross misconceptions.

He swivelled toward the window. Trademark paper and dried putty still stuck to the panes. But he could see almost the whole length of Manhattan. It was hard to understand how anyone could fail to experience the same autumnal joy. Tepper and the Tennessee boy were clearly psychiatric cases before they ever got to the Institute.

Ralph had become adjusted to his surroundings quickly enough, although, unlike other school years, a certain permanent sense of strangeness remained. He was perfectly at home during the lectures and laboratory work. It was all review, covering in a few months all four years of college mathematics and physics. His schedule was regular. After attending lectures all morning and lab all afternoon, he would allow himself a half-hour nap and a bite of supper before getting back to the books. Perhaps the persistent feeling of novelty could be attributed to the Institute buildings. They were certainly unlike any campus he had ever seen before: concrete skyscrapers separated by gravel courts. They completely occupied the north end of the Island almost to the water's edge. Although there were winding paths connecting the buildings, it was more convenient as well as time-saving to use the tunnels. They were well ventilated and lighted by sodium vapor lamps. The tunnel from his dormitory led a few hundred feet to an intersection of several tunnels posted with signs directing one to the classrooms, laboratories, and other dormitories. There was a curious thing about the tunnels. He had to admit to a small sense of embarrassment when approaching somebody. It was the same slight restiveness, multiplied several times, which one feels when approaching a person on a sidewalk. In the tunnel there was no scenery to engage one's eye, only the lines of shining tile converging on the other person. It must have been difficult for women. They solved it in different ways. They would look fixedly at a point in space a few inches from his left ear, or gaze with interest at the sodium lamps in the ceiling. Some few would stare into his eyes boldly, almost accusingly. It was undeniably a minor social crisis, and he always felt positively chivalric when he was able to get past a girl with just the proper mixture of looking at her and looking away. He often wondered what would happen if, as he neared one of the pretty technicians, he should gaze squarely at her, and as the gap between them closed, he should begin to walk at a slight crouch in the middle of the tunnel. She would face a terrible choice: either to keep going and try somehow to pass at close quarters or to cut and run.

To tell the truth, his life in New York had not fulfilled all expectations. Ralph had not thought about it much, but he had expected to divide his evenings between a group of fellow scientists and a second group, a sort of Bohemian coterie of impoverished students, artists, musicians, and chorus girls. He had easily visualized himself as one of an elite few invited to the rooms of the top man in quantum mechanics, a lean boyish sort of fellow, brilliant and erratic, the kind who would pay no attention to the ordinary conventions of lecturing but would wander all over the pit hooking an arm over the railing or sitting on the desk. He would soon recognize Ralph's qualities, and before long Ralph would find himself with a few others in the professor's rooms. There would be much good talk about philosophy, art, mysticism, and a thousand other subjects. He was no longer Mr. Budd, a first-year student who sat near the back of the lecture hall, but Budd: "I say, Budd, you're from the South. What do you think of —," some phase of the Negro problem. All eyes would turn to him, and he would stare thoughtfully into his mug of pilsener before answering.

Ralph only realized how complete a picture he had formed of New York when, as time went by, not a single detail materialized. There was, of course, no such person as Ralph's professor. The instructors were all bored-looking men who lived in Connecticut or Long Island and left as soon as possible after lectures. The only intercourse between student and teacher occurred immediately after the lecture when a few eager students would leap into the pit with well-put questions. Ralph knew their kind of old. He would leave the room alone, full of contempt for student and professor.

Nor was there an elite group of students, or if there was, he didn't know them. After six weeks his only acquaintance was his lab co-worker, a youth named Freddie from Muncie, Indiana.

Nor had he managed yet to fall in with a coterie of Bohemians. In this case, his preformed picture was not quite as clear. He only imagined that he would surround himself with many oddly assorted and carefree companions. They would frequent a regular rendezvous, perhaps a little-known bierstube in Yorkville. There might be on occasions a hoisting of steins, bawdy toasts, and rollicking drinking songs. But above all, there would be the women, the unattached, "unconventional" girls who had come to New York to escape life in small Midwestern towns. He would form a series of attachments with these independent girls. There were other couples who would invade their studio apartment, their arms full of French bread and wine bottles clad in little baskets.

Ralph probably got most of these notions from Dr. Goodbee at the university in Arkansas. Dr. Goodbee had spent a year at a German university at a time when it was good policy for an American professor. He used to tell Ralph about it over bottles of beer in the Campus Corner.

"They had the way of life all right," he would say, picking at the wet label. "The old German university towns before the war. The other war. Bonn, Tübingen, Freiburg, Heidelberg, though of course there were always too many Americans there. The leitmotif was comradeship. I remember the ski trains from München—." Ralph could almost see the young Bavarians sprawled in the aisles and hear the Sigmund Romberg songs, but he could never quite get Dr. Goodbee into the picture.

"But Paris!" With the word alone Dr. Goodbee could conjure up all manner of delights. He was fond of describing a class of women which he said existed in Paris, different from anything in Arkansas or this hemisphere. They were young, clean, attractive, affectionate, even loyal, and desired nothing more than to be mistresses of young American students. Dr. Goodbee would look sorrowfully at the coeds drinking cokes.

"There were no recriminations when time for goodbyes came and never any nonsense about marriage." At these times he wore a troubled expression, for all the world like a man hopelessly entangled with a number of young Arkansas girls who, in spite of his age and family, demanded marriage. All he appeared to want of life during these nostalgic moments was to be allowed to return to Paris for a short time and renew his friendship with another generation of these unusual girls or, even better, to introduce a similar system to Arkansas.

There was no sign of any of these activities in New York. Dr. Goodbee's account of university life was either greatly exaggerated or New York was a hopelessly different sort of place. Ralph knew only two girls and these in the most casual way: Miss Terhune and Miss Cassidy, secretary to the Dean. Miss Cassidy could be eliminated immediately. She lived somewhere in New Jersey and commuted. As for Miss

Terhune, it would be unthinkable to ask her for a date. Every other student in the Institute knew her at least as well. He spoke to her once a day and then only to say "good morning" briskly, with the air of a man totally absorbed in his work by day and busy at night with a large and cosmopolitan circle of friends. To approach Miss Terhune, who was, so to speak, part of the mesotron apparatus, would be humiliating. He didn't even know her first name. There seemed to be no way to expand their relationship. It remained static: a series of good mornings. He simply could not bring himself to say to her: "Good morning! I know a little out-of-the-way bierstube in Yorkville." It would be an admission of abject loneliness to approach a person who could not even be called an acquaintance, and worse, he would lay himself open to all sorts of devastating rejections.

Something had undoubtedly gone wrong in his calculations. It was a queer thing. For although he did allow himself romantic notions after the fashion of Dr. Goodbee, he had never really taken them seriously, had in fact resolved to tolerate nothing that interfered with his work. He had determined this year to put on the New Man in earnest. Fortunately, his surroundings encouraged him in this respect. The Institute was a house of pure science. There was no sentimental nonsense, no paraphernalia of tradition. He had once visited a medical student in Baltimore. His friend lived with several other students in an old house run by a motherly little woman. She attended to all their needs: nursed their colds, cooked Southern meals for them, arranged for them to meet girls of old Baltimore families. Miss Annie. One hardly knew her last name. Everything in the neighborhood was encrusted with tradition. There was the pub around the corner with the initials of the great carved into the booths and carefully preserved by varnish. Even the Baltimore dirt was hallowed. But the Institute got along without such sentimentalisms. There was very little dirt, only the faint acrid smell of burning garbage from the disposal plant across the river. There was no local movie inevitably nicknamed "The Axilla" or "The Perineum" and frequented by blocs of students who were obliged to hiss and cheer at the proper moments. And thank God there was no Old Pops, the janitor, who has been with us as long as anybody can remember. Since Ralph's class was the first to matriculate, there were not even upper-classmen to send one on fool's errands.

One day as he walked through the dormitory tunnel, Ralph had a strange thought. He was decidedly pleased with himself since a quiz paper had been returned to him with a very high mark. His thoughts flew ahead to the time of the triumph of his career. Although he was not yet a nuclear physicist, or even a student of nuclear physics, since he was still in the review course, he could easily imagine the day when, perhaps still a student, he would make an extraordinarily ingenious discovery (a cut in *Time* magazine of himself in white lab coat adjusting an apparatus). But for once his daydreams carried beyond the day of culmination. Then what? Naturally any job would be his for the asking, and he would accept the plum, a full professorship at the Institute. A lifetime of fifty years or more devoted to pure science. He looked at the gleaming tile of the tunnel. It was durable: no doubt it would be much the same fifty years from now. The yellow sodium lamps swam before his eyes. He was suddenly hot and nauseated. But anyone watching him would have only seen him pause a moment and touch the tile wall.

He took a cold shower and felt much better. Far below his window the ferry was warping in to the Institute landing. It heeled over dangerously as it turned against the current. A weight lifted from his heart. *I have been a fool. My error is simply a failure to apply method. I apply method with competence and success to mathematical and physical problems. Why should I imagine that my personal life is exempt, that it should work itself out with no conscious direction?* He cleared his desk top until nothing remained but a pencil and a sheet of paper. He wrote: *The problem: lone-*

liness. What a disgusting admission! How humiliating to be subject to such a demand! But already he was consoled by his discovery and by his forthrightness in facing it. How could he have been so stupid as to imagine that upon arrival in New York he would be automatically invested with a complete social life and a fake nineteenth-century one at that? Very well. What was the answer? He wrote: *Possibilities of meeting congenial people.* He realized with some agitation that he was getting unpleasantly close to the Dale Carnegie sort of thing. Nevertheless, he compiled a list:

1. *Freddie.*
2. *Miss Terhune.*
3. *Prostitutes.*
4. *Pick-ups in bars, night clubs, dance halls, parks, libraries, zoos, etc.*
5. *Social Agency which arranges meetings.*
6. *Call up relatives in Long Island City and meet their friends.*
7. *Church socials.*
8. *Arthur Murrays.*

He saw immediately that Freddie had no place in the list. He crossed out Miss Terhune next: in addition to the other objections, the truth was that he really didn't like her much. He crossed out prostitutes as inadequate to his needs. He realized that what he was looking for after all was one of Dr. Goodbee's girls, except that she would have qualities that Goodbee would never understand: a sensitivity, an intuitive understanding of him. What a tender relationship they would have! She would be a mild, dreamy girl, a constant and gentle presence in the studio apartment. His life would be a perfect balance of the Tender and the Abstract. He would burst in on her with armloads of foods and wines from exotic delicatessens. Perhaps a third ingredient was needed for the full life, an American equivalent of the drinking fraternity at Heidelberg. He permitted himself a short fantasy: a duel had been arranged, German style, with sabres. They wore special helmets which allowed only non-fatal cheek wounds. He was wounded repeatedly and honorably. The pain was fierce and exalted; his blood tasted salty and rich. The surgeon, standing by, stanched the hemorrhage, and he and his opponent, similarly wounded, drank a liter of beer through linked arms.

Suddenly, he developed a huge thirst for beer. He dressed and decided to go over to Manhattan.

He saw on the table, where he had emptied his pockets, a folded slip of pink paper. It was in his mail box when he came in. "Call GR 3-4454." He picked up the telephone and gave the number to the man at the switchboard downstairs. Presently a woman's voice said:

"The Betsy Ross Hotel. Good evening."

"Someone left a message for me to call that number."

"Do you know the name or room number?"

"No." He clicked the phone until the man downstairs answered. "Look. A call came in for me this afternoon."

"Yessir, Mr. Budd. I remember. She left her number."

She!

"The number is that of a hotel. Didn't she leave a name or anything else?"

"No, sir. I don't believe she did."

A woman's voice. He had to concede that it could be his aunt in town for shopping. But it was easier to think of Her as the Stranger, the archetype of all women, One mysteriously sent to him. Perhaps she was a lonely Memphis girl working in New York. She had seen his picture months ago in the *Commercial Appeal*: "Arkansan Wins Atom Post." She had not forgotten, and in a fit of desperate loneliness, she had called out to him as an ally in a hostile city.

It was one of those incidents in all likelihood trivial but which one would prefer to believe fateful and capable, if followed up, of changing one's entire life. Ralph looked up the address of the Betsy Ross and after a quick supper in the cafeteria took the ferry to Manhattan and the subway downtown.

The Betsy Ross was a huge brick affair the like of which he had never seen before. Across the marquee blazed the complete name: The Betsy Ross Hotel for Women. He gazed up at the solid bank of windows. *There must be thousands of them up there!* After some hesitation he entered the lobby. He reasoned that men would surely be permitted there, for how else could they call on their friends? There were, in fact, a few men sitting around the lobby, probably waiting for their dates to come down. A placard over the main desk read: No Gentlemen Guests Allowed Above Mezzanine. Ralph began to realize the hopelessness of his mission. He could not ask for anyone at the desk. He could, of course, sit in plain view until his unknown friend passed through. But that might take days, and even then she mightn't recognize him. Furthermore, the Betsy Ross management had undoubtedly taken stronger precautions than ordinary hotels against men loitering about the lobby with no legitimate business. He sat in a chair facing the elevators in the faint hope that she would emerge as magically as her telephone call. He looked at his watch frequently and assumed an expression of mock annoyance, as much as to say: "Women! They probably don't start dressing until we call for them." The elevators went up and down constantly and dozens of women came out, but no one paid any attention to him. After fifteen minutes he strolled idly across the lobby and mounted the steps to the mezzanine. At one end he found what he was looking for: a deep and poorly lighted recess furnished with writing tables and wicker chairs and sofas. It was a perfect vantage point from which to see the main desk, entrance, and elevator doors without being seen. Most of the women in the lobby were young. Some wore evening dresses. The elevator doors would slide back with their now familiar sound, and they would step out smiling. Their escorts would leap up to meet them. They would stand talking a moment and then walk out together. Some were middle-aged and older. They walked from place to place with the absentmindedness of long habit. Probably, Ralph thought, they were, in their youth, just like the others: out-of-town girls with jobs in New York. The only difference was that nothing had happened to them. They hadn't got married, or moved to an apartment, or gone back home. He wondered what happened when one of them died. They had come from the little towns in Tennessee and Iowa and had spent their youth and middle life and old age here in the Betsy Ross. It would certainly not be proper to ship them home to be buried in a place where they were no longer known. No doubt the hotel had foreseen such contingencies and could make appropriate arrangements. There would be services in a nearby place, a decent little chapel, with her friends in attendance: the other old-timers, the desk clerk, the doorman.

After more than two hours Ralph gave up his vigil. But far from being discouraged, he was convinced more than ever that he was on the right track. Logically, this was a lead that should be run down before starting on the list. Since no quiz was scheduled for several weeks, he felt free to spend several evenings at the Betsy Ross.

On Thursday, the night of his fifth visit, there was a dance in the ballroom off the lobby. He could hear the orchestra playing inside. Couples presented invitations at the door. He had not felt well lately, and tonight he was grimy and tired and his forehead throbbed. He held his face in his hands; they came away dripping with cold sweat. He let his head rest against the ridged back of the wicker armchair. After a while a girl came into the recess and, without seeing him, sat at one of the little desks and began writing letters. The yellow light fell on her bare arms. Her hand moved steadily back and forth across the page, the soft muscle rising and falling in her forearm.

"Look, Miss." Ralph stood at her side and gently touched her elbow. She was startled, but she looked up at him without alarm.

"Yes?"

He must have stood there too long gazing down at her without saying anything, or perhaps she realized that he could only have come from one of the chairs or sofas in the darkness behind her. She screwed the cap on her fountain pen and stacked her stationery quickly, as though this were really all the correspondence she had intended to do for the moment. When she was gone, Ralph moved to the mezzanine railing. The orchestra had stopped playing, and the lobby was filled with the dancers in their tuxedos and evening dresses.

"Hey, Miss." Ralph heard his voice unexpectedly loud, filling the whole room. The girl by now stood waiting for the elevator. At the sound of his voice, she moved closer to the elevator doors. Everyone was looking up at him.

He gripped the rail and leaned over, staring at their upturned faces.

"Hey you girls." He let his voice get louder than ever so that it trembled in the air and echoed from the walls. A girl just below smiled at him expectantly and nudged her escort. She evidently took him to be one of their crowd who was cutting up a bit. He saw her lips frame the question: Who is that?

"This is Ralph Budd in the mezzanine—." Rough hands seized him from behind.

"Hey down there," he cried as they pried his fingers from the rail. "Heyeeeeeee."

The two men hustled him down the steps and through the lobby. They seemed determined to make him look drunk or paralytic, for they propelled him forward with short jerks, lifting him almost clear off the floor so that his feet skipped along, touching only at the toes. His hat fell off somewhere in the lobby. He wondered if they were going to kick him in the buttocks when they got to the door and send him sprawling onto the sidewalk. But they came to a stop under the marquee as if undecided about the next move. The doorman joined them and said to one of the plainclothesmen:

"Is he one of the college boys?"

"Look at him. He ain't wearing a black suit. He was hollering around up in the balcony bothering the girls."

"Okay. I'll take him."

The men were satisfied. They released him and went inside. The doorman didn't touch him.

"Look, Jack. This is not the place for that kind of act. They could've put you in Bellevue with the pansies and the peepers. This place is full of girls, yeah. But you got to meet them right. Now just hold it a minute and I'll fix you up."

He blew his whistle and a cab came around the corner. He had a talk with the driver and held the door for Ralph, stepping back to a smart attention as though Ralph were a frequent and honored visitor at the Betsy Ross.

Ralph did not return to the Betsy Ross. He was too unnerved even to think about his list of "possibilities." As matters turned out, he could have spared himself all the trouble of the past few days. Not more than a week later, he found another folded pink slip in his box. He opened it with misgivings, and when he saw again that dreadful number GR 3-4454, he was seized with panic. *They have tracked me down. Despite the kindness of the doorman I will be exposed.* He was sure at first that the name below must be that of an official of the Betsy Ross, a person who was authorized to take legal steps against him in order to protect the girls from any more antics. "Call Miss Walterene Gross." So Walterene had the job. No no no no no. *She* was the girl who had called him the first time and was calling again because she hadn't heard from him. Walterene Gross.

She belonged to his past, a past twice removed, not the past of college years, which he had put behind him to start anew at the Institute, but the past before that, the years of living at home and going to high school. Ralph was still a very young man, yet it seemed to him that he had known her a thousand years ago in a different age, a different world.

They had not known each other well. He had probably not spoken two dozen words to her altogether. But after all these years, it was hard to imagine that they had not been good friends. People spoke of them together because they made the best grades in the class. Walterene Gross and Ralph Budd were the smartest girl and boy in school. It was conceded that Ralph was probably the smarter of the two, even though Walterene nosed him out to be valedictorian. Being a girl, she studied every night and never missed her homework while Ralph relied on heroic cram sessions the night before an exam. They spoke little, but there was (he thought) a silent camaraderie between them, a tacit understanding that they were the elite and nothing more needed to be said about it. They would pass each other in the hall or on the steps with carefully averted glances. She was a thin, dark girl with thick black hair cut in a precise bob which mathematically framed her face in three straight lines. She was forever carrying a tremendous double stack of books and craning her head forward to see the steps below. Incongruously, she had excelled in a minor sport. She was by no means athletic, but she had set a record in rope climbing, which probably still stood. Passing through the gym he would sometimes see her, scrambling agilely up the rope, her thin bloomered legs trailing passively behind.

She had all but died in his memory. When he went away to college he had expected somehow to meet better girls, a superior breed suitable to his higher academic status. He had heard nothing about her. He didn't even know if she had gone on to college.

There was a chance, of course, that she knew about his strange

behavior in the Betsy Ross. He had identified himself from the mezzanine. She may even have been in the crowd below. But if she said anything about it, he could make an excuse and hang up and that would be
the end of it.

He gave the number in the security of his room and asked for Miss
Gross. A voice finally said: "Yes?"

It must have been the wrong Walterene. There were overtones and
inflections in the one word, of which the old Walterene had been entirely
innocent.

"Is this Walterene Gross?"

"Yes?"

"This is Ralph Budd."

"Ralph Budd! I heard you were in New York. Imagine after all these
years."

He heard himself laughing and talking with a ready fund of small
talk. In a few seconds they had restored the tenuous bonds of their
old relationship and added many more. He kidded her about the rope-
climbing act which she denied laughingly altogether. But he still couldn't
associate this voice with Walterene Gross. There was no trace of an
Arkansas accent. When she said "silly," it was with the heavy lingual
L of the North: si-ully.

"I called you," she said, "because I happen to have two tickets to a
thing that might be a lot of fun. Have you ever heard of the Arkansas
Society? They have dinners and dances and make speeches about the
good old days. It's really rare. The only qualification you have to have is
that you hail from Arkansas and live in the big city. It might be amusing.
Imagine coming all the way to New York to get away from Arkansas
and then forming a tight little group of nothing but Arkansans!"

Ralph laughed loudly, hoping it would not occur to her that she
was doing just that.

"It sounds wonderful, Walterene. Do we dress?"

"Oh sure. We're uptown hillbillies now."

He was relieved. He would feel much more secure walking into the Betsy Ross dressed in a tuxedo.

Already he was transformed. The Ralph Budd of the past few weeks was a pitiful creature who bore no relation to him. He took out the list from the desk drawer and tore it up, averting his eyes from the shameful words. Yet a sense of misgiving remained. She was so confident and urbane. She had changed enormously, but had he? They would laugh at their fellow Arkansans, but after that, what was left to be said? He smiled: he was inventing trouble. She had just asked him for a date; naturally she had to make use of a special circumstance, take a particular line. What did he expect her to do?

He had a bad moment when he passed the doorman. But the fellow didn't recognize him or was kind enough not to show it. What a difference his new friendship made! He no longer had to devise means of getting to the mezzanine unobserved. He walked straight to the main desk.

"Miss Gross, please. Mr. Budd calling."

He sat in his old chair facing the elevators, holding the corsage box in his lap. He looked with serenity at his fellow men similarly disposed throughout the lobby. Every time the elevator doors opened, he started up anxiously. He tried to picture Walterene's face set above an evening gown. But he couldn't see her without the books. He decided that he could not positively recognize her, that he could only be sure when a girl was *not* Walterene. He sank back and waited for another car.

She stood in front of him, her hands clasped over an evening bag.

"Well, Ralph Budd."

He was caught off guard as she explained about living on the second floor and walking down; and he was further confused when she extended her hand, Northern fashion, to be shaken. He was so occupied with the business of giving her the flowers, getting out of the lobby, past the doorman and into a taxi, that it was actually a minute or two before he could register an impression of her. The doorman gave his arm a friendly squeeze as he helped him into the taxi.

"That's it, Jack. Now you're in."

She was Walterene all right, but in every respect *bigger*. Her thick black hair was still cut in a Dutch bob, but the lower corners curved forward in a bizarre and effective way. She crossed her legs and settled back into her fur coat.

"Say, Walterene—"

"Whup!" She said laughing and grimacing. "About that Walterene. I left that in Arkansas. Up here they call me René."

It seemed that at Wellesley her name had been something of a joke during her freshman year, and a few kind friends began to call her Rene for short. She dropped the Walter and used Rene even to sign her papers. Then one of her teachers in class had addressed her as René and it stuck. Ralph reflected that the slight modification of her hair-do was probably designed as a corroborative hint of a French influence somewhere in her past.

They went to the Astor Hotel where the Society had rented a private dining room. Several hundred Arkansans were there, none of whom Ralph knew. At the door they were handed lapel cards on which they printed their names and hometown. Ralph was pleased with Walterene because of her good looks and accent, or rather lack of accent. Some of the girls, it seemed to him, spoke with excessively Southern accents which would have sounded queer even in Arkansas.

After a plate of fried chicken, a man at the end of the horseshoe table rose and tinkled spoon against glass. He made a gracious little speech. He spoke nostalgically of the Southern way of life and told a joke about an Arkansas private and a Yankee general. He concluded ruefully that if "you cain't beat 'em, you have to jine 'em. If any more of us Rebs move up here, we'll make this a good place to live in yet."

René whispered to Ralph:

"If he thinks Arkansas is such a hot place to live in, why doesn't he go back? He came up here forty years ago, and he hasn't even been home for a visit."

"Why don't you?"

René bent over in a spasm; her hair fell forward and hid her face like blinders. Her shoulders heaved. For a second Ralph thought she had gotten sick. But she was laughing silently. He soon learned that this was a mannerism of hers acquired sometime after leaving high school.

He saw her often after that. He sought her company, feeling that he was lucky to know her and that, further, he was bound by his method to do so. But in one way the results were unforeseen. He had expected that Walterene would fill an empty place in his life, that at least she would dispel the loneliness. It wasn't true. His loneliness was only compounded. She shared it but didn't relieve it. Instead of wandering the streets of the city alone, he wandered them with her, and still alone. There was the added burden of forever adjusting himself to Walterene, the tedious chore of dealing with another person on a polite level. For she persisted in trying to extract something comic from every situation. And when he made a reply, however feeble, she would double up in silent laughter. It was hard to account for their unease. They had much in common. They were compatriots in an almost foreign country. They were "intelligent," "liberal" young people. And if they could be certain of anything, it was that both had a sense of humor. They discovered that they agreed enthusiastically on almost every subject. Yet each sally of conversation would leave them straining for the next. He often thought that she was as little to blame as he. It was something apart from them that gave them no peace. They agreed once that silence could be friendly and communicative, but their silences were self-limiting. They were contests, which after a few minutes, became unbearable. After long weary bus rides to obscure places in the Bronx and Washington Heights (they would certainly never go to Rockefeller Center or to the Statue of Liberty), he would feel when he got back to his dormitory room that he had walked the entire distance. *What is wrong?* he thought on the bus top with Walterene. He looked at a street number: ninety more blocks to the Betsy Ross. What he wouldn't give to be rid of her and to be on the uptown bus alone! To be able to close his eyes and rest his head in the corner of the window and seat back. To let his aching abdominal muscles relax. To be surrounded by strangers. It had something to do with the city, he decided finally. There was no place for them to go and be at home and with friends, except the lobby of the Betsy Ross. (And yet, he suspected that if a number of people should suddenly become their friends, it would be no different.) They belonged nowhere now, not even to their own families, except perhaps to the Arkansas Society. It was as if a malevolent force in the city had thrust them into the streets and public places and closed the doors against them.

One night they went to a night club which, as it turned out, made a specialty of making out-of-town people feel at home. A jolly master of ceremonies browbeat perfect strangers into playing parlor games like musical chairs. To break the ice he would go from table to table with his microphone, followed by the spotlight, asking people the name of their home state. Then the orchestra would play an appropriate number such as "Carry Me Back to Old Virginny," or "Alabamy Bound." When Ralph told him they were both from Arkansas, the orchestra was momentarily nonplussed and then for some reason began to play "A Boy from Texas." The spotlight shone full on them while the crooner sang:

> *A boy from Texas*
> *And a girl from Tennessee*
> *They walked down Broadway*

And were lonesome as can be
He said Howdy
And she said Hi you all—

It seemed hours before the spotlight moved on and he could let his face relax from its ghastly fixed grin. They left shortly after and went silently back to the Betsy Ross.

It would not be fair to say that Ralph "dropped" Walterene, for he was careful to maintain their friendship, though in a smaller way. She still figured as a positive, if not very promising, resource in his strategy, certainly not one to be discarded. To tell the truth, Ralph found her company much more tolerable now that his search had moved on. Nor did he despair when it became clear that his association with Walterene was not a success. He compiled another list.

As he studied his new list one winter evening, he conceived another possibility which was so good that it immediately took precedence over all the rest. Its virtue lay in the total absence of risk. Every other instance entailed in some degree the danger of rejection and failure. At some point in every projected campaign, whether it be a straight pick-up or a friendship at a young people's church meeting, he would have to make an overture, ask a question which could only be answered yes or no. His latest notion completely eliminated such perils. He was triumphant. Feeling that the mere conception of such an idea was a satisfactory day's work, he took a light work-out in the gym and went to a movie at Times Square.

Next day he submitted by mail an advertisement to a literary magazine. It read:

YOUNG NUCLEAR PHYSICIST, *22, with a fondness for good books,*
good music, liberal ideas, and unconventional situations desires

acquaintance with young woman of similar tastes. Wishes to
supplement the delights of research in pure science with the
enjoyment of the good things of New York in congenial company.

It struck the right note. There was the major ingredient proper to such advertisements: a genteel eroticism, plus an interesting fillip, science, that particular science which, next to psychiatry, would be most likely to intrigue the intelligent and liberal readers of the magazine. In addition to the notions of speeding neutrons and incalculable forces which the words *nuclear physics* conjured up, Ralph realized full well that there were also socio-political implications.

"Nuclear physics, eh?" one of his new friends might say. "Fascinating field. Pity you fellows have to be hamstrung by a bunch of politicians and gestapo agents."

Ralph would shrug philosophically, indicating long experience with these obstructions.

Although he was optimistic about his new venture, he was not prepared for the avalanche which followed. Within a week after the magazine appeared, he received nearly a hundred letters. He sat at his desk, cleared except for the neat stack of the latest batch of replies, and waited for his pounding heart to subside. His achievement was a triumph of method. He had succeeded in reducing a whole field of human relations to the arena of his desktop. He had imprisoned all those forces which had hitherto cast him about at will into a controlled experiment which could be treated as systematically as a textbook assignment.

Ralph reflected that he had discovered a new law in the economy of human relations: that one makes a gain in the social field only with a certain loss of personal dignity. Considered in the clear light of his method, there was, of course, no onus attached to the advertisement. All the same he would hate to admit to Walterene or to his family that he had advertised for love and friendship as others would advertise for a servant or a used car.

The letters showed an astonishing variety. A large number were written by girls who could not possibly have understood anything in the magazine except the advertisements. Their stationery was often tinted and perfumed. Some enclosed photographs showing the writers in bathing suits. Others were from ladies who, though no longer young, offered other compensating inducements. A few had taken Ralph's advertisement as a proposal of marriage.

But many were obviously written by girls of education and breeding. These nearly all began the same way: "Dear Sir," or "Dear Nuclear Physicist," or "Dear N.P.," "I have never done this sort of thing before but—," or "My friend and I would not think of answering this kind of ad ordinarily, but just for fun we were wondering if perhaps you too had a friend of similar tastes." His brain reeled. He was a sultan with a card-index harem.

A difficulty soon presented itself. These discerning girls from whom he would choose (one, or who knows, perhaps two or more) naturally avoided writing the "pen-pal" type of letter. They were not so vulgar as to describe their physical assets like the others ("my friends tell me I have a good figure") or to enclose a snapshot. This was all very well: beauty was not Ralph's primary objective. But he did not wish to go to the trouble of arranging a meeting only to find himself face-to-face with a monstrous-looking creature. It would necessitate a retreat painful to both. There was only one answer, of course: a reconnoiter before the interview.

After three weeks' accumulation of mail he had selected three letters. One was particularly promising. It was from a girl, twenty-one years old, named Nancy Brough. She wrote with dignity and precision. There were no apologies. She said simply that she had quite a few friends, none of whom interested her especially, and that she could see no harm in meeting the young nuclear physicist. But she wanted it clearly understood that she was not a sex-starved female looking for a man, or worse, one who wanted to exchange prurient letters. And since their meeting, if it occurred at all, would be unconventional, she saw no sense in prolonging it unnecessarily if one didn't happen to like the looks of the other. She was a poet and most of her friends were writers and painters and musicians. He was to reply to her letter, and then, if she still liked the idea, she would consent to a meeting. Her address was intriguing: 16 Coach Row. It didn't sound like Manhattan.

Ralph set out the following Sunday with a large map of the city. He found a bench near the ferry slip on the Manhattan side and spread out the map. Coach Row was a tiny blind alley off Fourth Street. Greenwich Village. He could no longer get excited about the Village. Before he came to New York, the name had always brought to mind narrow cobblestone streets and old gabled houses. But he had seen it. It was, if possible, more dismal than the rest of Manhattan.

Nevertheless, he boarded an open-top bus at Fifth Avenue with a light-hearted air of adventure. There was also the solid satisfaction of conforming to his method. The present action was a systematic elimination of uncontrolled factors. A reconnoiter in force. He couldn't help feeling a bit like Bulldog Drummond in his trench coat and slouch hat.

Coach Row was a surprise. Actually, it was nothing extraordinary: a double row of converted stables, but in contrast with the dreary tenements of the Village it seemed to him charmingly quaint. Number sixteen was nearly at the end of the alley opposite a little tavern. Ralph had formed a plan before he got to the stoop. In the vestibule there were four name cards with bell buttons. Number four was Miss Nancy Brough. No roommate. He pressed the button. Almost immediately there was an answering click in the lock of the front door. It was as if she expected him. He pressed the button again several times and walked quickly across the street to the tavern. He sipped a beer at the end of the bar and waited. Presently the door of number sixteen opened and a girl stepped out onto the stoop. His mission was successful. She was no beauty. Too thin. Her eyes were so dark that the pupil and iris merged into a single disc like a comic-strip character. She hugged her arms and looked up and down the alley. Already he felt a tender solicitude for her. "Get back into the house before you catch cold," he shouted at her silently. Finally, she shrugged and went inside.

Ralph turned back to his beer. The search was ended. All he had to do now was to go home and write a letter, a decent reserved letter with the merest hint of his love for her. He looked at himself between the bottles at the bar mirror and shoved back his hat brim with his thumb.

As he turned to leave, Nancy came in followed by a young man. Ralph was confused and ordered another beer. They chose a booth behind him and to one side. He could see them clearly in the mirror. *What am I worried about? She doesn't know me. If she does recognize me later it will only make a good story. I'll tell her about this anyway.* She drank coffee and smoked. Her movements were quick and nervous. *That's probably her breakfast. She smokes too much.* She held her lips pursed and gazed absently into her coffee cup. Her escort was a damp young man. He talked with great animation. Ralph couldn't hear him, but he shrugged frequently, flipping out a hand palm-up as if he were saying: "And, my dear, what else could I do?"

No wonder Nancy was not especially interested in her friends. He shouldered past them, scowling and exultant, hands thrust deep in his trench-coat pockets.

On the bus top again, he reviewed the situation. The groundwork was well laid. He could think of only one more thing to be done, and although this contingency would not arise for some time, it was well to be prepared. Her friends (and his-to-be) were all artistic. Each had an accomplishment. Perhaps even Nancy read her poetry aloud to a small group. Some had possibly formed a string quartet. Others no doubt were actors at the Village Playhouse. Nancy's friend in the tavern probably told clever risqué stories at the piano. The reality which had to be faced was that Ralph had no such accomplishment. Actually, he had even exaggerated his knowledge of "good music and good books." When Nancy presented him to her friends, he would arouse brief interest. There would be the usual remarks about atomic energy. But he couldn't rest indefinitely on his laurels as a potential nuclear physicist.

Before he reached Seventy-fifth Street he had the solution. It was simple and inevitable. When he examined his resources and his origins, he saw that they could be reduced to two prime elements. He had a good tenor voice, and he came from Arkansas. Folk songs. He would get a collection of Ozark Mountain ballads from the New York Public Library and go to work. Then, later, when the others had just finished a Haydn quartet, he might say quietly: "Here's one you never heard before," and sitting crosslegged on the floor of the studio apartment and staring into space, he would sing a haunting ballad about the sourwood trees and the stillness of the mountains.

Written in 1937; published first in The Oxford American,
January/February 1997

Sermon with Meath

BARRY HANNAH

YOU COULD SEE INTO THE BASEMENT QUARTERS through big glass sliding doors
the playroom, as they called it, of Webb Meath. Meath was seventeen
and I was only thirteen. I could see him putting 45 rpm records on a
machine and practicing dance steps by himself around the playroom.
I was going to enter Meath's world fairly soon. He was on the verge
of being a sissy, even though he was on the football team, not playing
much until all was hopeless or well in hand in the last quarter. Then
he would trot in with great earnestness and get some grass stain on
his uniform for when he met his girlfriend, who had almost made the
cheerleader squad and hung around these girls like an extra pal, no hard
feelings. She was almost cute, too. But Meath was built like a soft bowling
pin. Although tall, he didn't seem to have any strength to him, and he
slouched, with a high burr haircut on him and the red, bowed lips of
a woman, full and wet like that. Webb Meath was from Indiana, or
perhaps Minnesota. They were Methodists in a heavily Baptist town,
further alien.

    Meath wanted to be a Methodist preacher. He would bring a Bible
out where I and a couple of other buddies my age played at a wide board
rope swing hung from an oak at the bottom of our property, right where
the Meath meadow began, out there where we on Sundays had fierce
touch football games with fellows of all ages.

Meath would stand there with his Bible in hand, more than a foot taller, and watch our play sternly as if whatever we were doing was not quite right. For instance, plastic soldiers spread all out in attack with tanks, artillery, command bunkers, and fortresses of packed soil. We would air bomb them, too, with spark plugs, and fire into them with whitehead matches from shooters made of clothespins. Smoke and mouth gunfire and screams going on very seriously. Meath would observe us with pity on his face, but kind pity. We all liked Meath. He was gentle like a brother, and he was very strange. Meath would not interrupt, he would let us play ourselves out, then he would hunker down, peer at each of us sincerely, wet his lips, and begin preaching from the Book of Revelations, the Bible spread out in his big left hand. We would sit on our negligible butts with arms around our knees and listen for upwards of an hour.

The Eagle and the Bear and the Horsemen and the White Horse of Death and the minions and the princes and Joseph Stalin and the Hydrogen Bomb and the Daughters of Wrath. I don't think Meath had a very good grasp of all this, but he listed them well, and in that Northern voice somewhere between a whine and a song. His eyes would half shut as if it hurt to read these things. Many years later it would strike me that those who especially loved Revelations were nerds and dweebs and dorks who despised people and life on this planet, somewhat like the *Star Trek* crowd I saw at Iowa City who liked to get in elevators and discuss how this or that civilization was "utterly consumed." But I don't believe Meath hated this world. He wanted in it badly but something was very wrong. He was not winning and he had no joy being regular and mature. He did not dance well, his girl was not so special, he was awkward and had made only second team, and in the school halls he was galoot-like, slouching and puzzled as if lost among bad smells. Even we little guys noticed it.

That he had a good car and his people were well-off cut no ice. With another person it might have, but not with Meath. He stayed at the edge of the popular crowd, giving bad imitations of it. For instance, it was difficult for Meath to look casual. He seemed near tears often. I once saw him and his girlfriend having a quiet moment at the hall locker like you were supposed to, but both of them were red-faced and pouted-up as if nearly crying over some deep matter. It was my sense she wanted him to do things.

After Meath finished, he would begin playing with us and our soldiers, or whatever we had going, with more zeal by far than he had shown in the sermon. Meath would really get off into it, making machine-gun sounds and totally successful bomb explosions. His mouth would be red from wetting the kitchen matches on the head before striking them. You sailed them and they left true smoke like rockets, bursting into flame as they fell among the soldiers.

Then one afternoon he got very concerned and stared at his hands and we asked him what was wrong.

They don't think this is right, he said.

Who? What? I asked him.

Me hanging out with guys your age.

Oh. Why not?

It's queer, Dad said.

No. But we need your sermons.

Yes, that's true, said Meath, more confident now. He fell to playing with us again. Meath wasn't just hanging out with us. He was deeper in play than we were.

One other afternoon he said he thought we were mature enough to follow along in Revelations with our own Bibles, so I went up the hill to my house and got several Bibles. We had plenty. My mother was huge in the Baptist church. She was the president of the state Women's

Missionary Union. We had had Mexicans and Chinese people in our house.

Where are you going with those? my mother wanted to know. I told her Meath was preaching from Revelations and wanted us to follow. Mother peered down the hill where Meath stood with my other pals. She had that Nay look in her eyes. Baptists are the Church of the New Testament, they say, but in the South they tend to be severe as in the Old. My mother didn't believe in dancing or too much fun on the Sabbath. I never saw her affectionate with my Pa, not once. If the doors of the church were open, we were in it. With revivals, six days a week. She insisted on tithing to such a comprehensive extent that my father complained even to me. He was afraid she would give everything to the church in the event he died, so he lived a good long time. He was from the Depression where a nickel was serious.

Children shouldn't try to understand that book, she said.

But there's Meath.

Yes. He's a large boy, isn't he? She looked very doubtful as I left with the Bibles. I knew it didn't look right to her and was guilty, a common condition of young Baptists. My mother was from Delta planters. Somehow this made her consumed by appearances. The *appearance* of evil was as grave as, say, yelling *hell* at the dinner table.

Then another afternoon, a Sunday, Meath became entirely strange. We were playing touch football. Meath was far and away the largest out there. There must have been sixteen of us from junior high, and Meath, on his perfect sunlit property. My team did a sweep and I blocked Meath at the knees. I cut him down. I was shocked that this huge boy went over with only a soft rubbery give to him. We scored but we looked back and there was Meath rolling on the ground, holding his shins and howling. It was a thing I could barely connect with my block. I couldn't have weighed more than ninety or so. He was two hundred. But he wailed and then just began clinching up, all red and weepy, going on in an embarrassing, thin Yankee whine. It was a preposterous act. We all hung our heads. Soon we went home. All joy was gone, and it made us feel bad. My friends and I began to despise Meath. We watched his failures and cheered for them bitterly.

He and the girl broke up. Meath prowled around even sadder. We liked this. Some older boy pointed out that Meath had a low ass. This was true and we adored it. His voice, that we liked before, got on our nerves. We moved the soldiers back onto my property, abandoning the great forts in his, and watched the rains of the spring melt them down. We would jump bikes off a ramp and then leap from the bike at the peak of the rise and grab a rope that swung out forty feet high into a fir tree, and fall through the branches, usually hurt and even bleeding, which was the point. Meath came down and watched us from his swing. We knew he wanted to join us.

His mouth's connected to his butthole, whispered the older boy.

What?

No guts, the boy explained. This was a rich one and we barked the rest of the day about it, taking furtive glances at Meath, whose face with its big woman's lips just hung there sissy and wanting, a splendid annoyance to our play. We learned to cut Meath, just cut him, drop our eyes in the halls of the school when he came near. This was a sweet new social skill. High adolescence was going to be a snap.

Meath was ending his senior year this spring. I don't recall how we knew this in the small town, but it was understood Meath's father was failing in business. His Southern adventure had not worked out. They were moving back North. When I looked down into Meath's playroom, where he still practiced dancing, I saw the gray air of failure all around him. Somebody had caught him wearing a letter jacket he had not earned in the nearby capital city, Jackson, and this was his certain end. You could sink no lower.

In a frame asbestos-siding house on the street that Meath's faced, down just about five houses on the north side, lived a family that was not genteel poor. They were really poor. They were white, of course, and their father, in his forties, was studying at the little Baptist college in our town to be a grade-school teacher. He had many children and it was said they never ate much but cornflakes. He could not support them at whatever he used to do, so now he was educating himself to move up to the position of teacher, but the four years and odd jobs meant even direr straights for his people. Nevertheless he had them in church every Sunday, heads all watered-down with combing, in sorry clothes but clean. He and his entire family were baptized one Wednesday night at prayer meeting, there in the pool under the stained glass scene of the Jordan River. Everybody cheered him, and my mother became positively tearful about their goodness and conversion. Mother was stern, but she was loving, profoundly, about new church people. I understand the success of the Baptists in converting the South nearly wholesale, through my mother.

But Mr. Tweedy, the poor man, came out of the pool on the preacher's arm all choked up and fighting off the water. Here was an adult who feared water. I turned my head and grinned at another hellion down the pew. At Christmas I helped my father deliver boxes of hams and fruit and cheese to the needy. All of the families were black except the Tweedys, nearly on our own street. This was odd. I felt humiliated for them, even though they were most appreciative and showed no false pride. I knew this was biblical but it didn't sit right. I recall, also, the absence of damned near everything in the living room of that house. I believe there was a card table and orange crates.

So Mr. Tweedy was graduating, too. This spring he was getting his degree and already he was a substitute teacher in Jackson. Things were looking up. Mother and the neighbors applauded them. Providence, it seemed, was about to attend the new Christian Tweedys. Nothing could be better. The Lord had promised this.

But in April while Mr. Tweedy was driving his awful Ford to his school, a tornado came through Jackson, picked up only his car into the air and hurled him against something and killed him. All his plans and work meant this, and his children were now orphans, his skinny, bent wife a widow by celestial violence. I could not understand it at all. Although I played constantly at war with my pals, I could never, I thought, have devised anything this cruel. My mother was hurt, too. But she said it had a purpose. All had a design.

But I stopped going to church, scandalizing her and driving her into long prayer talks with our pastor. She went around teary and solemn. My father told me the same thing as when my terrier Spot died of jaundice: Son, everything dies. He could not know how viciously irrelevant he was then. I started growing up cynical. I believe, in the matter of Christians, I became a little Saul before the road to Damascus, Saul the persecutor of the faith, before he saw the light and became St. Paul of the Gospels.

My mother came in my room and told me Meath had called me and several of the boys to meet him down at the swing. He had a special testimony for us. I could not believe she was approving of Meath. She was truly desperate. But I went down, though sourly, already despising Meath as he stood tall among some boys who had already arrived. Nobody sat down. That was all over. We just sort of made a rank and stepped back from Meath. He had no Bible, but he clasped his hands together and was looking at the ground prayerfully.

What's giving, Reverend? said the older boy.

We're all confused by what happened to Mr. Tweedy, I know, said Meath. He was meek and humble, a hard-working Christian man, a resurrected man, who loved his wife and children. The meek should inherit the earth, the Savior said. But . . . Tweedy.

When Meath raised his face, there was one of those warm, evangelical smiles on him. He had let his hair grow out and it was swept back, all oily, and looked like black under shellac. I hadn't seen him lately and this was almost too much.

God has His reasons for poor Mr. Tweedy. He was using him as a testament to us. Mr. Tweedy is happy now.

Meath seemed to be imitating Tweedy in heaven with this insane, warm smile.

Tweedy is looking down telling us guys to just love and support one another and get right with the Lord!

There was a big gap of quiet then, and many of us looked down at the soil, too. Where the forts had been was only a dry mud. That was what God did to Mr. Tweedy, I recall thinking. Right back into the mud for daring to get better.

You only like Tweedy because he's lower than you, the older boy suddenly said to Meath. You love it that he was murdered by a tornado because it makes a creep like you feel lucky and right. You're using Tweedy to make us be your friend. But we ain't going to be your friends because you're chicken and a liar and that's the way it's always going to be.

I was astounded by what my friend said. He had really been winding up inside in his hatred for Meath, and I was shocked that I hated Meath almost this much, too. I had depended on Meath to be smooth and Northern-hip and a friendly guide to life.

Meath's warm new smile fell off and he just collapsed. He turned around and walked back to his two-story house with its glassed playroom. We could see him shaking with sobs. His mother was on the balcony waiting and watching him. We saw the sudden expression on her face, horror, and we left, to all parts of the subdivision. I felt a part of a mob that had stoned somebody and it was not that bad, it had a nice edge to it. That big Meath.

In college my roommate, a brilliant boy already long into botany and Freud, and I baited Christers at the college. Many of them were pre-ministerial students perfecting their future roles. They came on like idiot savants, quoting Scripture perfectly and at great length, but baffled by almost everything else. We especially went at a short boy with a wide, pale face and thick, ashy whiskers on him. He wore thick glasses and was a quoting fool, get him started. He was only eighteen but already like a loony old man. He roomed with a new Christian Chinese fellow, rail-thin and just out of starvation, who wrote this hesitant Christian poetry on the slant for the campus literary magazine. It was utter banal coonshit, and we loved to read it aloud. We played loud Ray Charles and much jazz on the machine, smoked and drank lab alcohol, and shouted out what we would do if challenged by one of the nude pin-up girls on our wall. The Christers gathered and put us on all the prayer lists. The dorm counselor, a giant, one-eyed Christer, broke down and told us nothing came from our room but crap and corruption. But we made A's, anointed thus. Once I hid in the closet while my buddy pretended to be in a spiritual crisis, weeping and gnashing his teeth for the loony thick-glassed guy who was overjoyed at his chance to save him. I finally howled out. The boy was so out of it, he thought I was in a fit of contrition, too. Then I went down and pretended to the Christian Chinese boy that his poetry had driven me insane.

I am not proud remembering this. Once I thrashed a skinny Christer, a senior, with boxing gloves in the hall. He had been wanting to prove that Christians were strong, too, but I routed him. I was cheered by the agnostic few around the hall, but this seemed cheap, at last, and I gave up open baiting. My roommate pal went straight to the state asylum for depression and alcoholism, and I felt so miserable and lonely I got married too early.

A couple of decades passed and I was in Chicago, reading some pages from my new book at the university, I think, when I saw something in the paper. That night I got a taxi and went out to see him. Meath was indeed a minister, Methodist, but in a small sort of hippie chapel on the edge of a bad and garish neighborhood where transvestites sported around nearly in ownership of the block. Meath was overjoyed to see me. He met me an hour before the service began and although I came wanting vaguely to apologize for our awful treatment of him twenty years ago, I never got the chance. He hugged me and acted as if we had been perfect boyhood chums. He bragged on good traits about me I didn't even remember, said he knew my imagination would pull me through. He too had been through divorce and bad times, although always a minister. He was stout, not much hair, but trimmer, more solid, and glowing with health. Mostly he was so delighted to see me.

At the service were some forty folks—some bums, some straight and prosperous men and women, and some truly ancient hippies, those phenomenal people who are fifty and have changed nothing. Meath began as if just chatting, then I sensed the sermon was in progress. He stood, no lectern, no altar, no height, in front of his flock, and spoke with a sane joy. Simply a good-looking, middle-aged man with a comfortable interior to him. He wore glasses. A loose hair sprang up at the back of his head and waved about. Everything counts, he said.

Everything counts but you must isolate this thing and not let it become mixed with others. You must look at it as a child would. You must not bring the heaviness of long-thinking and the burden of your hours to it. The lightness, the calm wonder and intensity of a child is what I mean. Picasso says at fifty, At last, I can paint like a child! That must have been paradise for him. Perhaps it waits for you.

Come unto me, all you that labor and are heavy laden, and I will give you rest. Take my yoke upon you and learn of me; for I am meek and lowly in heart. And you shall find rest unto your souls. For my yoke is easy, and my burden is light, speaks Christ.

Heaviness comes as you get older. But sufficient unto the day is the evil thereof, says the Savior. Look at the day alone and do not mix it with others. A child has no need of the future or the past. He is all times at once. You've only need of the day. The precious day. This day even more precious because my friend of long ago is here.

Meath pointed to me.

I can't remember, in my life so far, a happier time than this.

January/February 1997

Memories of a Dead Man Walking

SISTER HELEN PREJEAN

THERE SHE WAS DURING THE FILMING of *Dead Man Walking*, Susan Sarandon being me, going into the women's room in the death house, putting her head against the tile wall, grabbing the crucifix around her neck, praying, "Please God, don't let him fall apart." It's something to watch a film of yourself happening in front of your eyes, kind of funny to hear somebody saying that she's you, but I don't stay long with this mirror stuff. What happens is that I'm sucked back into the original scene, the white-hot fire of what actually happened.

There in the Louisiana death house on April 4, 1984, I was scared out of my mind. I had never watched anybody be killed. I was supposed to be the condemned man's spiritual advisor. I was in over my head. All I had agreed to in the beginning was to be a pen pal to Patrick Sonnier. Sure, I said, I could write letters. But the man was all alone. He had no one to visit him, and it was like a current in a river: I got sucked in, and the next thing I was saying was, Okay, sure, I'll come to visit you, and when I filled out the prison application form to be approved as his visitor, he suggested spiritual advisor, and I said, Sure. He was Catholic, and I'm a Catholic nun, and it seemed right, but I didn't know that at the end, on the evening of the execution, everybody has to leave the death house at 5:45 p.m. Everybody but the spiritual advisor. The spiritual advisor stays to the end. The spiritual advisor witnesses the execution.

People ask me all the time, What's a nun doing getting involved with these murderers? You know how people have these stereotypical images of nuns—nuns teach, nuns nurse the sick. I tell people: Look at who Jesus hung out with—lepers, prostitutes, thieves, the throwaways of his day. People don't get it. There's a lot of "biblical quarterbacking" in death penalty debates, with people tossing in quotes from the Bible to back up what they've already decided on, people wanting to practice vengeance and have God agree with them. The same thing happened in this country in the slavery debates and in the debates over women's suffrage. Quote that Bible. God said torture. God said get revenge. Religion is tricky business.

But here's the real reason I got involved with death row inmates: I got involved with poor people. And everybody who lives on this planet and has at least one eye open knows that only poor people get selected for death row. On June 1, 1981, I drove a little brown truck into St. Thomas, a black, inner-city housing project in New Orleans, and began to live there with four other sisters (with my scared Catholic Mama kneeling on crushed glass and saying her rosary, praying that her daughter wouldn't be shot). ("Kneeling on crushed glass" is just an expression. Read *fervently*.)

Growing up a Southern white girl in Baton Rouge, right on the cusp of the upper class, I had only known black people as my servants. I went to an all-white high school—this was in the fifties—and black people had to sit in the back of the bus and up in the balcony of the Paramount and Hart theaters.

I got a whole other kind of education in the St. Thomas Projects. I still go there every Monday to keep close to friends I made there and to keep close to the struggle. Living there, it didn't take long to see that there was a greased track to prison and death row. As one Mama put it: "Our boys leave here in a police car or a hearse."

When I began visiting Pat Sonnier in 1982, I couldn't have been more naïve about prisons. The only other experience with prisoners I'd had was in the '60s when Sister Cletus and I—decked in full head-to-toe habits—went to Orleans Parish Prison one time to play our guitars and sing with the prisoners. This was the era of singing nuns, the "Dominica-nica-nica" era, and the guards brought us all into this big room with over one hundred prisoners and I said, "Let's do 'If I Had a Hammer,'" and the song took off like a shot. The men really got into it and started making up their own verses: *"If I had a switchblade . . ."* laughing and singing loud, and the guards were rolling their eyes. Sister Cletus and I weren't invited back to sing there again. And the movie got this scene right, at least the telling of it. Sister Helen/Susan tells this story to the chaplain who has asked her if she's had any experience in prisons. He's not amused.

I wrote Patrick Sonnier about life in St. Thomas, and he wrote me about life in a six-by-eight foot cell. He and forty other men were confined twenty-three out of twenty-four hours a day in cells of this size, and he'd say how glad he was when summer was over because there was no fresh air in their unventilated cells, and he'd sometimes wet the sheet from his bunk and put it on the cement floor to try to cool off, or he'd clean out his toilet bowl and stand in it and use a small plastic container to get water from his lavatory and pour it over his body. Patrick was on death row four years before they killed him.

I made a bad mistake. When I found out about Patrick Sonnier's crime—he and his brother were convicted of killing two teenage kids—I didn't go to see the victims' families. I stayed away because I wasn't sure how to deal with such raw pain. The movie's got this part down pat. It really takes you over to the victims' families and helps you see their pain and my awful tension with them. In real life I was a coward. I stayed away and only met the victims' families at Patrick's pardon board hearing. They were there to demand the execution. I was there to ask the board to show mercy. It was not a good time to meet.

Here were two sets of parents whose children had been ripped from them, condemned in their pain and loss to a kind of death row of their own. I felt terrible. I was powerless to assuage their grief. It would take me a long time to learn how to help victims' families, a long time before I would sit at their support group meetings and hear their unspeakable stories of loss and grief and rage and guilt. I would learn that the divorce rate for couples who lose a child is over seventy percent—a new twist to "until death do us part." I would learn that often after a murder, friends stay away because they don't know how to respond to the pain. I would learn that black families or Hispanic families or poor families who have a loved one murdered not only don't expect the district attorney's office to pursue the death penalty but are surprised when the case is prosecuted at all. In Louisiana, murder victims' families are allowed to sit on the front row in the execution chamber to watch the murderer die. Some families. Not all. But black families almost never witness the execution of someone who has killed their loved one, because in Louisiana, the hangman's noose, then the electric chair, and now the lethal injection gurney, are almost exclusively reserved for those who killed whites. Ask Virginia Smith's African-American family. She was fourteen when three white youths took her into the woods, raped, and stabbed her to death. None of them got the death penalty. They had all-white juries.

Patrick tried to protect me from watching him die. He told me he'd be okay, I didn't have to come with him into the execution chamber. "Electric chair's not a pretty sight, it could scar you," he told me, trying to be brave. I said, "No, no, Pat, if they kill you, I'll be there," and I said to him, "You look at me, look at my face, and I will be the face of Christ for you, the face of love." I couldn't bear it that he would die alone. I said, "God will help me." And there in the women's room, just a few hours before the execution, my only place of privacy in that place of death, God and I met, and the strength was there, and it was like a circle of light, and it was just in the present moment. If I tried to think ahead to what would happen at midnight, I started coming unraveled, but there in the present I could hold together, and Patrick was strong and kept asking me, "Sister Helen, are you all right?"

Being in the death house was one of the most bizarre, confusing experiences I have ever had because it wasn't like visiting somebody dying in a hospital, where you can see the person getting weaker and fading. Patrick was so fully alive, talking and responding to me and writing letters to people and eating, and I'd look around at the polished tile floors—everything so neat—all the officials following a protocol, the secretary typing up forms for the witnesses to sign, the coffee pot percolating, and I kept feeling that I was in a hospital, and the final act would be to save this man's life. It felt strange and terrifying because everyone was so polite. They kept asking Patrick if he needed anything. The chef came by to ask him if he liked his last meal—the steak (medium rare), the potato salad, the apple pie for dessert.

When the warden with the strap-down team came for Patrick at midnight, I walked behind him. In a hoarse, childlike voice he asked the warden, "Can Sister Helen touch my arm?" I put my hand on his shoulder and read to him from Isaiah, Chapter 43; "I have called you by your name . . . if you walk through fire I will be with you." God heard his prayer, "Please, God, hold up my legs." It was the last piece of dignity he could muster. He wanted to walk. I saw this dignity in him, and I have seen it in the other two men I have accompanied to their deaths. I wonder how I would hold up if I were walking across a floor to a room where people were waiting to kill me. The essential torture of the death penalty is not finally the physical method: a bullet or rope or gas or electrical current or injected drugs. The torture happens when conscious human beings are condemned to death and begin to anticipate that death and die a thousand times before they die.

I'm not saying that Patrick Sonnier or any of the condemned killers

I've accompanied were heroes. I do not glorify them. I do not condone their terrible crimes. But each of these men was a human being, and each had a transcendence, a dignity, which should assure them of two very basic human rights that the United Nations Universal Declaration of Human Rights calls for: the right not to be tortured, the right not to be killed. To have a firm moral bedrock for our societies we must establish that no one is permitted to kill—and that includes governments.

At the end I was amazed at how ordinary Patrick Sonnier's last moments were. He walked to the dark oak chair and sat in it. As guards were strapping his legs and arms and trunk, he found my face and his voice and his last words of life were words of love to me and I took them in like a lightning rod and I have been telling his story ever since.

When they filmed the execution scene of *Dead Man Walking* on a set in New York City, I was there for the whole last week, watching Sean Penn, as the death row inmate Matthew Poncelet, get executed by lethal injection. It was tense, it was slow, it was hard. They shot each scene ten or more times. It took forever. Sean dying, Susan accompanying him, me remembering. Once, during a break, Sean stayed strapped to the gurney and Susan went to visit with him for a while. He's strapped at his neck, trunk, legs, arms, ankles. The cameras are over him. There's a hushed buzz from other actors and technicians. Susan's standing close and talking softly to him. I notice she's holding his hand. It's just a movie. He's not really dying, but there she is holding his hand. Even playing at dying and killing can be real, real hard on you.

Spring 1996

Jim White's Yellow Mind

LEE DURKEE

FOR TEN YEARS JIM WHITE LIVED IN ALPHABET CITY on the Lower East Side of
Manhattan and drove a cab and to this day suffers what he calls a "yellow
mind," which is a type of urban Tourette's where suddenly in the midst
of civil conversation he'll jut his head out the driver's-side window
and start barking obscenities at various cops, pedestrians, fellow time
travelers. Jim and I are in his dilapidated van, driving around Washington
Square Park an hour before soundcheck at the Village Underground.
We are, like so many others, looking for a parking spot, a place to rest
and talk. Jim is at the wheel. Tall and lanky with long, black hair and
sideburns, he looks like a gas station attendant from some music video
fantasy; his accent, more twang than drawl, is thick Pensacola, a city that
claims more churches per capita than any other in the South (and there-
fore the universe). One of its churches is a small Pentecostal one where
for a decade Jim was a less-than-fervent member not above faking the
occasional bout of glossolalia. Ten years as a Pentecostal, ten as a New
York cabbie. . . . Call it a wash.

When the obscenities subside, Jim's voice returns to a smooth, fast
river of observation, non sequitur, and storytelling that you can just ride
along on and watch its banks. For instance, you mention Pensacola, and
you get: "It's a beautiful, quiet, cheap place to live, but it's very con-
servative, and it's got its hands around the neck of life, and it's just slowly

choking you, and you don't really notice it when you first get there 'cause they're such pretty hands. . . . You're just thinking . . . what pretty hands . . . and you know what? *They're around-my-neck!*"

You mention Manhattan, and you get: "The great thing about New York is shit just flying at you from every direction. I was standing outside the Museum of Natural History today—my sweetie's here with our daughter, and we wanted to take her to see the dinosaurs—there it is, man, every cabdriver's nightmare: the woman throwing her door open into traffic—and this hip-hop kid came walking up to me and out of nowhere showed me a picture of Tyra Banks in a bathing suit and says, 'Man, what do you think about this?' He'd never seen me before. I said that I'd have to think twice before I even said a word, and he said, 'I can't even think about it not even once because it hurts too bad,' and he turned and walked away. New York's got this kind of thing where if you keep the windows open long enough, all kinds of interesting birds will fly in."

There are a few interesting birds flying around inside Jim's new CD, *No Such Place*, on Luaka Bop, David Byrne's West Village label. Although Jim has been forever cast as "alternative country," the fact remains that there is a strong urban wind of static, intercom, reverb, and police megaphone blowing through these thirteen songs that his own label calls "trip-folk" but which Jim likes to call "hick-hop." (Not to argue with the likes of Mr. Byrne, but this ain't folk.) Whatever it is, it's dark medicine, this music, dimly lit if at all, by its humor and desperate faith.

There are no parking spaces along Washington Square, which is an old haunt of Jim's, one of many here, not all of them kindly remembered. "It almost killed me," he says of New York. "I've been back a couple of times, three or four times since I moved and quit driving a cab, and I still got, like, this yellow mind I get in the city and start driving like a madman, cussing everybody." As he pauses, the various strange birds of the West Village flutter inside the van's open windows. Electronic whirls and twirls, a car alarm, some horn blowers, hollerers and hawkers, screamers and boomboxers. New York spring.

"Music is a real fragmented lifestyle," he suddenly picks up—I'm pretty sure not where we left off—then lays on the horn to assert us toward a fire hydrant. "There was a certain rhythm to driving a cab, at least. You pick up your fares, you drop off your fares, you pick up your fares. . . . You never know where you're going or anything like that, but there's a rhythm to it. But there's no rhythm to this at all, and it's funny because it's rhythm that's what you're doing you're doing music, which is supposed to be rhythmic—*No, I'm not honking at that thing you're shaking there, honey, I'm honking at your bad pedestrian skills!*—Sorry. The New York cabdriver just comes flying out of me. People are so astonished when they're riding around with me and I seem like a fairly polite person, and then suddenly I start calling someone f—head," he sticks his head out of the window, "YO, F—HEAD! GET OUT OF THE WAY!" He shrugs. "It's reflexes. Anyway, my sweetie made a real good living here so her memories of New York are Edenic. It's just this paradise. Meanwhile, I lived here for ten years hand-to-mouth, driving a cab and making movies on shoestring budgets, and I think of New York, and I taste dirt in my mouth because it was so hard on me here so many times I was sick to the point of death and guys with guns threatening to shoot me when I was driving a cab and taking shit from people all the time and having to ride my bike home across the Manhattan bridge. . . . I don't know if you've ever had to ride a bike home across the Manhattan Bridge at three o'clock in the morning, but *it-ain't-no-fun.*"

We park illegally, doing what Jim calls the alternate-side-of-the-street-Watusi near the giant, cement arch flanked by two statues of George Washington: soldier and statesman. A tall hurricane fence surrounds the entire structure so that no one can pass underneath it, which I think is kind of the purpose of an arch, being passed underneath. The fence was built to discourage the local artists-at-large, who are having a hard time of it these days, especially since some scientist, probably Giuliani's sister, invented the Teflon subway car. My girlfriend was raised in Queens and remembers the good old days when every square inch of every subway car was art.

Eyeing that arch, Jim says, "Yeah, even though there's a big sign on that thing that says, LET US RAISE A STANDARD TO WHICH THE WISE AND HONEST CAN REPAIR, they still sell crack right under it. I used to laugh like hell about that."

He laughs nostalgically now while I watch a drug peddler searching the crowd for a hungry eye. We talk a little more about New York and how hard it can be on the artist soul. Jim was a student at the NYU film school and used to finance his films on cab tips, working fifty-hour weeks for months, then quitting and spending it all in one week of production. He's earned money in stranger ways, too: as a professional surfer in Florida, a professional model in Europe. But whatever hardships he has endured, he has at least put them to good use in *No Such Place*, his second album, two years overdue. (Jim looks to be in his late thirties, like me; anyway, we both call them albums.) *No Such Place* is a haunted collection of songs, it's poetry filtered between realms, leaving Jim's voice with the lonesome and, at times, disembodied sound of a Patsy Cline record played over a PA system to an empty midway on the closing night of the state fair.

When I was a kid, a friend once told me that you could listen to dead peoples' voices on the shortwave radio. I believed him and used to sneak out of bed and into in my dark closet late at night and slowly spin that dial listening to all the static-eaten ghosts. This notion that voices never die has stuck with me, and it's not too far removed from what you get listening to Jim White's broken ballads. This ghost-in-the-machine effect is strongest in the dusky remake of Roger Miller's "King of the Road." As Jim tells the story, he first performed the song while deathly ill, battling disease and depression in a Florida beach house. Some friends had come over to cheer him up, they claimed, and after a while they demanded he join in the reverie. Half delirious, Jim dragged himself out of bed and moments later found himself speaking in tongues for real.

"Somebody shouted, 'Sing something!'" he recalls now. "And like I was possessed, I suddenly started singing 'King of the Road' like David Byrne." Here Jim belts out a few lines in that shouting delivery that trademarked Talking Heads. "I'd been playing guitar for twenty-five years, and I'd never learned one song by another person. I don't know how to do it. I just don't have the patience to sit and learn. It's a form of narcissism, like the only thing you're interested in is yourself. I learned half of 'Stairway to Heaven,' and I learned the first half of 'Fire and Rain.' Anyway, the record company hated it ['King of the Road']," he adds, smiling grandly. "It was like pouring vinegar in their eyes."

It wasn't the only battle won over Warner Brothers, the parent company of Luaka Bop. Four years earlier, during the production of Jim's first CD, *Wrong-Eyed Jesus*, Byrne got worried that Jim's music might be coming across a bit too hostile and remote instead of swampy and mystical, so he advised Jim that what that first album needed was a "handshake to the world."

"Yeah, David told me it was a strange, interesting album, but you need to think of a handshake for the world because if people know you, they're going to like you, but if they don't know you, they're not going to like you. And I thought about it—I went to film school here at NYU, right behind you—and I remember that during the first film I showed, there was a kid in the class who said, 'I feel stupid watching this film, and I don't like feeling stupid, so I don't like the film.' Now there were a couple of people in the class who knew me and the way my mind works and loved it and were dedicated to it, and I thought, Well how can I get people to know me? If they know me, maybe they'll understand all these surrealist hillbilly references, for lack of a better term. So I sat down and wrote 'Wrong-Eyed Jesus.'"

"The Mysterious Tale of How I Shouted Wrong-Eyed Jesus" is of all things an accomplished short story included with the liner notes inside that first CD, and it went on to receive rave reviews. Even the one mixed review I found conceded high praise for the story, which tells the saga of a teenager, hitchhiking home from a minor drug deal one night, who gets picked up by a dirt-farming pervert. The inclusion of the story does exactly what Byrne had hoped for: it helps ground the music, which at times tends toward the ethereal, into the very solid, Southern land-scape of Jim's childhood.

"Anyway, I presented the story to the record label, and Yale, the guy who runs the label, said no. Warner Bros. was never going to pay to have a story in a first album. Then David read it and said, 'Let's see what we can do about this.' So we fought this big inter-nesting war where we were fighting against our own people. We were shooting each other at Warner Bros. because there were people ready to lose their jobs for the sake of keeping the story in the album, and there were people who were willing to lose their jobs—you know, *over my dead body that thing's going in there*—and we got away with it in the end, and I'm glad we did."

In fact, Jim has always considered himself a writer first and a musician second. He is faithful to both William Faulkner and Cormac McCarthy, but above all to Flannery O'Connor: "I didn't have a clue about my quote-unquote literary voice until I read Flannery O'Connor, and once I read that, particularly a story called 'The River,' I felt like I knew—like you'd been lost for fifty years, like the Israelites in the desert, and suddenly you see Israel, and you say, *Okay, that's where I have to settle.* That's how I felt when I read Flannery O'Connor."

His favorite novel, however, is a bit more obscure, a little-known Mexican classic called *Pedro Páramo*, written by Juan Rulfo, the grand-father of magic realism. Jim shows me the copy stashed in his van. By coincidence it's one of my favorites, too, a novel told through a series of ghost ruminations arising out of a Mexican graveyard. Of the book, Jim says, "[Rulfo's] wandering back and forth between the ghost world and the literal world, and I got to a point where I was doing that a lot. Lots of times people kind of romanticize this idea of ghosts, and I learned the hard way—I talk about it in 'Ghost-Town of My Brain'— you can't take comfort in ghosts. That's not the point of their presence. You can learn from them certainly, but don't snuggle up with them too much because the physics of it will lead to disaster."

"Ghost-Town of My Brain" gives you a pretty good glimpse into Jim White. Performed almost somnambulantly, it is a song that didn't quite make it into this world, the spectral lyrics played against a heavy mix of percussion and a subtle background of banjo and lap steel. The delivery is full of lull, more subliminal than real, and groaned in a dark Waitsian voice.

But in spite of its ghosts, the new CD is balanced—more so than Jim's first one—with humor and even some lively tunes that could be called half-pop. One troubadour number, "God Was Drunk When He Made Me," is even a bit reminiscent of Jimmy Buffett (that is, young Buffett, before he started recording white-rap rants against popcorn prices and then opened up a chain store celebrating himself). Further balancing the album is its tenacious optimism, what I would call optimism-in-the-face-of-considerable-evidence-to-the-contrary, as witnessed in the beginning lines of the opening track:

> I'm handcuffed to a fence in Mississippi.
> My girlfriend blows a boozy good-bye kiss.
> I see flying squirrels and nightmares of stigmata.
> Then awakening to find my Trans-Am gone.
> Still I'm feeling pretty good about the future.

Yeah, everything is peaches but the cream.
I'm handcuffed to a fence in Mississippi,
Where things is always better than they seem.

"Handcuffed to a Fence in Mississippi" pretty much sets the tone for the CD. It's a song that refuses to wallow, its music pulsating, Jim's voice seedy and bluesy and at times crooning. In true John Prine manner, the song doesn't feel it has to explain itself too much. It's also one of the tracks where you can hear the lingering possession of David Byrne loud and clear when Jim starts chant-lamenting: "My Trans-Am is missing / I guess there's no more kissing the girl who loved my car." The song's optimism is reinforced by a shaa-naa-naaah backup, and the irony of this optimism is reinforced by a police PA system repeating the refrain: "Things is always better than they seem."

Morcheeba, a British trip-bop trio, produced the second track, "The Wound That Never Heals," a spooky, sad ballad about a woman serial killer. But it's not the production that carries this song, it's more the absence of too much production that allows the grim beauty of its lyrics and distant almost-spoken vocals to create this touching and haunted portrait of the murderess. Jim wrote the song after reading an unauthorized biography of Aileen Wuornos, a prostitute who killed seven men in Florida. But it's not a song solely about Aileen Wuornos, he points out. "None of the actions in the song parallel her actions." The song, as Jim tells it, was also written with a few former girlfriends in mind, women who had been victims of sexual abuse. "The Wound That Never Heals" begins with the stunning lines:

Long about an hour before sunrise she drags his body down to
the edge of the swollen river,
Wrapped in a red velvet curtain stolen from the movie theater
where she works.

Quiet as a whisper, under the stanchions of a washed-out bridge,
She cuts him loose and watches as the flood waters spin him
around once then carry him away. . . .

Jim's lyrics are filled with the strongest, darkest poetry I've come across in music since the likes of Tom Waits and Shane MacGowan.

The third and last Morcheeba track is the catchiest song on the album, the upbeat "10 Miles to Go on a 9 Mile Road," which contains the trademark, preacherly lines:

From the splinter in the hand,
to the thorn in the heart,
to the shotgun to the head,
you got no choice but to learn to glean
solace from pain or you'll end up cynical or dead.

These vocals are gruffly sung over a line of static that sounds, at times, like a computer going on-line. It's a bent, warped, wonderful song, almost like two diametrically opposed songs somehow welded together.

There are more subtle moments, too. Among them is the beautiful Sohichiro Suzuki–produced "Christmas Day," where again the music takes a step back and lets the songwriting have the floor, deservedly so, in this soft, understated number, another detached tale of grief and woe that has a couple parting at a Greyhound station. Strange electronic chimes haunt this song whenever the vocal pauses, which it does frequently and to great effect, in this meandering anti-serenade:

I remember quite clearly . . .
a bad Muzak version . . .
of James Taylor's big hit . . .
called 'Fire and Rain'. . .

was playing as you crouched down . . .
and tearfully kissed me . . .
and I thought, 'Damn, what good fiction I will mold from this
terrible pain.'

When I ask Jim about that line—and it's a line that doesn't need much explaining to any writer—he smiles and says, "Yeah, my sister told me not to put that in. She said it makes it sound like you're not present in an emotional sense, you're thinking about the future, and I said, 'That's the point of the song.' It's that there's this emotional maelstrom all around me, and I'm thinking, How can I turn this into a story?"

Before Jim leaves for sound check, I ask him if, when touring Oxford, Mississippi, last week, he had visited Faulkner's house. (I'd noticed the Faulkner quote on the new CD, "Between grief and nothing I will take grief.") But no, Jim didn't have the time or desire. He'd rather find the ghost in the books.

"The town seemed like it was frozen in a way. It was frozen in the intentionality of showcasing Faulkner. I don't know if it was, but it kind of felt that way. I don't want to slam Oxford, but I had this hope of coming to Oxford and seeing this new metropolis of subversive thought . . . like a new epicenter of confusion and charm blending together and creating—"

"In Oxford?" I interrupted.

"Yeah, and it didn't feel that way—the thrift stores there are real over-priced!—but what happened to me in Oxford, and please write about this because any eccentric in Oxford will identify with it. We were in that bookstore in Oxford, which is a really nice bookstore, and me and the keyboard player were in there, and sometimes those oak worms fall on you, and he had one just crawling across his shoulder. And when I was a little kid I read *Horton Hears a Who* by Dr. Seuss, and so I have an extended sense of the universe and think that all life forms have some kind of right to live, and there he was, this worm. He didn't do anything wrong. He just happened to fall on somebody's shoulder, and so I picked him up off Clint's shoulder, and I started talking to him," he extends index finger in front of nose. "You know, like, *You're going to be okay. I'm going to take you and find you a nice bush,* and I walked out the store, and I'm walking along the sidewalk—I guess I was dressed kind of scruffy—and I'm talking to the worm like this, and people are staring, and I don't care, go ahead and stare, and I get to a nice row of bushes off the Square, and I'm saying, *You want to get on this bush right here, and it wouldn't go,* and I'm saying, *C'mon just do it,* and it won't. So I get in this big, long negotiation, and finally the worm gets off, and I'm telling it, *See that wasn't so bad, and you thought I wasn't going to be your buddy, and here I am helping you out,* and I get done talking to it, and I look up, and there's a cop right there just staring at me. And all he saw was this guy talking to his finger, talking to a bush. That f—er circled me for hours, waiting for me to throw a brick through a window." Jim pauses for breath, for thought. "Yeah, when I was deathly ill, I read Faulkner, and that shit will get inside your soul if you're deathly sick."

After Jim leaves for the Village Underground, I wander around Washington Square. I have a few hours to kill before the show, and so, while watching the drug deals of dusk, I put my flask to use with a dollar can of Coke. The cement lawn is filled with the usual parade of riffraff, and I'm feeling kind of sad and nostalgic because the previous day I'd given notice on my Lower East Side tenement. I'd been borderline leaving New York for months—I simply couldn't afford it. And now I sip my Coke and start thinking about returning to ice-shackled Vermont and getting back my old job bartending. I had finished my first novel and moved to the city in a gust of romantic optimism. Well, now I'm moving back. Which isn't so terrible, except after over a decade of bartending, it hurts to even think about cutting off another drunk, and I mean physically hurts, like my heart's wincing at it.

I wander over to check the inscription on that big arch, to see if Jim got it right. Sure enough, above the statue of General George, who had so successfully slaughtered the Hessians on Christmas, it states: LET US BUILD A STANDARD TO WHICH THE WISE AND HONEST CAN REPAIR. And sure enough, as I'm standing there, a short black guy with long, beaded dreads introduces himself as Medusa and asks if I am in need of anything.

I'm a bit late for the show, and my girlfriend is waiting for me outside the Village Underground. She is looking especially beautiful but is wearing diabolical shoes and so isn't in the best of moods. "Your eyes look funny," she says. I haven't yet told her about breaking my lease— I'll tell her tomorrow or the next day. Maybe she'll go with me to Vermont, but I doubt it—it's real hard to imagine her existing outside of New York City—and leaving without her, that hurts my heart to think about, too. We descend into the club and are steered toward the reserved Luaka Bop seats. The tavern is filled with white people of all ages, thrift-shop art on the walls, the obligatory net of smoke, the musicians on stage tuning. We settle in, get some drinks, and I'm probably the only person in the club who doesn't notice when David Byrne sits down right next to me. My girlfriend elbows me, whispers at me, and a few seconds later, I glance over. Sure enough. No big suit or anything, but David is looking himself, fit and healthy. "David, by the way, is a sweet, wonderful person," Jim had told me earlier. "He's a nice guy. He's a very distant person, and he has an angular mind, and if you take those two things as givens, you will not meet a nicer person."

Being quiet and shy, I am not about to bother him, but then Byrne leans over and holds out his hand and says, "Hi, I'm David."

I raise my palm in high-five position and say, "Dude!—Burning down the house!"

No, not really. I was happy to shake his hand, though.

Jim onstage is a master of self-deprecation. "I am doomed as a performer," he announces at one point. His shyness offsets his good looks and tallness. He's lost his straw cowboy hat, but he's still wearing the gas-station-attendant shirt. His version of "Handcuffed" is much livelier and more infused with humor than the recorded version. This is pretty much true straight through the set. It's a great show that ends with a randy encore of "God Was Drunk When He Made Me," not Jim's best song, but it's a good one to march them home on. (The CD ends in a more thematic fashion, the last track on the album being a reprise of the imagistic "Corvair," a song about an old car being overgrown by nature and becoming something other than a car.) Jim is up there enjoying himself, belting out in drunk-reverend fashion:

> *If it was God that saved the miracle child from the peril of the*
> *   fiery flame*
> *Well then it musta been Him killed the two hundred others*
> *   just to glorify His name.*

People are clap-dancing and shouting for more, but it's the third encore already.

The house lights go on, and we escape upstairs to the street, the diabolical shoes causing us to opt for the F train on an otherwise beautiful night. We hold hands waiting for the F, which never comes quickly, but luckily on this night there is an old Japanese man playing the subterranean violin. He is wearing thick, taped glasses, and propped in front of him is a similarly duct-taped music stand. I don't know what he's playing, but it is very spring-sad and flight-filled, and whatever it is, the old Japanese guy appears utterly lost inside it, his eyes shut behind the thick lenses, a small smile playing on his lips. Two F trains roar in at once, converging at the station in an onslaught of noise so loud that parts of you disappear, but the old man keeps playing, even though not a soul can hear him now, except maybe the rats. We get on the F and leave him there, his eyes shut, his bow hand dropping down to turn a page of sheet music.

Summer 2001

Banjo

STEVE MARTIN

THE FOUR-STRING BANJO HAS FOUR STRINGS. The five-string banjo has five. The five-string banjo has a truncated string running halfway up the neck. It is called the fifth string and is rarely fretted. It creates a drone. Conventional history places the addition of the fifth string around 1855, but I saw a five-string banjo, by all rights an American instrument, in the Victoria and Albert Museum in London that dated back to the 1820s. The five-string is the banjo I'm interested in.

The four-string banjo is generally strummed, and the five-string banjo is generally picked. The four-string is associated with Dixieland music, and the five-string is associated with bluegrass or Appalachian music. Some bluegrass banjos are open-backed; some are closed in the back by a resonator. The resonator-backed banjos are louder and sharper than the open-backed. An open-backed banjo is softer and mellower. The five-string open-backed banjo is played in a style called "frailing." I have lost many games of Scrabble by using the word *frailing*. It is not in the dictionary, but I assure you it's a word as valid as *oscillococcinuin*. Frailing is a combination of strumming and picking, sometimes called "drop-thumbing." The thumb drops from the fifth string to whatever string it chooses, while the forefinger plucks upward and the rest of the fingers strum across the strings. It is highly rhythmic and strange. Even when

I was immersed in learning the banjo, there were some frailing rhythms I could not duplicate or fathom.

The resonator-backed banjo, or bluegrass banjo, is not strummed. It is picked by three fingers, usually at lightning speed. The style was invented by Earl Scruggs in the '30s. He is still the consummate *artiste* of the bluegrass banjo, because he understands that the player must always make music first, and show off second.

The sound I most like, of which Scruggs is a master, is that of a rolling, endlessly punctuating staccato that is at once continuous and broken.

I first heard Earl Scruggs on record in 1962 when I was seventeen years old. I was living in Orange County, California, about as far away from bluegrass country as one could get and not be in Taiwan. The sound penetrated me, however, and I borrowed my girlfriend's father's four-string banjo in order to learn it. I did not know that I was one string away from nirvana.

Knowing nothing about music, I bought a chord book and meshed my fingers into the steel wires, using my right hand to place my left-hand fingers onto the frets. The first attempts I made sounded like a car being crushed in a metal compactor. I was so ignorant and untrained musically that when I finally learned to play several chords, I could not discern any difference between them.

I had a high school friend named John McEuen, who was also interested in the banjo. He is now one of the finest banjo players in the world. It was at his house in 1964 that a friend, Dave, came over and played the banjo live. Dave sat in front of us and intoned "Flopped Eared Mule," a song whose high point came when the strings were struck behind the bridge, emulating the sound of a donkey's bray. Emulating the sound of a donkey's bray may not be your idea of music, but to us, Dave was Menuhin.

Dave showed us some simple picking patterns and wrote them down in impromptu hieroglyphs on a torn piece of paper. These patterns could be practiced not only on the banjo but also on your school desk and on the car steering wheel and on your pillow just before sleep.

I scraped together two hundred dollars and bought Dave's spare banjo from him. I still have it today, an open-backed frailing banjo, a Gibson RB-170. Its tones have mellowed nicely through the years.

The first song I ever learned was "Cripple Creek." The advantage of learning "Cripple Creek" was that it could be played over and over and over and over into the night, endlessly, forever. We could play it fast, then we could play it slow. We could modulate from fast to slow. We could play it quiet and then play it loud. It had lyrics that we could sing, and when we came to the end of a verse, the banjo would take over, and I would play it extra loud, believing the increased volume created excitement. Then, after hours of playing "Cripple Creek," we would look at each other and decide it was time to end it, and we would blunder to a coda, stop, and take a break. Then it would be time to play again, and someone would suggest "Cripple Creek," and the whole thing would start all over. To this day, I cannot stand to play "Cripple Creek." I can barely write its title.

Finally, I was ready to play for my high school girlfriend, Linda. I put the banjo on my knee and played in all earnestness. She burst out laughing. The reason she burst out laughing was not my playing, but rather that my lips moved with each finger movement.

Worried that this involuntary twitch would signal the end of my embryonic two-chord career, I tortured myself trying to keep my lips still while playing.

Obsession is a great substitute for talent. I had several 33 rpm banjo records by the Dillards and Earl Scruggs. The Dillards boasted the fastest and most thrilling banjoist alive, Doug Dillard. They played live in Orange County in those days, and watching Doug Dillard was like watching God, if God were a fingerpicking madman. Doug, thin as a rail, had a grin that Lewis Carroll could describe, like a piano keyboard stuck on the end of a reed. But the sound of the banjo accelerating from zero to sixty in a nanosecond, in a town that had heretofore heard only lazy folk guitar, made us freeze. Doug was generous, too, and he would teach us various licks (slang for finger and chord sequences). My obsession was such that I would hibernate in my bedroom and slow down the 33 rpm records to 16, and figure out the songs note by note. This process took days. I would have to downtune the banjo until it was in the same key as the down-shifted recording, which caused the strings to become so slack that they would oscillate like a slow-motion jump rope. It also drove my parents crazy. Imagine the muffled sound of a banjo being clunked, insistently and arhythmically, through the paper-thin walls of a tract home, of a song being played so slowly that any melody was indecipherable. My understanding of how annoying this must have sounded led me to park my car on the street after dinner, close all the windows—even in the baking Southern California summer—and practice into the night. By the time I had closed myself in my '57 Chevy, however, I was getting somewhere, and I was entranced with the sounds I could make. One tone from one string could send me into ecstasy, and here I was, making thousands of notes in thousands of combinations. The songs that I worked on in the Chevy were "Doug's Tune," "Fireball Mail," "Earl's Breakdown," "Foggy Mountain Breakdown," and "Old Joe Clark." I'm sure if that car were unearthed today, my little tunes could be found trapped in the cellulose of its seat cushions.

My interest in the banjo was also heavily fueled by David Lindley. David played in a group at Disneyland called the Mad Mountain Ramblers. During my last two years of high school, I worked at Disneyland performing magic tricks in the magic shop. I arranged a deal with Patty, who worked there with me, where we would cover for each other when she wanted to sneak away to rendezvous with her boyfriend or when I wanted to sneak away to hear the Ramblers. In the summer nights at Disneyland, with the fairy lights in the trees, I would listen amazed as Lindley's authority over his instrument drove the music. I spoke with him once, and he explained the frustration of having his mind outpace his fingers' ability to move. I was still learning to put the fingerpicks on properly. He had an eccentricity of standing on his tiptoes as he played, which I copied for years afterward, thinking it was cool. I was also pleased to see that he moved his lips when he played. I intentionally redeveloped my old habit. Lindley later became a renowned rock 'n' roll guitarist.

Some bluegrass instrumentals are called "breakdowns," which simply describes a song that is played very fast. When a song had the word *breakdown* in its title, it acquired a mystical oomph that sent the adrenaline rushing and the fingers pumping, whether they were quite ready to play that fast or not. It had the same cache that the word *raptor* had after the movie *Jurassic Park* was released. Breakdowns were the meanest and baddest of the banjo tunes. Whenever I played a breakdown, I wanted everyone who was in listening distance to understand that this was something very special indeed. I would convey this by standing on my tiptoes and getting a very serious look on my face and moving my lips.

The Topanga Canyon Banjo and Fiddle Contest took place in the summertime in California, and the contest was held under trees in the dry forests of the Santa Monica Mountains. Carrying my banjo in its case, I walked down the long road to the tree-shaded bowl and could hear the tinkling of fifty banjos, all playing different tunes. As there were no seats, the audience spread themselves out on blankets. One could wander away from the contest itself and find, hidden away in the trees, an occasional clump of musicians, all whizzes compared with me, who had found one another and who expertly played the tunes I longed to know. The sound was so pure and exhilarating, it cleansed me. I had about three songs in my repertoire. I entered the contest in the beginner category and vaguely remember winning something, either first or second place. I have a clipping of me onstage that appeared in the local newspaper. Later that day, I heard the blues artist Taj Mahal, in the professional category, frail the song "Colored Aristocracy" so vibrantly that I actually wanted to *be the song, to* be the notes that wafted into the air under the broken sunlight filtering through the trees.

He won.

By the time I got to college, I had discovered another quality of the banjo, which came to dominate my initial desire for speed: melancholy. By then I had found recordings of frailing artists both young and old, who wrung from the banjo an echoing sadness. The banjo had a lonesome sound, reminiscent to me of Scottish and Irish pipe music. One of my favorites was a song written and played by Dick Weissman called "Trail Ridge Road" (later, the title was changed to "Banjo Road"). I learned it the usual way, by slowing down the record. There are odd rhythmic passages that still elude me, but it is one of the few songs that I still play today. I had also become proficient enough to write my own songs. I went to Nashville with my soon-to-be manager, Bill McEuen, and the Nitty Gritty Dirt Band, of which Bill's brother, and my old high school friend, John, was now a member. Catching the coattails of the Dirt Band's recording time, I taped five original songs with the best bluegrass musicians around: Vassar Clements on fiddle, Junior Husky on bass, Jeff Hanna and John on guitar. Years later, I put the songs on the back of my last comedy album. I still take pride in these early efforts at creativity.

Some of the records I loved were *Livin' on the Mountain* by Bill Keith and Jim Rooney (Bill Keith stood banjo playing on its ear with his two-finger rendition of "Devil's Dream"); *Bluegrass Banjos on Fire* by Homer and the Barnstormers (because I have never heard of this group before or since, I believe they were created as a one-shot to satisfy the banjo-recording demand created by the popularity of "Foggy Mountain Breakdown," the theme song to *Bonnie and Clyde*); *New Dimensions in Banjo and Bluegrass* by Marshall Brickman and Eric Weissberg (Marshall Brickman is now a friend and the talented screenwriter who cowrote *Annie Hall*); *Old Time Banjo Project,* an assemblage of various artists; and my favorites, *The Banjo Story* and *Five-String Banjo Greats,* available these days on one CD, under the title *Feuding Banjos.*

I played the banjo in my stand-up comedy act, largely using it as a prop but sometimes playing a full-out bluegrass song, which the audience tolerated. When I stopped performing live in 1981, I also stopped practicing consistently, though I still pick up the banjo periodically and get my thick fingers moving again. Occasionally, I'll learn a new song.

Several months ago, I went out to the garage and sat in my Lexus and put in a CD of Bill Keith playing his whizbang version of "Auld Lang Syne." I plucked it out note by note on my banjo, just like the old days.

Nothing had changed but the price of the car.

Summer 1999

Note in a Bottle

TOM PIAZZA

[The pattern] imposed by a circular image of this kind compensates the disorder and confusion of the psychic state—namely, through the construction of a central point to which everything is related, or by a concentric arrangement of the disordered multiplicity and of contradictory and irreconcilable elements. This is evidently an attempt at self-healing on the part of Nature, which does not spring from conscious reflection but from an instinctive impulse.

—C. G. JUNG, *MANDALA SYMBOLISM*

SUNDAY AFTERNOON ALONG THE RIVER ROAD heading west from New Orleans; low clouds over the levee. I was in the passenger seat, for once, as we passed under the giant, rickety Huey P. Long Bridge and out through Harahan, where the housing subdivisions creep outward, like a fungus, from Metairie. I always expect to see a billboard reading TIRED OF SURPRISES? LIVE HERE. A wasteland of time and space spreading out in all directions.

That day I had been feeling edgy for no reason I could name, and I was no fun to be around. I remembered the feeling all too well from when I was a kid, returning home from church on a gray afternoon, watching the leaves tossing fitfully along the curbs, the feeling of being in exile, somehow, from someplace I had never seen, and which would have been a lot better than where I was.

So we decided to take a ride, a time-honored way to put the blues off for a few hours. We had made it out into Kenner, passing modest brick houses built on cement slabs with lawns that were turning brown, dogs in groups of two and three, when the car slowed sharply and pulled to the shoulder.

"What happened?" I said, jolted out of wherever I was in my head.

"You want me to prove I love you?" she said. It wasn't an entirely rhetorical question, but she was smiling mischievously, looking into the side view, waiting for the car behind us to pass. Then she made a U-turn and started back toward where we'd come from, slowed immediately, and I saw the sign, tiny, stuck into somebody's lawn: FLEA MARKET, with an arrow pointing down the side street, away from the levee. Usually I am the one who notices these signs. I must, I thought, be slipping. She pulled into the street, and we made our way along, guided by more tiny signs that took us over the railroad tracks and along behind some giant Quonset huts.

Eventually we found it, a permanent building almost the size of an airplane hangar. It would have been hard to imagine a more out-of-the-way location. We parked and strolled in together through an open garage door beneath the dim fluorescent lights high up under the corrugated metal roof, through the aisles and alleys of forgotten junk. You train yourself not to get optimistic in these circumstances. Flea markets often mean factory-second clothes, cheap, shrink-wrapped tools. But this place had a promising mix of older furniture, display cases with military medals and advertising pens, stacks of sheet music along with hideous ashtrays and baby strollers, computer equipment from the late 1980s, ancient boom boxes.

And then I saw the 78s and felt the immediate surge in my pulse that they always elicit. There were several stacks of the shellac discs in bins, next to some LPs and 8-track tapes. I squeezed Mary's hand and walked over to the bins. The old 78s have fascinated me for as long as I can remember. Each one is a little world of its own, a ten-inch-wide mandala in which the grooves spiral gradually inward to the central point, which is the ending, a disappearing center consisting of the hole through which the turntable spindle fits.

The 78s contain about three minutes of recorded sound on each side, three minutes in which every detail counts, as in good fiction. For the three minutes between the recording's beginning and its ending, the blues singers and jazz bands and old-time string bands cast their thoughts, their whole style of approaching reality, out into the world without being able to know exactly where it would all land. Such wit, such intensity, such heartbreak, such style, such care with the expressive detail. Each record is like a note in a bottle. They made the records, and the records landed in places no one could predict, and they added oxygen to the world. Finding a good one is like experiencing grace itself descending upon you. Time itself is redeemed, to live again and again, expanding infinitely.

Now, standing on the cement floor under the high, dim lights, I looked through maybe one hundred records in various small stacks squirreled away under tables and on shelves. While the 78s were from the period that I favored—the late 1920s and early '30s—most of the records offered more or less inconsequential dance or pop music of the time by performers like Jesse Crawford, Seger Ellis, Art Gillham, Nat Shilkret— the now-forgotten artists who were the Bee Gees and Ricky Martins of their period. I found one or two things that were marginally interesting, but the search was basically a washout. As a formality, I asked the proprietress if she had any more 78s laying around anywhere.

She gave a short, almost derisive laugh. "Sure," she said. "Come on over here." I frowned and followed her around a corner, and stacked up against a wall were at least thirty boxes big enough to hold fifty records each.

"Holy smokes," I said.

"Yeah, well, when you get finished smoking, there's just as many boxes up front."

Mary was standing nearby when this exchange took place. I looked at her, and she said, "I'll be outside. Don't worry. I have the paper. Have fun." She gave me a reassuring smile and headed out. I sat on a stool and started looking.

Quantity, in Engels's famous remark, changes quality, but not to a shellac collector. Each new record you pull from the stack is a potential New Beginning, as fresh as the pull of the lever on a slot machine to a confirmed gambler. The records were grouped together in boxes roughly by label—Victor, Brunswick, Columbia, OKeh. Again most were from that late twenties, early thirties period. There were multiple copies of certain titles, which suggested, along with the extraordinary quantity, that they came from a store stock. But store stock tends to be in new or nearly new condition. Many of these had clearly been played repeatedly. A puzzle.

It took about forty-five minutes to go through every box. The proprietress loaned me a red Magic Marker so that I could check off the boxes I'd looked through. I turned up nothing. Some of the records were tantalizingly close—duds by pop singers who occasionally recorded with jazz accompaniments, items by well-known personalities like Maurice Chevalier or Fanny Brice, which might have interested another collector but not me. Still, the time frame was right. I could almost smell the scent of what I was looking for. But the fact that there was almost nothing was discouraging; it suggested that someone else had gone through the boxes already and beaten me to the good stuff.

When I was finished in back I stood up and made my way around front ("You didn't find anything?" the lady asked as she pointed me in a new direction), where I was now confronted by a small mountain, an Aztec pyramid, of similar boxes, at least forty of them. The prospect of looking through all of them and again turning up nothing was momentarily demoralizing. Yet there was always the possibility. The possibility. Guiltily, I peeked out the door toward the car, where Mary was engrossed in the newspaper. I sat down on a stool with the Magic Marker and opened the first box.

It wasn't long before I pulled up a record that sent a jolt through me— "The Only Girl I Ever Loved" by Charlie Poole with the North Carolina Ramblers—Columbia 15711-D, from 1930, one of his last records, one side of which is not even available on CD. This one was in almost new condition. I fought the impulse to yell out. It's like catching a good trout. You don't want to spook the whole river. You unhook the fish, place it in your pack, and keep fishing. I quietly set the disc to one side and kept looking. Before long I pulled the next good one: a fine copy of "Nehi Mamma Blues" by the Memphis blues singer Frank Stokes, a very rare record. Breathing deeply through my nose I set it on top of the Poole record. A few records later I turned up a copy of "Got the Jake Leg Too" by the Ray Brothers, a Mississippi string band, a rare Victor 23500 series from the bottom of the Depression, also in fine condition.

Now I was getting excited; this had the markings of a major haul. I went out to tell Mary that I might be awhile. She had moved the car into the shade of a tree and was reading the paper with the door open. She nodded indulgently. I told her, sotto voce, that I'd found a copy of "Got the Jake Leg Too." "That's good, honey," she said, reading.

I felt like Walter Huston in *The Treasure of the Sierra Madre,* setting up his scaffolding and sluice gates, concentrating feverishly, separating the gold from the bulk of the rock and clay. I went through every single disc, and before I was finished I'd also found a beautiful 1932 blues record on Columbia by Lonnie Johnson under the pseudonym Jimmy Jordan; a Depression-era Carter Family on Victor ("Dying Soldier"); something by the old-time guitarist Henry Whitter on the Broadway label entitled "There Was an Old Tramp," which turned out not even to be listed in any of my discographies; and several records by Gid Tanner and His Skillet Lickers, Riley Puckett, Kelly Harrell, and Fiddlin' John Carson.

By the time I finished, I had looked through at least three thousand discs and had whittled down my stack to thirty-five. I paid two dollars apiece for them ("They always find some good ones," the proprietress said as she counted out my change from a wad she kept in the pocket of her housedress), and I walked out slightly overstimulated, a little toasted around the edges, but with a sense of satisfaction and even of gratitude for being able to retrieve these records from the mountain of chaos where they had languished. That my own emotional cloud cover seemed to have evaporated was not lost on me, either.

Mary had been reduced to reading the automotive supplement of the *Times-Picayune,* and I felt a little sheepish. She looked tired, and I didn't blame her. She had, after all, been sitting there for almost two hours. Between the lines, her smile said, "Love costs." I didn't go into much detail about my finds. She understands and she doesn't understand. The important thing is that where understanding leaves off, she has the faith to hang with me anyway. Grace, I thought as we drove off, is not something anyone has a right to expect in this life. But when you find it, you can at least say thank you. Which I did.

January/February 2001

Feet in Smoke

JOHN JEREMIAH SULLIVAN

ON APRIL 21, 1995, THE ANNIVERSARY OF MARK TWAIN'S DEATH—a date that now seems not entirely coincidental—my brother, Worth, put his mouth to a microphone in a garage in Lexington, Kentucky, and was electrocuted. His band, The Moviegoers, had stopped for a day to rehearse on their way from Chicago to a concert in Sewanee, Tennessee, where I was at college. Just two days earlier, he'd called to ask if there were any songs I wanted to hear at the show. A newer song came immediately to mind, one that I'd heard him play late at night, on an acoustic guitar, after a holiday meal at our grandparents' house. I don't remember which holiday, probably Christmas; they all end the same way, with my brother and me half or wholly drunk and trying out our songs on each other. There's something almost biologically satisfying about harmonizing with your brother. We've gotten to where we communicate through music. I don't mean we speak in notes—we're not twin savants or anything like that—but we use guitars the way fathers and sons use baseball: as a kind of emotional code. Worth is seven years older than I am, an age gap that can make siblings strangers, and I'm fairly sure the first time he ever felt we had anything to talk about was the day he caught me in his basement room at our house in Indiana, where I was trying to teach myself how to play "Radio Free Europe" on a black Telecaster he'd forbidden me to touch.

The tune I requested on the phone, "Is It All Over?," doesn't sound like a typical Moviegoers song; it's a bit simpler and more earnest than the winningly infectious geek-pop that is their specialty. The changes were still unfamiliar to the rest of the band, and Worth had been about to lead them through the first verse, had just leaned forward to sing the opening lines—"Is it all over? I'm scannin' the paper/for someone to replace her"—when a surge of electricity arced through his body, magnetizing the mike to his chest like a weak but obstinate missile, searing the first string and fret into his palm, and stopping his heart. He fell backward and crashed, already dying.

Forgive me if you knew most of this. I got my details from a common source: an episode of *Rescue 911* (yes, the one hosted by William Shatner) that aired about six months after the accident. My brother played himself on the show, which was amusing for him, since he has no memory of the real event. For the rest of us, the re-creation is difficult to watch, and it took me three years to get around to it. In fact, it was only as a kind of research for this essay that I played the tape, but I'm glad I finally did. Though it tells a different story from the one I know to tell, one that ends at the moment we realized my brother would live, the show offers a healthy reminder of the danger involved in talking too much about "miracles." I'm not down on the word—the staff at Humana (now Jewish Hospital) in Lexington called my brother's case miraculous, and they've seen any number of horrifying accidents and inexplicable recoveries—but it tends to obscure all the human skill and coolheadedness that go into saving somebody's life. I think of Liam Davis, my brother's best friend and fellow Moviegoer, who refused to freak out while he cradled Worth in his arms until help arrived, and who'd warned him to put on his Chuck Taylors before they started practicing, the rubber heels of which were the only thing that kept Worth from being zapped into a more permanent fate than the six near-deaths he did endure. I think of Captain Clarence Jones, the fireman and paramedic who brought

Worth back to life, ironically with two hundred joules of pure electric shock (and who responded to my grandmother's effusive thanks by giving all the credit "to the Lord"). Without people like these, and doubtless others whom Shatner forgot to mention, there would have been no miracle. My brother would have met his Maker in a scene that played like cutting-room footage from *Spinal Tap*, except that it would have left dozens of people devastated and lost.

The first word I had of the accident came from my father, who called me from Florida that afternoon to tell me that my brother had been hurt. I can still hear the nauseating pause before his "I don't know," when I asked him if Worth was dead. My girlfriend drove me from Sewanee to Lexington at ninety-five miles an hour, getting us into the city at around ten o'clock that night. We were met in the hospital parking lot by two of my uncles from my mother's side—fraternal twins, both of them Lexington businessmen—who escorted us to the ICU and filled us in on Worth's ambiguous condition. They very calmly explained that he'd flat-lined five times in the ambulance on the way to Humana, his heart locked in something Captain Jones called a "systole," which Jones describes on *Rescue 911* as "just another death-producing rhythm." As I understand him to mean, my brother's pulse had been one continuous beat—like a drumroll—but feeble, not actually sending the blood anywhere. By the time I showed up at the hospital, Worth's heart was at least beating on its own power, but a machine was doing all his breathing for him. The really bad news had to do with his brain, which displayed one-percent activity—vegetable status.

One of the nurses who'd been there when they brought him in, a heavyset woman who introduced herself with the pleasingly thick accent you hear in small towns around Lexington, led me through two automatic glass doors and into Intensive Care. My brother was a nightmare of tubes and wires, dark machines silently measuring every internal event, a pump filling and emptying his useless lungs. The stench of dried spit was everywhere in the room. His eyes were closed, his every muscle slack. It seemed at once that only the machines were alive, possessed of some secret will that wouldn't let them give up on this particular dead man.

The nurse spoke to me from the corner in a tone of near-admonishment that angered me at the time and that I've never been able to understand since. "It ain't like big brother's gonna wake up tomorrow and be all better," she said. I looked at her stupidly. Did she think the situation didn't look quite grim enough?

"I know," I said, and asked her to leave the room. When I heard the door close behind me, I walked to the side of the bed. Worth and I have different fathers, making us half-brothers, technically. Although he was already living with my dad when I was born, so that I've never known life without him, we look nothing alike. He has thick dark hair and olive skin and was probably the only member of our blood family in the hospital that night with green, and not blue, eyes. I leaned over into his face. The normal flush of his cheeks had gone white, and his lips were parted to admit the breathing tube. There were no signs of anything, of life or struggle or crisis, only the gruesomely robotic sounds of the oxygen machine pumping air into his chest and sucking it out again. I heard my uncles, their voices composed with strain, telling me about the "one-percent brain activity." I leaned down farther, putting my mouth next to my brother's right ear, and spoke his name: "Worth . . . it's John."

All six feet and four inches of his body came to life, writhing against the restraints and what looked like a thousand invasions of his orifices and skin. Then his head reared back, and his eyes swung open on me. The pupils were almost nonexistent, the irises sea-green with flecks of black. His eyes stayed open only for the briefest instant, focusing loosely on mine before falling shut. But my God, what an instant. When I was a volunteer fireman, I once helped to pull a dead man out of an overturned truck, and I remember the look of his open eyes as I handed him to the next person in line—I'd been expecting pathos, some ember of whatever thought had last crossed his mind, but they were just marbles, mere things. The eyes into which I'd just caught a glimpse had been nothing like that. If anything, they were the eyes of a madman. It occurred to me then that a condition parallel to the systole, which had seized Worth's heart and nearly killed him, must have effectively taken over his mind. What the machines were reading as vegetable activity was really chaos, the fury of an electrified brain fighting to reassemble itself. I had seen all that unmistakably, and it had been like looking down on a man trying to climb his way out of a moss-grown well; the second he moves, he slips back to the bottom. Worth's head fell back on the pillow, motionless, his body exhausted from its efforts at reentering a world that his mind couldn't possibly fathom. I put down his hand, which I had taken without realizing it, and ran back into the hallway. I remember burning to tell my family what I knew, but quickly deciding against it, trusting my instincts but not my ability to deliver the news convincingly. I spent the night in another hospital room with my sister, my girlfriend, and my mother, who prayed us all to sleep.

Worth spent that night, and the second day and night, in a coma. There were no outward signs of change, but the machines began to pick up indications of increased brain waves. A doctor explained to us (in what must have been, for him, child's language) that the brain is itself an electrical machine, and that the volts that had flowed from my brother's vintage Gibson amplifier and traumatized his body were in some sense still racing around inside his skull. There was a decent chance he would emerge from the coma, but no one could say what would be left; no one could say who would emerge. That day of waiting comes back to me now as a collage of awful food, nurses' cautious encouragement, and the disquieting presence of my brother supine in his bed, an oracle who could answer all our questions but refused to speak. We rotated in and out of his room like tourists circulating through a museum.

"On the third day" (I would never have said it myself, but Shatner does it for me on the show), Worth woke up. The nurses led us into his room, their faces almost proud, and we found him sitting up—gingerly, with heavy-lidded eyes, as if at any moment he might decide he liked the coma better and slip back into it. His face lit up like a simpleton's whenever one of us entered the room, and he greeted us by our names in a barely audible rasp. He seemed to know us all, but he hadn't the slightest what we were doing there, or where "there" might be—though he came up with several theories on that last point over the next two weeks, chief among them a wedding reception, a high school poker game, and, at one point, some kind of horrifyingly Kafkaesque holding cell.

I've tried so many times to describe for people the brother who emerged from that electrified death, the one who remained with us for about a month before he went back to being the Worth we'd known and know now. It would save me a lot of trouble to say, "It was like he was on acid," but that's not quite true. Instead, he seemed to be living one of those imaginary acid trips that we used to pretend to be on when we were in junior high—you know, "Hey, man, I think your nose is, like, a monkey or something"—only better, and scarier, and altogether more profound. My father and I kept notes, neither aware that the other was doing it, trying to get down all Worth's little disclosures and moments of brilliance before they faded beyond recapture, or became indistinct against the backdrop of their own abundance. I'm sitting here now with my own list. There's no appropriate place to begin, so maybe I should just transcribe a few things:

Squeezed my hand late on the night of the 23d. Whispered, "That's the human experience."

While eating lunch on the 24th, suddenly became convinced that I was impersonating his brother. Demanded to see my ID. Asked me, "Why would you want to impersonate John?" When I protested, "But Worth, don't I look like him?" replied, "You look exactly like him. No wonder you can get away with it."

On the day of the 25th, stood up from lunch despite my attempts to restrain him, spilling the contents of his tray everywhere. Glanced at my hands, tight around his shoulders. Said, "I am not . . . repulsed . . . by man-to-man love, but I'm not into it."

Day of the 26th. Gazing at own toes at end of bed, remarked, "That'd make a nice picture: Feet in Smoke."

Referred to heart monitor as "a solid, congealed bag of nutrients."

Night of the 26th. Tried to punch me while I worked with Dad and Uncle John to restrain him in his bed, swinging with all his might and missing by less than an inch. The IV tubes were tearing loose from his arms. His eyes were terrified, helpless. I think he took us for some kind of fascist goons.

Evening of the 27th. Unexpectedly jumped up from his chair, a perplexed expression on his face, and ran to the wall. Rubbed palms along a small area of the wall like a blind man. Asked, "Where's the piñata?" Shuffled into hallway. Noticed a large nurse walking away down the hall. Turned and muttered, "If she's got our piñata, I'm gonna be pissed."

The whole spectacle went from tragedy to tragicomedy to outright comedy on a sliding continuum, so it's hard to pinpoint just when one let onto another. He was the most delightful drunk you'd ever met— I had to follow him around the room like a shadow to make sure he didn't fall, because he couldn't stop moving. He was a holy fool. He looked down into his palm where the fret and string had burned a deep red cross and said, "Hey, it'd be a stigma if there weren't all those ants crawling in it." When the doctor asked him the year, he smugly replied, "Um, wouldn't that be 1994, Doctor?" Asked if he knew how to spell his name, he said, "Well, if you were Spenser you might spell it W-o-r-t-h-e." Everything was a giant, melting metaphor in which the tenor and vehicle had become equally real. He looked at the wall sockets and said, "Look, the Axis armies fighting the Allies!" Examining his hospital gown, he wanted to know if he'd be allowed to "keep the cool jumpsuit."

A nurse, when I asked her if he'd ever be normal again, said, "Maybe, but wouldn't it be wonderful just to have him like this?" And she was right; she humbled me. I cannot imagine a more hopeful or hilarious occasion than spying on my brother's brain while it reconstructed reality. Since roughly the age of sixteen, I had assumed that the center of the brain, if you could ever find it, would inevitably be a dark place. Whatever was good or lovely about being human, I figured, had to be a result of our struggles against everything innate, against physical nature. Worth changed my mind about all that. Here was a consciousness reduced to its matter, to a ball of crackling synapses—words that he knew how to use but couldn't connect with the right things; objects that he had to invent names for; unfamiliar people who approached and receded like energy fields—and it was a fine place to be; you might even say a poetic place. He had touched death but seemed to find life no less interesting for having done so.

Yes, death. There is one little remark that I didn't include in my notes, since I wasn't at all worried about forgetting it.

Late afternoon of April 25th. The window slats casting bars of shadow all over his room in the ICU. I had asked my mother and father if they'd mind giving me a moment alone with him, since I still wasn't sure if he knew who I was. I did know that he wasn't aware of being in the hospital; I believe his most recent theory at the time was that we were all back at my grandparents' house having a party. Neither of us was speaking. He was jabbing a fork into his Jell-O, and I was just watching, waiting to see what would come out. Earlier that morning he'd been scared by having so many "strangers" around, and I didn't want to upset him any more. Suddenly, very quietly, he started to weep, his shoulders heaving with the force of whatever emotion had brought on the tears. I let him cry. I didn't touch him. A minute went by, and I asked him, "Worth, why are you crying?"

"I was thinking of the vision I had when I knew I was dead."

Had I heard him right? I knew I had. But how could he have known where he'd been, when he didn't even know where he was? And yet he'd said it.

"What was it?" I asked.

He looked up. The tears were mostly gone. "I was on the banks of the River Styx. The boat came to row me across, but . . . instead of Charon, it was Huck and Jim. Only, when Huck pulled back his hood, he was an old man . . . like, ninety years old."

He cried a little more and then seemed to forget all about it. I believe the next words out of his mouth were, "Check this out, I've got the Andrew Sisters in my milk shake!"

There it was. We've never spoken of it. How could we? My brother has a month-long lacuna in his memory that starts the second he put his lips to that microphone. He doesn't remember the accident, the ambulance, having died, having come back to life. Even when it came time for him to leave the hospital, he had only managed to piece together that he was late for a concert somewhere, and my last memory of him from that period is his leisurely wave when I told him I had to go back to school. "See you at the show," he called across the parking lot. When our family gets together now, the subject of his accident naturally comes up, but he looks at us with a kind of disbelief. It's a story about someone else, a story he thinks we might be fudging just a bit.

But what he can't remember, I can't forget. I've spent nights puzzling out that vision. The closest I've been able to come is a sort of quasi-Jungian reduction, based on the knowledge that my brother was never much of a churchgoer (he proclaimed himself a deist at age fifteen, meaning that I proclaimed myself one at eight) but had been an excellent student of Latin. His high school Latin teacher, a sweet and brilliant old woman with the undeserved name of Rank, had drilled her classes in classical mythology. So maybe when it came time for my brother to have his "near-death experience," to reach down into his psyche and pull up whatever myths would help him make sense of the fear, he reached for the ones he'd found most compelling as a young man. For most people, that involves the whole tunnel-of-light business; for my brother, the underworld.

Where he got Huck and Jim from, though, defeats my best theories. I'm just glad they decided to leave him on this side of the river.

Summer 1998

Notes on Contributors

RICK BASS has published numerous nonfiction books, including *Brown Dog of the Yaak: Essays on Art and Activism;* a novel, *Where the Sea Used to Be;* and a collection of short fiction, *The Hermit's Story.* Born in Mississippi, he lives with his family on a remote ranch in Montana.

OA columnist **ROY BLOUNT JR.**'s essays, humor, and sports writing have appeared in over a hundred periodicals including *The Atlantic Monthly, The New Yorker,* and *Esquire.* He has written sixteen books, many plays and screenplays, and covered the 1992 Democratic and Republican national conventions for Comedy Central. Raised in Decatur, Georgia, he lives in New York City.

WENDY BRENNER has written two books of stories: *Large Animals in Everyday Life,* which won the Flannery O'Connor Award for Short Fiction in 1996, and *Phone Calls from the Dead.* Her stories have appeared in *Mississippi Review, Ploughshares, Seventeen, Southern Exposure, Story,* and *Travel & Leisure.* She teaches creative writing at the University of North Carolina at Wilmington.

LARRY BROWN served sixteen years in the Oxford, Mississippi, fire department. He has four novels, two collections of short stories, and two books of nonfiction to his credit. A two-time winner of the Southern Book Critics Circle Award for fiction, Brown received a three-year Lila Wallace–*Readers Digest* Writers' Award in 1999. He lives on a cattle farm in Yocona, Mississippi, with his family.

Grammy Award-winner **ROSANNE CASH** is the author of a short story collection, *Bodies of Water,* and is the editor of *Songs Without Rhyme: Prose by Celebrated Songwriters.* Her work has appeared in *The New York Times, Rolling Stone,* and *New York Magazine.*

BILLY COLLINS's recent poetry collections are *Sailing Alone Around the Room: New and Selected Poems* and *Nine Horses*. His poetry has appeared in *The Atlantic Monthly, Harper's Magazine, The New Yorker,* and *The Paris Review*. A former Guggenheim Fellow and Literary Lion of the New York Public Library, he was appointed United States Poet Laureate for 2001–2003.

OA columnist **HAL CROWTHER** is the 1992 recipient of the H. L. Mencken Writing Award, and his third collection of essays, *Cathedrals of Kudzu: A Personal Landscape of the South,* was awarded the 2001 Lillian Smith Award for Literature. He lives with his wife, the writer Lee Smith, in Hillsborough, North Carolina.

Born in Hawaii, **LEE DURKEE** grew up in Hattiesburg, Mississippi, and now lives in Vermont. His stories have appeared in *Harper's Magazine, New England Review,* and *Zoetrope: All-Story*. He is the author of the novel *Rides of the Midway*.

TONY EARLEY's fiction and nonfiction have appeared in *Esquire, Granta, Harper's Magazine,* and *The New Yorker*. An *OA* contributing writer, Earley is the author of the novel *Jim the Boy* and the collections *Here We Are in Paradise* and *Somehow Form a Family: Stories That Are Mostly True*. He teaches English and creative writing at Vanderbilt University.

OA columnist **JOHN T. EDGE** is the director of the Southern Foodways Alliance at the Center for the Study of Southern Culture at the University of Mississippi. His books include *Southern Belly* and the James Beard Award-nominated *A Gracious Plenty*.

WILLIAM FAULKNER (1897–1962) was born in New Albany, Mississippi, and lived most of his life in nearby Oxford, never graduating from high school or earning a college degree. He won the Nobel Prize in 1949. The story that appears in this anthology was not published during his lifetime.

Born and raised in Morgan City, Louisiana, **TIM GAUTREAUX** has been anthologized in *Best American Short Stories, New Stories from the South,* and *Prize Stories 2000: The O. Henry Awards*. His third book, *Welding with Children,* was a *New York Times* Notable Book in 1999. He is a professor of English at Southeastern Louisiana University.

After years of travel, **WILLIAM GAY** once again lives in his hometown of Hohenwald, Tennessee. His work has appeared in *The Georgia Review* and *The Missouri Review,* and he has written two novels, *Provinces of Night* and *The Long Home.*

MARIANNE GINGHER has twice been awarded the North Carolina Literary Fellowship Award for Fiction. She directs the creative writing program at the University of North Carolina at Chapel Hill. Her memoir, *A Girl's Life: Horses, Boys, Weddings, and Luck,* was published in 2001.

Best-selling author **JOHN GRISHAM** has published *The Oxford American* since 1994. His novel *A Painted House* was serialized in the magazine in 2000. He lives in Charlottesville, Virginia.

BARRY HANNAH grew up in Clinton, Mississippi, and received the Chubb Award for Fiction in Honor of Robert Penn Warren in 1999. The author of twelve works of fiction and many essays, he is a writer in residence at the University of Mississippi and teaches regularly at the Sewanee Writers' Conference in Sewanee, Tennessee.

Novelist, anthropologist, and folklorist **ZORA NEALE HURSTON** (1891–1960) grew up in Eatonville, Florida. Her works include *Jonah's Gourd Vine, Their Eyes Were Watching God, Tell My Horse,* and *Dust Tracks on a Road.* She died in poverty and obscurity but, due largely to the advocacy of Alice Walker, her talent and contributions were rediscovered in the 1970s. The story that appears in this anthology was not published during her lifetime.

DONALD JUSTICE was born and raised in Miami, Florida. He has published eleven books and chapbooks of poetry, including his 1979 Pulitzer Prize-winning *Selected Poems,* and is the recipient of the 1991 Bollingen Prize.

ANDREA LEE's fiction has appeared in *The New Yorker* and *The New York Times Magazine,* and she was the second-prize winner in *Prize Stories 1993: The O. Henry Award.* Her books include *Russian Journal,* which was nominated for a National Book Award, the story collection *Interesting Women,* and the novel *Sarah Phillips.* She lives with her family in Turin, Italy.

STEVE MARTIN won an Emmy Award for his television writing at age twenty and has since won two Grammy Awards for comedy albums. He has written a novel, *Shopgirl,* a collection of comic essays, *Pure Drivel,* and several plays, including *Picasso at the Lapin Agile.* He lives in Los Angeles and writes frequently for *The New Yorker* and *The New York Times.*

After the death of his parents, **WALKER PERCY** (1916–1990) was raised by his cousin William Alexander Percy in Greenville, Mississippi. His first novel, *The Moviegoer,* won the National Book Award in 1962. His other novels include *The Last Gentleman, Love in the Ruins,* and *Lancelot.* The story that appears in this anthology was not published during his lifetime.

TOM PIAZZA's books have won the James Michener Award for Fiction and the ASCAP-Deems Taylor Award for music writing. He is a regular music contributor to *The New York Times* and has recently completed his first novel, *My Cold War.* His *OA* essay on Gillian Welch was included in *Best American Music Writing 2000.*

Four-time Nobel Prize nominee **SISTER HELEN PREJEAN** is a member of the Sisters of St. Joseph of Medaille. She is the author of *The New York Times* bestseller *Dead Man Walking.* She was born in Baton Rouge and has lived and worked in Louisiana all her life.

MARK RICHARD grew up in Virginia and Texas. His short stories have appeared in *Antaeus, Esquire, Harper's Magazine, The New Yorker,* and *The Paris Review.* He has written *The Ice at the Bottom of the World,* a collection of short stories that received the PEN/Hemingway Award, as well as *Charity: Stories* and *Fishboy,* a novel.

CYNTHIA SHEARER left the curatorship of William Faulkner's home, Rowan Oak, to devote more time to her writing and to teaching English at the University of Mississippi. Her first novel is *The Wonder Book of the Air.*

JOHN SIMPKINS has contributed to *The New Republic, The New York Times Magazine,* and the *South African Yearbook of International Law.* He is an attorney in Washington, D.C., and lives in Baltimore.

SUSAN SONTAG's most recent novel, *In America,* won the 2000 National Book Award for fiction. A collection of essays, *Where the Stress Falls,* was published in late 2001.

JOHN JEREMIAH SULLIVAN was born in Louisville, Kentucky, and graduated from the University of the South in Sewanee, Tennessee. A former *OA* associate editor, he lives in New York City where he works as an associate editor at *Harper's Magazine.*

DONNA TARTT has been a frequent contributor to *The Oxford American* since its second issue in 1992. She is the author of *The Secret History* and *The Little Friend.* Her work has appeared in *GQ, Harper's,* and *The New Yorker.*

MATTHEW TEAGUE lives in New Orleans and is a writer-at-large for *GQ.* His first writing job was for his hometown newspaper, *The Vicksburg* (Miss.) *Post.* His stories have appeared in *Esquire, GQ,* and *Men's Journal.*

Born and raised in Pennsylvania, **JOHN UPDIKE** began writing for *The New Yorker* soon after graduating from Harvard College. He is best known for his series of four novels chronicling the life of Harry "Rabbit" Angstrom. Among Updike's many other books are *Olinger Stories, Roger's Version, Collected Poems,* and *In the Beauty of the Lilies.* His novel *The Centaur* won the National Book Award in 1964.

STEVE YARBROUGH is the author of three story collections—*Family Men, Mississippi History,* and *Veneer*—and two novels, *The Oxygen Man* and *Visible Spirits.* He teaches at California State University, Fresno.